Table of Contents

Introduction 5

New Year's Eve, 2019. Part 1. by 7

New Year's Eve, 2019. Part 2. by 12

A train journey to remember by ' 19

Haitian Boat People by Lally Brown 24

If I may... by Ronald Mackay 27

When the Going Gets Tough – The Tough Need Laughter by Tina Wagner
Mattern 34

Dreams, Drama and Dolphins by Amy Bovaird 37

Dog Days in Uruguay by Syd Blackwell 45

The Kindness of Strangers by Robyn Boswell 51

High Tea in Colonial Williamsburg by Patricia Steele 54

Elspeth by Andrew Klein 59

Still the English Teacher by Patty Sisco 63

My Year of Nothingness by Susan Mellsopp 69

Prick of Conscience by Ronald Mackay 72

In the Library by Mary Mae Lewis 81

The American smugglers in Cuba by Denis Dextraze 85

Maywood by Tina Wagner Mattern 92

While the Roses Still Bloom by Malcolm D. Welshman 99

A Lamb, a Dog and a Haircut by Irene Pylypec 103

Raining Cowboys and Injuns by Mike Cavanagh 107

It came from above by Alison Alderton 110

O'er the Bridge that Spans the River by Ronald Mackay 113

The Cuddle by Elizabeth Moore   120

Going Batty by Frank Kusy   123

Gertrudinous by Robyn Boswell   126

Espressivo by Vernon Lacey   132

Summer Faith by Tina Wagner Mattern   137

Rambo, the ex-U.S. Marine in Cuba by Denis Dextraze   141

My Silvery Friend by Susan Mellsopp   148

The 'Keeper wi the Lauch by Ronald Mackay   150

In Caring for my Ficus by Liliana Amador-Marty   159

American Cemetery by Neal Atherton   163

Luxury Limo Surprise by Robyn Boswell   166

Life Changing Moments by Ronni Robinson   169

Mom – Some Thoughts and Memories by Syd Blackwell   173

My Mother's Last Gift by Tina Wagner Mattern   180

Nervous Night in Nevada by Leslie Groves Ogden   183

Unto the Haven by Ronald Mackay   187

Family Love and a Dog named Bruce by Carolyn Muir Helfenstein   194

The Cyprus Affair (Final Scenes) A Screenplay by Susan Joyce   201

CONTRIBUTORS   213

Thank you!   245

Travel Stories and Highlights Series   247

40 Memorable Life Experiences   249

About the Editor   251

Books by Robert Fear   253

40

Inspirational

True Stories

2021 Edition

Originally published on the *Fred's Diary 1981* blog

Edited by Robert Fear

Introduction

A warm welcome to this fifth annual anthology of real-life stories.

In case you do not know the history to this series of books, here is a brief recap.

While working on the second edition of my memoir *Fred's Diary 1981* in early 2015, I began a blog to help with the editing process. To encourage people to visit my website fd81.net, I started a travel story competition. It was such a success that I ran another one for travel highlights. That went well too, and a selection of these were self-published in a book called *Travel Stories and Highlights*.

In 2016, I repeated the contests. Again, there were lots of fantastic entries, and I released a 2017 edition, which included the best contributions from the first two years. 2017 and 2018 saw the competitions have continued success. This led to publication of the 2018 and 2019 editions of *Travel Stories and Highlights*.

In 2019, I changed the format, and introduced an Authors Showcase. An anthology entitled *40 Memorable Life Experiences: 2020 Edition* was the result. This year (2020), the subject for the showcase was *Inspirational True Stories*. This release includes the most powerful of these.

I hope you enjoy this compelling new collection.

Robert Fear

December 2020

New Year's Eve, 2019. Part 1.
by Mike Cavanagh

The house phone rang just after 6 a.m. on New Year's Eve and my wife Julie got out of bed to answer it. In a doze, I could just hear her say,

"Hello?"

Then nothing further. As she came back, she said,

"It was a recorded message from the Rural Fire Service. The fire's crossed the highway and heading our way. We should be prepared to leave."

Strange thing, we'd been expecting this call, yet when it arrived it just didn't seem real. Julie came back to bed and booted up her laptop to check the online fire information. I got up to make the coffee; something real, at least.

* * *

From as early as the beginning of August 2019, a month before Spring, it was clear that unless the heavens opened in a prolonged drenching, this fire season would be one of the worst on record. Sadly, the heavens remained closed for business, and by early September south-east Queensland and north-east New South Wales were littered with fires; some small, some big, but all growing. By October, a fire had sprung up between Canberra and Braidwood, some 60 kilometres north-west of where we live, and a number of fires in the Blue Mountains, west of Sydney. Then in early November, a fire began in the State Forest near a place called Currowan, some 25 kilometres north-west of us. As the fire front bore down towards the coast some ten kilometres north of us, it was clear as November headed towards December that the coastal townships in its path were in dire straits. We knew and loved these places; Depot Beach, Durras North, South Durras, Pretty Beach, Kioloa. Our adult son, Dan, who lives with us, had some friends with properties up there. Crowded places in summer and school holidays, but otherwise peaceful and leafy retreats for the residents, local day trippers (us) and surfers (Dan). Those who lived there looked like they might pay a heavy price now for the beautiful coastal bush that surrounded them.

Where we live, in Catalina, a suburb of Batemans Bay (population 17,000 odd), we'd been experiencing the distant reach of the fire for some weeks already as 'smoke haze likely' became part of our daily weather forecast. We rarely saw stars at night, washing was hung to dry inside on the bad days and working in the garden restricted to the better days, usually when a nor'easter blew in from the sea. As rare event as it was a welcome one. On the days when the wind was from the north-west, fine grey ash flakes floated down, their gentle rocking as they drifted along belying the fury behind their origin.

Checking the RFS fire mapping was now a daily routine for me, and often several times a day as things were moving so quickly. Julie kept daily tabs on her laptop on what was happening via the local news and media websites, and Dan often came in to sit with me while we perused the online fire maps, trying to figure out what the likely scenarios were.

Somehow, no, not somehow, but through the amazing efforts of the RFS and National Parks and State Forests fire crews, the coastal townships and properties were in the main saved as the fire swept down to the coast. In the end only stopped by running out of things to burn, scorching all right down to the water's edge. In particular, the efforts of the RFS crews were epic and it would be a disservice to call their efforts 'tireless' as they battled well beyond fatigue, well beyond being tired, exhausted, choked on smoke, smeared in ash, and sweltering within their life saving but bloody hot and heavy suits and helmets.

By the 3rd of December, the fire had stopped at the sea, and the coastal townships in the main saved, we felt like we might have 'dodged a bullet'. Yet we knew the fire season had barely begun, and the long-term weather reports could only suggest the chance of any significant rain by late February or early March. The highway north remained closed as fire crews continued to mop up and still smouldering trees were brought down along the road.

But while the fire front had stopped at the coast, its north and south flanks continued to spread slowly. The southern flank soon reached the Kings Highway (which headed west to Canberra) about 14 kilometres away, and we were cut off now, both north and west. The road south remained open, but that wouldn't last for long.

We were in a cycle of weather that seemed to have been locked in for months; hot dry nor'westers for three or four days, then a rapid swing around to a brief, blustery southerly, before perhaps one day of respite with north easterlies. Then the nor'westers swept down again, and each time the fire took off with a vengeance. It had already burned through over 50,000 hectares and along its northern front, some 90 kilometres away, it was now threatening the towns and villages further north along the coast. And it wasn't the only fire burning along the eastern ranges, not by a long shot.

By mid-December it felt like the whole east coast was ablaze, and we watched the nightly news with growing awe and anxiety. We were barely into the fire season and already lives and many homes had been lost. From the size of the areas now burning, it was inconceivable that there could be enough fire fighters to even begin to countenance saving every threatened property. It was equally inconceivable how the women and men of the RFS were still standing, let alone able to drag their sleep-deprived, energy sapped bodies into another battle. In the face of such conflagrations there was no way these fires could be stopped. All that those on the front line could do was turn up at the next life or property threatened, do the best they could, then head off without respite to the next crises situation. I can't help but shake my head even now, thinking about it. Bloody marvels, each and every one of them.

For more than a week beforehand, the RFS and Bureau of Meteorology had been issuing warnings about 'catastrophic' conditions predicted for 31st December. Temperatures were due to soar well into the 40s (approx. 105F) with hot dry westerlies for the day before and leading into New Year's Eve, with a southerly change predicted to head up the coast from mid-morning. From my training and experience fighting fires as a ranger, the words 'wind shift' in the context of wildfires still make my stomach twist in a knot; flight or fight response kicking in, I guess. The problem with wind shifts is that they turn what were more slowly and less fiercely burning fire flanks into far hotter, speedier, and much more dangerous fire fronts. The time you thought you had to get yourself out shrinks from a half-hour to a handful of minutes, and from minutes to mere seconds, if you can make it out at all. It can catch even the most well trained and well prepared.

In preparation for the 31st, Julie, Dan and I began a regime of hosing down the house and the surrounding garden and garden trees. We love our place, but it's a 1970s expanded beach cottage with wood-fibre Hardy-plank walling and a large timber framed and decked front verandah. We've got a small bush reserve behind us and a number of shrubs and trees overhang the fence. A lot of ground 'litter', dead, dry plant matter, had built up on the other side of our old timber fence. I cleared and cut away what I could but could do nothing about my greatest concern, a twelve metre high, crusty old dying black wattle that leaned towards our yard, its main upper branches arching high and well over the fence.

We hooked up two of the garden hoses together so I could hop over the fence and water into the reserve for up to 10 metres, and I paid mind to wet the trees as best I could. Water was precious in the ongoing drought, but not compared to our home and lives. The wetting down wouldn't stop a fire if it started up in the reserve, but it might slow it down enough, if it came to it, to give us time to save the house, or ourselves, if needs be.

On the evening of 30th December, reports had come through that the township of Mogo, about nine kilometres south-west of us along the Princes Highway, had been evacuated as the fire raged towards it. A spur of the main fire further to the west had jumped containment lines and curled down south through the bush to the west of the highway, and when the daily nor'wester blew, it changed course and headed east and straight for Mogo. Wind shifts. Can be a yachter's blessing and a firefighter's curse.

Dan and I sat at the computer that night of the 30th and pulled up the Rural Fire Service fire mapping, and as the outline of the fire appeared, Dan pointed at the screen.

"What's that about?"

On the map, the main front of this southern extension of the fire was at Mogo, and it didn't look good at all for the township. But this wasn't what he was pointing at. Fire mappers try to match the on-screen mapping as accurately as possible, so that anyone viewing the information has the best possible idea of where the fire edges are. But what we were looking at was a bold, elongated, black rectangle extending north of Mogo straight out for two kilometres to the east.

"Looks like the fire has obviously jumped the highway," I replied, "and I'd say it's travelling too rapidly for the mappers to accurately map. If that's the direction it heads tomorrow, we might be in trouble, depending on when the southerly kicks in."

"That's not good."

"No," seemed to cover it.

We went to bed on the 30th, wondering what the next day would bring. One thing we knew it would bring was a southerly wind change, sometime in the morning. If the fire was south of us when it hit...

We were cut off by road, soon to be surrounded by fire. No, whatever tomorrow would bring, it wasn't going to be good.

The phone call the next morning on New Year's Eve would confirm that.

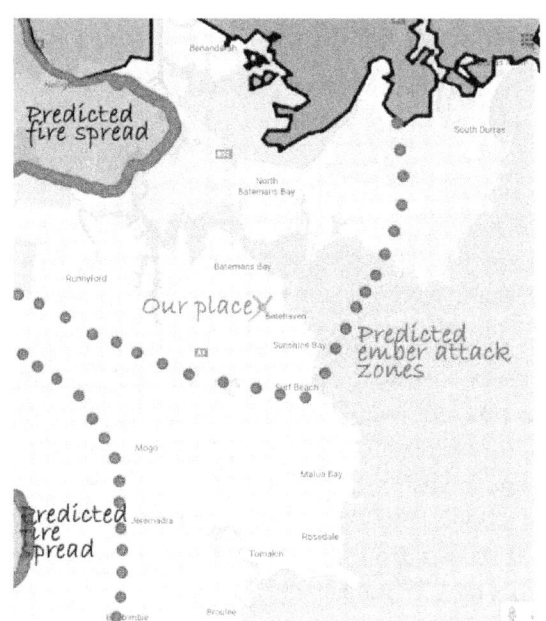

Predicted spread for New Year's Eve

New Year's Eve, 2019. Part 2.
by Mike Cavanagh

After the evacuation phone call from the RFS and a quick morning coffee, Julie began to pack, and I went upstairs and woke Dan. Our plan, as we'd discussed and agreed, was to stay and defend at least until the southerly hit. At that point we would reassess and either stay on or leave immediately.

Our house lies on a south facing slope in a shallow bowl. A curving, low ridge surrounds us, open only towards the south-east, a channel that funnels any southerly winds our way. Today's southerly was expected around lunchtime; forty, fifty kilometres an hour. While we live in a suburban area, there are three linear bush reserves around us, more or less following the ridges and down slope some ways, that adjoin the extensive forests to the south and west. If the fire front swung with the southerly before it reached the coast, we could be surrounded by a ring of fire and cut off from escape. We wanted desperately to defend our quirky little home, but as they say, houses can be rebuilt, people can't.

Around 7:30 a.m. we got another message from the RFS; it was too late to leave. Shelter where we could. An hour later roiling orange smoke rolled across from the ridge to the south-west, spiralling wildly into the sky, driven by the ferocious heat of the fire we couldn't yet see. But we could hear it.

We went out onto the front verandah, scanning the ridge top in the direction of the rushing, snarling growl.

"Is that the noise of the fire?" Julie asked.

"Yep. It's here."

I've heard the sound of a raging fire described as like a jet engine, or a train. Yes, it has some resemblance to these, but in essence the only sound that is like a large, really angry wildfire is the sound of a really angry wildfire. It hits your stomach, your chest, as much as your ears; a deep, threatening growl that seems far too loud, too purposefully destructive, to be anything natural.

Within seconds we could see the flames writhing up and over-topping the trees at the end of the ridge to the south, less than 400 metres away, whipped along by the hot, dry nor'westerly. Majestic eucalypts, twenty-metre-high trees, were mere match sticks now, lighting up one after another within seconds. We couldn't see the houses we knew were there, at the end of Vista Avenue that ran all along the ridge to our west. We could only hope that somehow those houses were not part of the flames.

Then we heard the first explosion, from somewhere over in that direction, and shortly after another, but this time directly west of us. There's no gas pipeline to this region and all gas is delivered by 45kg LPG bottles that are placed against house walls and connected to the appliances inside. I thought the explosions we now heard might be gas bottles, but in really hot, fierce fires, trees explode too. Over the next couple of hours, we continued to hear them intermittently; nerve wracking every time, knowing that if it was a gas bottle, then that house had gone. I still don't know, and I think I don't want to now. Julie organised a woollen blanket to cover our two bottles and we kept them constantly wet, mitigation against the bottles heating to blow point if the fire got too close.

We went back inside, made sure everything was ready to go if needed. Julie took what she could of the things we'd packed down to the carport and packed the cars. If we had to evacuate, we were heading to Corrigans Beach, less than a kilometre away. There was a large open park in front of the beach, and if even more hard pressed, the beach itself to seek safety on. Dan and I went back out into the yard, and the reserve, watering madly whatever we could reach.

What do you take, if you think it might be all you have left come nightfall? We had three vehicles and while we made sure we had what we'd need as a family, water, food, money, we also individually packed what we could, and needed to. I brought down two of my guitars and my two computers; years and years of writing, researching, and recording music on the hard discs I was not going to leave behind. We left the photo albums, knowing we had digital copies on the computers. In the end, we didn't even fill the cars. Somehow in the face of potentially fighting for your life, material things diminished in importance.

Earlier this morning, this fire had been still five kilometres away. Fires invariably settle down over night and take a while to pick up again. It shouldn't be here yet, it couldn't be here, yet here it was.

All morning, from around 6:30 a.m. we'd heard fire brigade sirens, and soon helicopters and fixed wind aircraft flying overhead. One chopper carried a large water bucket, another had a large camera on its undercarriage, mapping the spread, reporting to crews on the ground and back to some central operations point. At least three fire trucks with attendant crews were in the immediate vicinity, their sirens blaring as they raced from threatened home to threatened home. Every now and then we could hear other sirens further off; this was but one of many battles going on that early morning. As the flames took hold at the end of Vista Avenue the water bucket chopper and plane were in constant motion; down to the inlet to pick up water, blessedly only 800 metres away, back to drop it on the fire, then again, and again, and again. A larger plane came over low, dropping pink fire retardant across the ridge and behind it.

Somewhere on the ground, standing between us and the inferno, brave women and men were desperately trying to save homes, lives. As they'd been doing now, virtually non-stop, for weeks, months. All we could do was prepare ourselves and our home, and will them on, to keep fighting; and stay safe themselves. It was something that was drummed into me through fire training for National Parks: don't become a casualty. Don't be a hero. You can't help anyone if you're dead. Stay alive. Stay safe. We hoped they would.

Across the ridge to the south, the fire had moved through the line of trees, leaving them still burning and smoking. We couldn't see where the fire front was now but were thankful that what we'd seen was the flank of the fire. But I've learned to be wary of being 'thankful' in such circumstances; our good fortune so far meant that someone else's fortune was worse, far worse.

We were all back inside pulling the last of the goods we were going to take if needed when we noticed the branches of the palms against the south side of the front verandah were swaying in all directions.

"The southerly's coming," said Julie.

This was the moment we'd known would come. It's one thing to be prepared to stay and defend when the threat is still some way off. When it arrives at your door is a very different matter. I'd told Dan the night before as we sat looking at the fire map, it all depended on where the fire front was when the southerly hit. If the inferno reached the coast beforehand, then the southerly would blow the fire back north, into already burned ground, lessening its potential impact on us. However, if the wind change occurred while the fire front was still raging directly south of us, then our wonderful surrounding bush would go up in mere minutes and we'd be surrounded by fire and fighting not just for the house, but for our lives.

Julie told me later that she knew as soon as she looked out that whatever the fire was doing, wherever it was, was impossible to tell. Bearing down on us, and enveloping the house within seconds, a roiling, mad, orange wall of smoke swept up from the south, blotting out the sky. We could only see

14

about 30 metres through it. Black bits of burned leaves and bark were swirling down.

It took a second or two for my brain to process what I was seeing, then I turned to Julie and Dan and said,

"We're getting out of here."

Without hesitation we were moving, grabbing the few remaining bags, shoving complaining cats into their cages, and heading out the front door to the cars. The southerly was now a roar, the sky blotted out, just this dark, angry, orange smoke now consuming our world.

As we drove away from our quirky, demanding but much-loved home, we had no idea when we might return or what we might come back to when we did.

* * *

We drove through an eerie world of dense, orange smoke, hearing screaming sirens, near and far, and the sound of a helicopter or plane from somewhere above us. Now part of a small convoy of vehicles, we pulled into the beach reserve car park where a man in a hi-vis jacket directed us down to the grassed sandy area at the beach a hundred metres further on. Everywhere was full; of cars, of people sitting staring in their seats, of some walking around, wearing masks or scarves or holding handkerchiefs on their faces. Eyes squinting in the acridity of the smoke, their faces held the same anxious and dazed countenances that I'm sure ours did. The cats in their cages were with me, and their intermittent cries seemed to reflect what I was feeling: what hell on earth had we been condemned to?

Julie and I managed to park near each other, but Dan had been shunted off further back up the car park, onto the verge on Beach Road. I got out and went to check Julie.

"Dan's parked further back towards the road," she said as soon as she wound down the window, loud to be heard over the still blustering southerly. "Could you please go check on him? Here, take this face mask."

"OK, be right back."

I donned the mask and kept my glasses on as some defence against the smoke and sand being whipped up. I found Dan and told him there was some space near where we were and to come down. As his car was packed full, I walked back to the beach and Julie.

We were alive and safe but, along with the other three hundred or so people, disoriented, anxious, helpless. Some folks were walking their dogs, putting water bowls out for them behind their cars. Most people were wearing masks, and a few couples and groups had headed down to wait on the sand. What else could you do? We were all isolated with our fears, but also joined by them, everyone wondering the same thing: do we have a home to go back to?

After an hour, the southerly dropped back to a stiff breeze and the smoke pall eased off to a thick haze. Visibility improved to around 300 metres, and we could see as far as where Beach Road curved up over the low headland south of us. Jules and I were in her car when she said,

"I think we should head back to check on the house."

"I don't think that's a good idea. There's still fire trucks moving around, I don't want to get in the way."

"The smoke has lessened, and a number of cars are leaving. We should go back to check on the house."

Our discussion was interrupted by the scream of sirens and looking across to Beach Road we could see two fire trucks and a support vehicle speeding south, and the sound of another siren from over the ridge between the beach and our place heading in the same direction.

We watched the trucks disappear, wondering, fearful for the lives and homes down that way.

"Michael, we need to go check on our house."

"OK."

Dan offered to stay and mind the cats, so we moved them into his 4WD and Julie and I set off in her car, back to what we hoped was still our home. We drove in silence through the dense, unworldly smoke haze, each in our own thoughts, quietening our own fears, comforted though to be with each other.

As we turned the corner into our street we breathed out, deep, long, letting some of our built-up anxiety go. It was still there. As far as we could tell the RFS had managed to hold the fire at the ridge; from here we could see no houses burned, just the charred remains of the trees along the skyline. Only later would we learn that half a dozen homes had been lost along the ridge and down into the gullies. Julie went inside to grab some things we'd left behind in our rush to leave, and I went back around the house with the hose. I was down the front hosing the roof of the garage when I heard a loud, crackling bang, then a woman's voice screaming, then other voices shouting. About 400 metres away, south, I saw the top of a tall

16

roadside tree raging into flames. I stopped watering and headed back to see Julie.

"A tree's just exploded across the way. We need to get out of here again."

"OK."

We grabbed the odds and ends (including kitty litter for the cats) and bolted back to the car then back to the beach.

So we waited, again, back on the beach. While the tree exploding was disconcerting, we'd seen no signs of a fresh fire line while we'd been back home. We still had reason to be anxious, but less so, finding reassurance that for now, at least, we'd escaped the maw of the beast. But we also knew one stray glowing bit of tree bark could destroy our house as surely as a whole wall of flame, and blackened scraps of leaves and ash were falling steadily.

After an hour or so we could see other cars leaving, people heading back to their homes, hoping their houses were still there. We'd still seen no further sign of a blaze, so when Julie suggested we head back home with Dan, I agreed.

Thankfully our home was still there and we unpacked what we required for the night, leaving some bags in the cars in case we needed to evacuate again. We had no power though and the evening was drawing on, but it was somehow comforting to know a bright summer sun was sinking through a blue sky somewhere above this still angry, smoky world below.

Exhausted, with only candlelight to see by, we went to bed early. Sleep for both of us was fitful at best, and I kept waking during the night with every noise, immediately alert and straining to hear any hint of a fire crackling. None were, thankfully, but each time I was also thankful as I drifted off again; thankful that we had a bed, we had a home, and we had our lives.

* * *

There was more to this fire season before it was over, and we had days on end without power, and food stocks ran short as supermarkets struggled without power. Contacting family was problematic, and we are very grateful to a young girl who had intermittent service and loaned us her mobile so we could text our family back in Wollongong. Our youngest, Sarah, posted on her Facebook page that we were safe; the first news anyone had had for three days.

The next day I went up onto the roof to hose the overlapping flashing where the steep upstairs roof meets the shallow slope of the living room. Black water streamed out, filled with burnt leaves, burnt twigs, bits of charred bark, obviously blown under there when the southerly hit; three buckets worth by the time I'd finished. How had none of this stuff burned the house down? I couldn't help but wonder if that trip back, the one that Julie had insisted on, had helped save the house. I sat on my haunches and gave thanks that it's also the angels, not just the devils, who are in the details. Then I went inside and hugged my wife.

* * *

While tragically 25 lives were lost and 3,500 homes destroyed in Australia over the five long months of this 'Black Summer', more than 9,000 homes and who knows how many lives were saved directly by the efforts of the firefighters. To the Rural Fire Service fire crews, sleep deprived, worn to the bone, staggering from crisis to crisis, and the National Parks and State Forest crews who assisted, in awe and profound gratitude, we have no words but these.

Thank you.

Epilogue

Four days later we had another catastrophic weather day. We had our drill worked out now, and by day's end all was safe, although we had no power. In the early evening a southerly hit, and we heard a thud on the roof. The old wattle out the back had fallen down, over our back fence and onto our bathroom roof. Very little damage though. But we also knew that had the fire hit our reserve on New Year's Eve, this tree would have fallen, burning, onto our house.

We know we have so much to be thankful for. Every day.

Estimated fire spread at end of New Year's Eve

A train journey to remember
by Val Poore

It's hot in Cluj Napoca. Very hot. The mercury's hovering somewhere around 37C in the shade in this beautiful Romanian city. We sit wearily on the station platform with our backs against one of the columns supporting the overhanging roof. Other passengers, mostly young people, sit in circles on the paving, talking animatedly. Meanwhile, they're using anything available to deflect the heat from their faces: magazines, pieces of folded paper, newspapers and even real Spanish-style fans. I'm using a train timetable. It serves the purpose, but not all that effectively.

My partner, Koos, and I chat quietly about the trip we're about to make. We're on a ten-day tour of Transylvania and we're waiting for the train to Timisoara, a journey that will apparently take some four hours. We're supposed to have left at three forty-five, but it's already after four. I muse briefly on the wisdom of our decision to go by rail; we could have hired a car and been halfway there by now.

"I wonder why it's so late," I comment, looking at the schedule. "It must be quite slow if it only gets to Timisoara at eight. It's not all *that* far, is it?"

"It's somewhere around 330 kilometres, I think, so yes, four hours is quite a long time!" Koos agrees.

In our home country, the Netherlands, we're used to main line trains travelling at 160 kph, so we'd normally expect to do this sort of distance in well under three hours.

"Well, I hope it's got air conditioning, anyway," I sigh, wafting the timetable up and down in front of my cheeks.

About half an hour after the expected departure time, our train finally crawls into the station, disgorging dozens of exhausted looking passengers. I'm a bit shocked at the state of the train. This is supposed to be a major inter-city service, but the locomotive and carriages look ancient, as if they've been dragged out of the back of a museum, and a very dusty and dirty museum at that.

We've reserved our seats, so we climb aboard the carriage that bears the number on our tickets and squeeze our way along the passage until we find our compartment. This type of carriage is like something from my childhood. It's old and shabby and the window is so grimy we can't see out of it at all. There's condensation trapped between the double glazing, which adds to the problem, and the opening part at the top is stuck closed. Still, at least we have seats.

When it eventually leaves, the train is forty-five minutes behind schedule, but then Koos tells me it's already come more than five hundred kilometres through the mountains from Iasi on the other side of the country. Is that a reason to forgive it? I suppose so.

We seem to crawl the first hundred and fifty odd kilometres, but the upside is that it's through stunning mountain scenery. We can only see the views by peering out of the sliding window in the passage, taking turns with the other passengers who are also desperate to inhale some fresh air. The poor train lumbers heavily up hills pulled by its old diesel powered (or under powered) locomotive. For me, it's like going back in time. I haven't been on such an old-fashioned train since I left South Africa in 2001.

As might be expected on such an antiquated system, there's no air conditioning. The afternoon temperature is rising, and it's becoming almost unbearable in the close, fetid air of our compartment. If it's 37C outside, it must be well over 40C in the train. The heat thickens the air, making it hard to breathe. Perspiration pours off us and my summer dress clings to my legs and back, but there's nothing we can do except endure it. We take our cue from the young Romanians by using anything we have as fans. My Cluj guidebook is bigger than the timetable and comes in very handy; Koos uses a map of Romania.

To find some relief we spend as much time as possible alternating with our fellow passengers at the windows in the passage. Then someone, a young student type, has the bright idea of opening an outside carriage door to smoke a cigarette. It's a long journey and he's desperate. Some of our compartment companions follow suit and after hesitating only a moment we join them. I'm not a smoker, but the lure of the fresh air is irresistible. I glance at Koos and grin.

"No one at home would believe this," I say, gesturing to the gathering by the open carriage door. Our partners in crime laugh.

"Where are you from?" one of them asks.

"The Netherlands," Koos says.

"Ah, I expect they don't allow this on the trains there," he winks.

"You have great trains in Holland," another young man says, flicking his ash onto the tracks passing beneath us. "Fast and clean; not like this. I've been to Amsterdam. Such a beautiful city."

This illicit activity proves great for contact and conversation and friendships, however ephemeral, are formed. We share stories round the open doorway, laughing at the contrast between our respective countries: the Netherlands, so fresh, modern and efficient, and then Romania, a bit ramshackle and unorthodox but somehow more charming. What also strikes me is how nice these people are and how it takes very little to make real and warm connections, even if we don't know each other's names.

As we turn to go back to our places, a female conductor approaches us along the passage. We all shuffle past her guiltily, but she realises immediately what's been happening. "No comment," is all she says, with a smile. It's too hot for admonishments.

The carriage door remains open, swinging on its hinges and banging intermittently against its frame.

Sitting down again in the sweltering compartment, I realise we've run out of water. Never imagining it would be so hot and take so long, we haven't brought anything like enough with us. My gesture to show Koos my empty bottle is noticed by the girl sitting next to me.

"Have some of mine," she offers. "Here, I've got plenty."

How incredibly kind. I smile and accept gratefully. Once again, the contact leads to more conversation. The girl tells me she's going to Arad, the last stop before Timisoara.

"The diesel train ends there," she says. "The last part of your journey will be much faster as it's electric from there to the end of the line." She smiles as if to comfort me.

After Oradea, the land flattens out and we follow the Hungarian border south to Arad. The train picks up a bit of speed on the level ground, but whereas before we were just plodding slowly through the mountains, now we stop at several villages along the way. I'm fascinated by the stations. They look like private homes and the platforms are just a few short metres of wooden planking near the line. The only things that distinguish them as stations are the name boards and the smartly uniformed station masters standing to attention like soldiers on parade. Most passengers have to climb down from the carriages onto the grass between the tracks and walk to the station yard across the rough terrain. The young people help the older folk over the humps, but there's no official assistance for the elderly or disabled. Clearly, EU regulations haven't reached Romania yet. As for Health and Safety, well, we won't mention that.

By now we have our own club in our compartment: sharing water, snacks and more illicit visits to the open carriage door. The heat has provided the cohesion, and we feel united in endurance. But at least the conversation is lively, and we learn more about our new friends. Four of them are students; the other two work in Cluj and are on weekend trips. Life in Romania is improving now they're in Europe, they say, but there's still a long way to go before they can achieve the same standard of living as we're accustomed to. We listen with interest to their accounts of how things are developing here.

At Arad, where we change from diesel to electric, we lose most of our lovely fellow passengers.

"So nice to have met you," they say with big smiles before leaving the compartment. "Have a great holiday!"

"Keep this," says the girl, handing me the bottle of water. "You'll need it."

Each of them shakes hands with Koos and me on their way out. I find myself beaming with the pleasure of it all, although I'm sad to see them go.

The two remaining passengers keep us entertained for the rest of the trip. They are students at the university in Timisoara, and they tell us stories about their country and their city, of which they are very proud. It's uplifting to hear their enthusiasm and optimism for the future of Romania. Then the discussion takes a new direction into more philosophical areas. One of the pair is studying psychology, but he looks more like a top tennis player than a social sciences student. "If you could have a choice between living inside someone's head for a day, or flying for five minutes a day, which would you choose?" he asks. It's that kind of conversation, both exploratory and fun.

We eventually arrive to a stifling, humid night in Timisoara six hours after leaving Cluj. It's ten thirty, we're two-and-a-half hours late, and it's still around 30C. But apparently this is normal, or so our companions tell us; both the lateness and the temperature.

The trams to our hotel have stopped for the night, so the students lead us to a nearby taxi rank.

"If you catch one outside the station, it will cost twice as much," they say before waving goodbye and disappearing off into the sultry gloom.

Our Romanian travel companions have been so friendly and so full of goodwill I don't think I've ever enjoyed a train ride as much; nor, I admit, have I ever been quite so hot and sticky. But somehow the physical discomfort has contributed to the emotional satisfaction of this unique journey.

"Wow," I say to Koos, pulling my damp dress away from my back and legs. "What a simply amazing trip!"

"Yes," he nods, "truly memorable."

"It was incredible, wasn't it? So much kindness and interest from total strangers. That would never happen at home. Mind you, neither would that train... " I shake my head and laugh.

"That's why travel like this is so good for us," Koos says. "It's such a unifier."

And he's right. It was criminally uncomfortable in that hot, airless compartment, but somehow it brought out the camaraderie in all of us; we were united in our suffering, so to speak, regardless of age, background and nationality.

In fact, despite the awful conditions this train ride has been one of my peak life experiences. We've learnt things about Romania and its people we'd never have discovered by being cocooned in an air-conditioned car. We've shared our lives, albeit briefly, with some lovely, charming and generous individuals, and I wouldn't have missed it for the world.

"Come on," Koos nudges me. "Time to move on to the next phase. Timisoara, here we come!"

And so, gathering ourselves and our bags together, we head for the line of waiting taxis.

Haitian Boat People
by Lally Brown

Back in the 1990s I was living in the Caribbean on Providenciales, an idyllic little island in the Turks and Caicos. This group of rocks and cays nestles at the southern tip of the Bahamas and is administered as an Overseas Territory by the British Government. 150 miles to the south of Providenciales lies the island of Haiti.

During the early years of the Nineties, poverty-stricken Haiti was in political turmoil and the country in crisis. The elected President had been overthrown by the army and fled to the US. There was rioting in the streets, no food, no money and life for the ordinary Haitian became so unbearable that they were taking to boats in their hundreds and trying to escape to the Bahamas or Cuba to start new lives.

Providenciales was also the island of choice for some of the refugees, and out of a total population of 5,000 people we had 3,000 Haitians. They were good workers and contributed well to the life on the island, but it was estimated that two-thirds were 'illegals' with no work permit who lived in the bush at the northern end of the island. Providenciales was happy to have these extra workers, but as the crisis worsened in Haiti and more and more 'boat people' arrived, the little island could not cope. We had one doctor, no Red Cross, only a small clinic and no hospital and we simply did not have the facilities needed.

It was decided to build a refugee camp on the main island of Grand Turk and any 'illegals' who arrived on Provo, or who were 'rounded up' and found not to have a valid work permit, were to be flown across to Grand Turk and 'processed' to check if they were political or economic refugees for either return to Haiti or granted refugee status. Every person in authority was given an official Government leaflet entitled *'Instructions in case of a Haitian Emergency'*.

I remember one incident vividly. The wind was blowing from the south and the sea was calm. We knew this was the perfect combination for the boat people to attempt the crossing to Cuba or the Bahamas. Sure enough, UK authorities received information from US Intelligence that several boats were preparing to sail from the north coast of Haiti.

One week later a small boat was spotted heading for Providenciales. The helicopter pilot identified it as a Haitian fishing vessel and estimated there were forty to fifty people on board. It was escorted to south dock where we were waiting.

The little fishing boat was no more than forty-five feet long. They were standing on the deck, packed like sardines, no room to move, or sit. There was a central mast roughly hewn from a tree trunk and painted a faded peppermint green. A large, homemade sail was draped across the wooden deck, black patched with brown pieces and sewn by hand with green twine. The boom was a long and twisting piece of tree which bent first this way and then that, but followed a sufficiently straight line to be pressed into service as a boom. Two huge rough-cut flat paddles lay on the deck, carved in haste but adequate. She was an old maid. Somehow, she had been jollied, mended, bandaged, and pushed into service for this one last heroic trip. They had set off from Haiti seven days earlier, hoping to reach Nassau. But the wind had blown them off course and they had run out of water after three days. A small cone-shaped cooking grill rested above the hold, and charcoal chunks nestled underneath.

One hundred and six dehydrated, malnourished, exhausted, and weak men, women and children were helped ashore from this tiny fishing boat. It was an astonishing sight. We simply could not believe the little boat could hold so many people. Fifty clung to the main deck area and another fifty-six were discovered cramped together in the dark and smelly hold. It was a miracle no-one had died, and it was a miracle the vessel had crossed 150 miles of ocean without sinking. Did this vessel actually bring to safety one hundred and six people? After seven days at sea, three with no water, I would have to say 'impossible', unless I had seen it for myself.

'Fast Eddy' a local restaurant owner joined us on the dock. He had heard about the arrival of the Haitians and donated a burger and a glass of coke to each Haitian. A welcome meal, although perhaps not the most appropriate nutritional snack for the starving refugees. A bus quickly transported the 106 Haitians to the airport to be flown to the island of Grand Turk where a refugee camp had already been prepared. A local charter company made their newest plane available, a sixteen-seater 'Dash' which was redecorated with plastic sheets and forty refugees at a time were squeezed in and airlifted to Grand Turk.

Grand Turk was expecting the refugees and quickly had them at their makeshift camp – part of an abandoned US Army Base. They received medical and health checks, decent food and a bed until the authorities could decide what to do next.

Only one of the refugees had a passport. After two weeks on Grand Turk they all asked to be returned to Haiti saying they did not want political asylum in the Turks and Caicos Islands. They were immediately flown back to Haiti on specially chartered flights.

There was no doubt in our minds they would try again for Cuba or Nassau. The popular choice for the fleeing Haitians was the US base in Cuba, which housed 14,000 refugees, and it was a growing humanitarian problem for the United States.

There was a rumour circulating at the time that the Military Government in Haiti was actually encouraging the boat people to exodus the island in large armadas in order to put pressure on the US Government and the UN to give the island economic aid. But I couldn't possibly comment!

Haitian refugee boat

If I may...
by Ronald Mackay

"If I may say so, Mrs Mackay, your invoice entries are..."

Try as she might, Pearl was unable to read the company secretary's expression.

After three weeks with this London firm, Mr Chadwick's social niceties, suspenseful pauses and unfinished sentences were still unsettling to Pearl. It was as if he constantly struggled to avoid giving offence. In her previous post at home in Scotland, she'd welcomed the frank evaluation of her work and thereby had learned much and expanded her book-keeping skills. Here, she noticed that the women in the office – little more than girls, to her and much in need of guidance – sheltered their unnecessary errors behind his reluctance to be forthright.

"Your entries are neat and accurate, Mrs Mackay." He stopped, watching this Scottish woman who puzzled him. This recently arrived bookkeeper who added columns in her head just to make sure that the mechanical calculator had not erred.

Do I hear a reservation in his compliment; need I now dread a 'but...'? Pearl held her breath.

Since her first day, she had been conscious that the figures entered into her daybook were under scrutiny, so she double and sometimes triple-checked them, a silent finger running up and down the columns. As company secretary, Mr Chadwick had every right. The girls revelled in trying to alarm her in the colourful way they had with their rhyming slang.

One Jaffa Cake and you'll be Jeramiahed. A right Peter Crouch is our Mr Chadwick!

She understood that Mr Chadwick didn't care for mistakes (*Jaffa Cakes*) and, as he was such a grouch (*Peter Crouch*) careless errors could easily result in her being fired (*Jeramiahed*).

Their giggled warnings, however, didn't overly alarm Pearl. *Despite their causal errors, the five of them are still employed, aren't they? Didn't this suggest he was less fierce than they suggested?*

She suspected, rather, that they cradled the hope that this middle-aged newcomer with the peculiar accent might be dismissed and replaced by someone closer in age to them; a person more able to join in their carefree banter, less focused on work, on precision. For Pearl, the finance department was that vital centre of a business where fun could be permitted, but only if it did not interfere with scrupulous attention to detail. *These girls have their priorities awry and there's nobody to guide them.*

"Thank you, Mr Chadwick, neat, legible and accurate is how I learned to keep the daybook in Scotland." He failed to respond, so she added, "Accuracy is everything in book-keeping."

His continued silence suggested that, after the mollient compliment, he was now trying, uneasily, to summon up the courage to break the bad news that she had to go. She was saddened. She wanted to stay with this company. Mr Chadwick's English formality pleased her, told her that they shared a common respect for the traditionally strict demands surrounding the recording of revenues and expenditures. His reluctance to wield authority, however, served neither him nor his employees well. That aside, she'd come to enjoy the banter of the girls despite being unable, so far, to join in as freely as she would have liked to. London was their home. Cockneys born and bred, with quick minds and ready wit. They had such potential! If rightly channelled, it would add a much-needed accuracy to their work, justifying the gaiety.

I want to keep this job. Another week of searching will simply cripple my budget. Vivian is already carrying more than her share of the expenses. Cripple her budget it might, but she knew it would never, ever, force her back north of the Firth of Tay.

"I'd like to ask you a question or perhaps two, if I may, Mrs Mackay. Then I may make a suggestion."

Mrs Mackay nodded. "Of course." *Why the constant 'if I may' when he has the right to demand? How will he camouflage the suggestion that I look for work elsewhere?*

"For over a decade you worked for a contractor."

Pearl nodded.

"What kind of contract work?"

"We bid on small public works mainly. Road construction to improve physical access to rural properties owned by municipalities."

"Ah, civil engineering projects?"

Civil engineering sounded much too grandiose for the work of Horsburgh Murray, so Pearl expanded. "Our crew did the road excavation, added and compacted the base, graded, drained, levelled and finally rolled the asphalt."

28

"How many of you worked in the accounts office?"

"Me, alone. I handled the correspondence, kept the books and made up the wages weekly." *I can't read what he's thinking.* So, she continued. "Mr Murray showed me everything during my first year. Then, he left me to get on with it."

"By yourself?" Mr Chadwick's expression didn't alter, but his cultured voice rose.

Is he disappointed by a business so small that the office could be run by one middle-aged woman with no formal qualifications? She braced herself for the dismissal that she imagined coming, the suggestion that she seek employment with a firm more in keeping with her limited experience than with a long-established company trading triumphantly across the Commonwealth from the heart of London.

In the silence, Pearl allowed her mind to wander.

* * *

She was back under the protection of a sweet autumn day in 1948, in the friendship of the maturing sun beneath the tree that provided *Homebank* with cooking apples. Daughter and mother sharing together, in that love-affirming way the task of coring windfalls as they had done autumn after autumn, throughout the lengthy rumble of distant war. Daughter from mother absorbed the counter-intuitive wisdom that silence can offer the most certain way to share the things that matter.

Mother broke the companionable silence.

"Pearl, my Lass, you're no happy." Empathy the more easily voiced in the quiet cadence of her birth.

Pearl's continued silence was confirmation enough. Neither needed to name the source of the unhappiness – a husband who had returned from the front, an undeclared war raging inside, a war waged unrelentingly on his wife and off-spring.

In the evening sky, gathering swallows swooped and twittered.

"Listen to me, my Lass. Ye've nae need to stick to a road that'll lead but deeper into grief. As He has warned us, *a crushed spirit dries up the bones*."

Pearl felt her mother's hand clasp hers, inhaled the aroma of bruised apples. Their combined warmth spread to her very heart and seemed, oddly, to hone and relieve the aching that was in it at one and the same time.

"There's a better road, my Lass. When the time's right, ye'll find the courage to take it."

Comforted, Pearl raised her eyes to receive the embrace offered in her mother's.

They finished coring the windfalls.

* * *

Sixteen years it had taken her to find that better road, and by then she had buried her mother, though never as much as a day passed that her heart did not weep from the missing of her.

Pearl had tried to bridge the gulf that yawned between her and George, attempts that were met with anger or vilification. Any common ground they might once have shared was consumed in the rage he nursed. To shield herself from such a wasteland, she reared and nurtured her children, read joyfully for them and for herself, and escaped into the luxury of imagined worlds offered, for a few short months each year, by the Repertory Theatre.

She learned that people wedded to the error of their own bitterness cannot bear reconciliation. So, shouldering her burden, she had educated her three children in what it means to live honestly in the world: that we must strive to accept a legacy that we did not create and to amend it only once we have understood it. From their earliest years, she introduced them to the consolation of daily praise. She raised them to be compassionate, independent, and self-reliant.

She'd seen all three of them set out on careers before boarding that train to London together with the loyal daughter who had chosen to accompany her, bearing a one-way third-class ticket, £200, and a light suitcase – the material wealth rescued from 25 years of a burdened life.

No resentment did she carry for she had learned that gratitude is a must if we are to experience joy and despite all, Pearl was grateful. She was grateful for the true home she had known in the modestly genteel west-end of Dundee, for caring parents and for a boisterous houseful of siblings who were friends and family rolled into one. She was grateful for her mother's move to the village of Coupar Angus, where the pace of life accompanied the seasons and the cycle of growth and harvest on the surrounding farms. In an inexpressible way she was grateful for the years of War that had intermittently separated her from a callous husband, allowing her to mother children with thoughtful love in the company of one who had done the same for her.

Pearl had been taught to avoid the mistake of assuming that the good things of life are ours by right. When they came her way by chance combined with the result of her own efforts, she was grateful.

It was in this frame of mind that she and Vivian had alighted from the train in Kings Cross Station and taken temporary lodgings in Sussex Gardens near Lancaster Gate tube station.

As a dental nurse, Vivian had accepted a prearranged position in a practice with three dentists and started work immediately, as the breadwinner. Lacking such an approved training that provided a recognized professional standing, Pearl was initially reliant on her willing daughter but wholly resolved to accept whatever work her assorted experience might fit her for.

To her unexpected delight, on her first full day in London, she had discovered that her comfort with numbers, lined columns and financial records ideally fitted her to serve as a bookkeeper. She'd jumped at the first offer the employment agency made her as the only employee in the small import business owned by a resentful refugee from the Russian Civil War. His failed daily attempts to humiliate her for whatever she did or did not do added to his rancour.

Inured to petty reproach, Pearl sealed her being off from the guttural carping until she and Vivian had found an apartment, a church to worship in and a community to embrace and be embraced into.

The urbane and gentle streets of St. John's Wood where wisteria and ivy-clad walls spoke of an age in which dignity and authority declared itself unashamedly while seeking to honour the community provided a sense of belonging.

She joined an early morning Saturday class to explore London's historical past. With infectious enthusiasm, the guide was able to gratify his group with sights and the sounds, and to flesh out the city's narrative with anecdotes from a history hitherto unknown to her. Thanks to these peaceful walking tours, the City's history arose slowly around her like a great cathedral, defining a place where everything connected and where everything possessed a significance that made making London's friendship a welcome adventure. London quickly became her spiritual home.

Then, comfortably established and confident that she had found the lost haven for which she had been searching, Pearl turned her back on the guttural entrepreneur from South Russia and stepped into Mr Chadwick's finance department with its promise of comforts and puzzles to be mastered.

In London, Pearl relished that it was sufficient just to *be*. Together, she and Vivian began to thrive.

Yes indeed, I would like to have kept this job, but if it is not to be, I will search further.

* * *

"By yourself, Mrs Mackay?" Mr Chadwick's repetition extinguished Pearl's reverie.

"By myself, Mr Chadwick. I kept the daybook, then transferred the entries from the daybook into the ledger. In the first quarter of the year, I drew up the trial balance in preparation for the chartered accountant's annual audit."

Mr Chadwick raised his eyebrows. "If I may be so bold as to inquire, might there have been anything else you undertook?"

Was he suggesting her workload had been overly light or was he gently mocking?

"I also prepared the documents for the tenders we submitted."

He accepted this in silence.

These English gentlemen can be so hard to read, but I'm learning.

"When Mr Murray inherited the company, he shrank it to satisfy his own needs. He preferred fishing and shooting to work, so long as the business covered essential expenses, he was satisfied. The company stayed small and my workload was manageable."

"Thank you, Mrs Mackay, for your candid answers to my questions."

Now he's ready to suggest I move on. Pearl steeled herself for the inevitable but satisfied that she was beginning to grasp the Englishman's oblique manner of conversing. Such knowledge would prepare her for the next job interview.

Mr Chadwick drew a deep breath. "I am an accountant, Mrs Mackay, comfortable with financial statements but less so with managing..." He gestured ruefully towards the giggling girls.

Pearl heard Mr Chadwick's admission with alarm. *Did I speak my thoughts about his weakness aloud? Has he the power to read my mind?*

"I need an assistant willing to organise the work of this office, to supervise the staff so that the work gets done to the standard required. You, Mrs Mackay, possess the qualities to provide that assistance."

Pearl had seldom reflected on the skills she had mastered while raising a family and resolving the daily challenges faced by a business whose owner preferred casting flies or shooting pheasants to scheduling the maintenance of earth-moving equipment. *Do I?* She asked herself for the first time and immediately knew the answer.

"You possess the personality, the discipline, the practical knowledge of keeping track of financial transactions. Moreover, if you will permit me, your age and demeanour permit you the authority necessary to supervise and mentor a capable but overly playful staff."

'If you will permit me.' There he goes again!

They both somehow seemed to know, without her even answering, that she accepted the offer.

"Oh, and Mrs Mackay. One last thing, if I may?"

And again, she thought. *'If I may.'* But now she appreciated the diffidence as the respect due from a conservative gentleman to a middle-aged conservative woman.

"When you use the calculating machine, you may rely on its accuracy, odd as that must appear to you."

As Pearl walked from the tube station, she turned into Loundoun Road for the sole joy of allowing her soul to be renewed by the fragrant purple wisteria that clad the symmetrical brick walls of Arnold House School. Then she retraced her steps to Grove End Road and to the flat so that Vivian could share her good news. She gave silent thanks for Mr Chadwick's offer, confident that she could fulfil his expectations. *I can bring the girls round to a more sober work ethic without halting their fun,* she reflected. *I'm not convinced, however, that I can abandon my mental check on the accuracy of the mechanical calculator.*

Pearl breathed deeply and smiled. For the first time in many years, she was truly happy.

Mum (Pearl Mackay Sword)

When the Going Gets Tough
– The Tough Need Laughter
by Tina Wagner Mattern

In these uncertain times, when each day can, and often does, bring worrisome news, I try to remind myself to focus on all the blessings in my life instead of the negative things that may be going on in the world. Mark Twain, inarguably one of the world's greatest humorists, once said, "The human race has one really effective weapon, and that's laughter." Let me just add to that, "Love makes the world go round, but laughter makes the trip so much more fun."

With that reasoning in mind, I have to say that a relationship with humor as one of the foundational underpinnings is one sure way to get through tough times. This has definitely been the case in my marriage; I have been with my best (and weirdest) friend for almost 40 years now. His name is Fred; he is 63 years old. His inner child, Freddie, however, is about 8. It is this character who keeps our marriage fresh and endlessly entertaining. He keeps me laughing even in those times when the world feels like it's spinning out of control.

I'll give you a for instance: You know how boring grocery shopping is? Not with Freddie. When he comes with me, this is usually how it goes: We walk into the market and Freddie says, "I wanna push the cart!"

"Why?"

"I'm the man."

"So, you're the man. What does that—?"

"I have qualifications. I have muscles."

"I guess you could call them that. But what does that—?"

"AND I have hair on my chest."

"You have hair on about 90% of your body, Freddie. You're more bear than you are man. It still doesn't explain why you should—"

"I am the man and I push the cart."

I can see that I'm never going to come out on top of this ridiculous dispute.

"Okay. Whatever." I let him push the cart but each time I try to put something in; he runs about 10 feet ahead. This continues until I am literally chasing him up and down the aisles and the other shoppers are laughing out loud. A woman who's been watching this whole debacle laughs. "I have one of those at home," she says. "Of course, mine is 3." I shrug, smiling. "He seemed so normal when I met him."

I'm 6 years older than Fred, which delights Freddie no end, giving him an opportunity to spout endless old lady wisecracks. For instance, I walked into the kitchen one winter day, rubbing my arms. "I'm cold!" I said. He turned around and perfectly deadpan replied, "Well, honey, you've just been alive a really long time."

He ducked just in time to miss the sponge flying at his head.

When our kids were little and Fred and I found ourselves short of alone time, we started taking a nightly bath together after the kids were safely in bed and asleep. It was here that my husband and I discussed our days, talked about the children and dreamed of upcoming vacations. It was also here that Freddie liked to come out and play.

"Quit splashing me, Freddie!"

"I'm helpin!"

"You're not helping anything, you're just splashing me!"

"I'm helpin you rinse."

"I haven't even washed yet."

"Whatever!" This would usually be followed by him winding up his toy frogman and setting it loose in my direction.

After one particular bath, I was trying to pull up my pajama bottoms while Freddie was trying equally hard to tie the legs in a knot. Exasperated, I shouted, "Knock it off!" He ran out of the room before I could throw something at him but then from the bedroom I heard, "Ha-ha!" Peeking warily out the door to see what he was up to, I said, "Ha-ha, what?" In his best Bart Simpson voice Freddie said, "Ha-ha, you're married to *me*!"

I couldn't help it, I laughed. Later, however, I regretted encouraging him because as we were watching TV, I had one of my routine hot flashes. When I reached for the little portable fan I keep by my recliner, Freddie suddenly turned to me with a devilish gleam in his eye. "You look cold!" he announced.

"No, I'm not," I said.

"Seriously, you do! I need to help you!" Grabbing a big fluffy blanket, he wrapped me securely in it, and then draped himself over me like a 180-pound octopus. "There! Isn't that better?"

I called him a name I can't use here.

Over the years of being married to this one-man circus, I've learned some things to expect/not-be surprised-by/avoid at all costs where Freddie's concerned:

- All toothpicks and/or sticks found while on a walk are pokey-things.
- A bra, which is not where I would expect to find it, will likely turn up repurposed as earmuffs.
- Never, ever precede Freddie up a flight of stairs.
- Hugs, no matter how tenderly they begin, will usually turn into wedgies. (He just can't help himself.)
- Wearing a sweater that zips down the front is (according to Freddie) just asking for trouble.
- At bedtime, my pillow will often disappear just before I lay my head down.

By now I'm sure you're rolling your eyes and thinking this might be the weirdest relationship you've heard of so far, and that I might have the patience of a saint. Possibly, but that's not to say that I'm entirely innocent either. Being around Freddie will more times than not inspire my own inner 8-year-old to come out and play. *She* is rarely at a loss for words. For instance: Freddie lost most of his hair by the time he was 40, so now (as payback for all the old lady jokes), when he says, "I need a haircut," I smile sweetly and ask, "Which one?"

So, with all that said, I hope that all of you out there who feel like the world is in chaos right now, has at least one bonefide character in their life, someone who keeps things interesting, who can be depended upon to lighten their spirit with laughter. I count myself blessed because I'm married to mine.

Dreams, Drama and Dolphins
by Amy Bovaird

In 1997, I moved to the United Arab Emirates (the UAE). Living in the Middle East fit in with my plan of seeing more of the world—while I could. For the past decade, I had struggled with a progressive eye condition, stealing my vision a little at a time. Though I was hush-hush about my sight loss back then, my "mission" was to live out my travel dreams in as many ways as possible.

I arrived on a wave of international English teachers brought in to educate the locals. This small country had only been a nation for twenty-six years, and its citizens were coming to the forefront of change. The president, His Highness Sheikh Zayed bin Sultan Al Nahyan, looked to technology to accomplish this.

I lived in Ras Al Khaimah (better known as RAK), the northernmost of the seven emirates. The culture revolved around camels, goats and sheep, thousands of date palm varieties, traditional shipbuilding and, at one time, pearl diving. RAK had everything I wanted—the mountains, the desert and the sea.

In contrast to the rural setting, my job focused on teaching Business English to Emirati women. The Higher Colleges of Technology (HCT), seen as a cutting-edge higher-level institution with branches in each emirate, gave me a front-row seat to change. For RAK, sending women into the workplace broke new ground, though it focused on schools or hospitals. One cultural line would never be crossed: HCT was divided into two separate campuses, one for the men and one for the women.

I loved teaching and living in the UAE not only because I could witness change first-hand but also because it threw me into a smorgasbord of international cultures. It gave me the best of all worlds.

I lucked out with Roger, our laid-back Canadian director of both campuses in RAK. He provided ample opportunity to immerse ourselves in culture around the Arabian Gulf.

One Thursday morning—the first day of the weekend in the Middle East— Roger drew our joint faculty meeting to a close. He ran a hand through his sparse white hair and loosened the collar of his short-sleeved polo shirt, sending out the message that, like us, he'd had enough of being cooped up.

At nearly seven foot and lanky, Roger looked unassuming but had no trouble leading because we saw him as "one of us." A man of few words, he held our monthly staff meetings to a minimum—strictly administrative details. Today, his blue eyes gleamed as he touted yet another cultural activity for us, an excursion on a dhow—a traditional handcrafted wooden boat typical of the Arabian Gulf.

"Now don't everyone sign up at once. Let the new staff go if you've been there before." Roger smiled. "Take advantage of the opportunity to explore the region. Several of you have four-wheel drives. If you don't, find someone who does and pool a ride with them."

Used to problem-solving for rides since I could no longer see well enough to drive, I recalled the librarian and her husband owned a 4x4. They might agree to take me.

Roger continued, "We're headed to Dibba, where we'll rent the dhow for the day. Be sure to take your swimming suits as we'll drop anchor. You can swim, snorkel or even scuba dive at the site. If you're lucky," his face crinkled into a lopsided smile, "you'll be able view a dolphin or two before we're through."

I caught my breath. *Dolphins! Oh, I wanted to go.*

As the meeting broke up, I found the librarian.

"Dibba is our Omani neighbor," Janna explained, "and is only a few hours from RAK."

"That's great," I enthused, "I hope I can catch a ride."

My name made the list and so did Janna and her husband, John, so I was *in*.

The next morning, I strained to see the headlights of the promised vehicle. A quick *toot-toot* let me know my friends had arrived.

At the roundabout, we met more drivers. Pre-dawn darkness shrouded the landscape as our 3-vehicle caravan headed toward Dibba.

While we jounced along, I reveled in the chance to glimpse Oman and Musandam Peninsula. I knew little more than Iran was to the north and the Gulf of Oman, to the south. We were headed to the Strait of Hormuz.

Janna turned to me. "Did you know the Strait of Hormuz is a strategically important sea passage on the Persian Gulf? It's the only channel to the sea. Navy vessels from several different countries travel through. If you pay attention, you may see one."

"Wow, no, I didn't know that." Riding with a librarian had its benefits.

"Navy vessels, blah! I'd much rather spot a frolicking dolphin in the waves," John interjected. He pulled the vehicle to a stop. "This is us." He exited to consult with the other drivers while the rest of us stayed put. Outside the window, I saw a large commercial dock and a few more faculty members.

Momentarily, John returned, and we all headed for the wharf.

A few men carried ice chests filled with food and beverages. Roger and his wife, Maggie, brought on their scuba gear. I carried only my backpack with my beach towel, sandals and a book. I hadn't decided if I would swim or not.

Roger motioned us forward. Our entourage fanned out as we stepped onto the flat wooden planks that made up the crude bed of our dhow. To one side was an airy cabin framework, and the other side came to a point that tipped up. The cabin was brightly painted, for tourists I supposed. The damp wood attested to the dhow's seaworthiness. These beams would never be in port long enough to dry out.

As we prepared for our journey, I took a seat on the starboard side. The water gently lapped at the ship. *How heavenly the sun feels on my bare arms. I will never tire of tropical climates.* Leaning my head against the side of the boat, I closed my eyes.

Janna gave my shoulder a small shake. "Amy, you're missing some spectacular scenery."

I fought to open my eyes. Even under the protection of prescription sunglasses, the sun seemed to burn a hole through the lenses and force them shut. They were so sensitive to light. Once my pupils adjusted, I could see again. A small price to pay for a day of adventure.

I watched the huge rock mountains as they paraded into view on both sides of the dhow. The mountain range with its sharp angular lines appeared as if drawn with bold strokes of a child's marker. The caves inside resembled heavily penciled dots.

We stopped near Lima Rock, where divers and snorkelers prepared their gear. It looked deep. "Watch out for the current," warned a Kiwi diver. He pointed to surprisingly rough waters at a distance. "Stay on this side of the boat."

A snorkeler gave him the thumbs up and replied, "Right, matey," which prompted me to guess at his nationality as I watched several more faculty members enter the water. Was he an Aussie, Kiwi or Brit?

It hadn't taken me long to pick up the expat lingo delineating our international colleagues. *Kiwi* – from New Zealand. *Aussie* – Australian. *Scot* and *Brit seemed* easy enough nationalities to match. Tougher were sorting out the myriad of Arab and Eastern countries on the staff.

While we sunbathed, I brought up the topic with a few faculty members I recognized from the Men's college. "There's Egyptian, Iraqi, Syrian, Pakistani, Bangladeshi, Indian... and the nationalities break down to staff members within various countries. South India is different from North India... It's so fascinating."

The time passed pleasantly. Topics changed, and I became better acquainted with my colleagues. The dhow rocked pleasantly, and I couldn't stop smiling. Here I was hanging out in a native-made boat chitchatting with people hailing from half a world away.

I felt as if were filled with champagne and it bubbled out of me in effortless laughter. I wanted to hold on to this feeling forever. Every country I lived and taught in had a unique national culture and beauty that enhanced my life. But never had I taken a job where so many different nationalities converged. We even had a name: expatriate. Expat. And I was *one of them*. We talked about different foods, travel, politics and local Emirati values.

The Maths teacher said, "You'll have to go to Liwa, a real desert gem near Abu Dhabi," She yawned. "Guess it's about time for a dip." She stood up and motioned to her Economics sidekick, then turned to me, "Ya' comin' in, Aims?"

'Aims.' I liked that. It fit me. I was aiming for my best life.

I glanced at the water and considered. The sun made me lethargic. "Nah, I don't think so. Not right now."

After they left, my mind wandered. So many new terms, even among the western staff—small differences, such as how they referred to Math, as Maths, the European way. I never tired of discovering these subtle language differences.

I started to read a few pages of my book before turning it over and napping.

"Someone is tugging on our emergency line!" The tense voice woke me from my slumber.

I sat up, and like others, turned my attention to the water. In a short period of time, the sky had turned dark, and the wind had kicked up a notch. Of course, no surprise to me, I didn't see much on the water. Tiny blobs. For all I knew, they could be seals. I looked on as the New Zealander and a few of the other men jumped to action.

"Two females," another confirmed. He moved with lightning speed toward the rope. "We'll pull 'em up here." His voice infused calm. The rescue took only minutes, and the women were pulled aboard.

"Than–Thank you for the leg up," the first one said, ashen. "That current is wicked."

The second woman coughed up seawater. Her eyes darted from person to person without recognition. "Um, who… are you?"

After a few startled looks back and forth, someone laughed and the Kiwi, who had become our spokesperson while Roger was out scuba diving, grinned. "You're safe, matey, but you're on the wrong dhow, are ya'?"

The two women blinked, sputtered and coughed as it became apparent that is exactly what had happened. As red as their faces were from embarrassment, the women did not test the water again.

With the rescue behind us, the mood turned lighter. When the sun came out, I must have closed my eyes and drifted off again. I woke up and contemplated fishing a bottle of water out of the cooler when the Kiwi cried out, "There's someone else out there on the rocks and they're tugging on the line!"

One of the divers said, "It's Roger and his wife."

Fear darted through me. *Oh no! Not Roger and Maggie.*

The current must have carried them past the boat. It was likely even stronger in deeper water.

An anxious murmur ran through the group. Cocky members grew silent. Talk became terse. Several staff hung over the side, trying to catch a glimpse of where the couple could be stranded.

Janna had said the Strait led to the open sea. My stomach clenched. *It'll be okay.* Of course, I expected the rescue to go as quickly as the first one had gone, but it didn't.

Squinting, I tried again to locate them, but the wind whipped the water around in high waves, and I couldn't see either one. The sky darkened even more and suddenly huge drops of rain pelted our dhow. Those in the water clambered aboard and offered their help in the crisis.

We'll bring 'em in. We have to.

"The line is broken!" someone shouted.

With a flurry of movement, the crew tied on a thicker rope to the dhow.

I heard cursing. But still no rescue. Hushed voices spoke. Tense words passed between the men and women on board. Precious minutes ticked away.

"They're drifting away from the rocks and into the sea!"

"What are we waiting for?" shouted the Business instructor.

"It's been about thirty minutes since the first tug on the distress line. What the...? We need to catch up to 'em."

The two dhow drivers kicked the motor into high gear. They shouted back and forth in Arabic. Had they spotted Roger and Maggie?

The boat circled out in wide arcs and drew close enough that a diver could throw out the thicker rope. He then jumped into the churning water and swam toward them. We all waited with bated breath.

The staff crowded by the side of the ship, preventing me from seeing what was going on. *With my vision loss and my own tendency to tumble into danger, this rescue business is something I should probably know more about.* If I had gone out on the water, it could well *be* me. No time to ponder. The charged atmosphere and shouts turned triumphant. They were rescued!

Maggie came first. Then Roger. Everyone on board burst into cheers.

Roger smiled, gave a half-wave and muttered, "Helluva current out there."

Someone wrapped a towel around Maggie and handed one to Roger. An exchange of tales flew between the two parties as they hashed out the harrowing event. Roger said, "We wondered for a while if you saw us."

"We'd a pulled ya' in sooner but the damn line broke–"

Maggie interrupted, "Thank God, it did! As we drifted farther out, that rope wrapped around my wrist. It kept getting tighter and tighter, like a vise. It hurt like hell. The rope was cutting off my circulation. I thought I might lose my hand."

The crowd leaned in to examine her wrist, blocking off my view of it. Would she need a doctor's care?

"I'd have rather gone out to sea than go through that agony." She shuddered.

"Glad that didn't happen." Roger slid an arm around Maggie's waist. His eyes, which seemed a paler blue, still held gentle humor.

When we didn't turn around, I figured the injury didn't require immediate medical attention. Then I heard Maggie laugh. What a seasoned traveler she was! Any woman who could handle being washed out to sea, survive almost losing a hand, and laugh afterwards was a trooper.

Someone handed them cans of beer.

Roger took a long draught. "I need this about now." He still wore his wet suit and flippers but looked more relaxed, seated on the rough planks toward the center of the dhow. He suddenly noticed the two strangers on board.

"We're the first rescue," one woman volunteered. "We got back on the wrong dhow."

Roger chuckled. "Don't blame ya' there." He shook his head and motioned to the cooler. "Have a cold one on the HCT. You deserve it."

Now that everyone was safe, we all turned to the great comforter in any crisis—food.

Raindrops still bombarded us, but with everyone on board, the sound felt oddly comforting. I finished eating and downed another bottle of water. With my legs warmed by my towel, I observed my colleagues. So many new faces, my *mates* now. They carried on with jokes and jibes as if nothing had happened. How different it could have been. A peril on the sea. Relief flooded through me that it ended well.

"Ya' look like you're havin' a good time," Roger said with a smile as he brushed by me.

I grinned back, thrilled that after all my director had gone through, he still noticed how others around him felt. That's how Roger was.

In late afternoon, with the ship gently bobbing in the placid water once again, someone called out, "Looky there, matey, after two rescues on this long crazy day, what do ya' know, the sun's shining and we got our dolphins."

Everyone grabbed their cell phones to photograph them. It was the perfect cap to the drama we had experienced earlier.

While my sight loss keeps me from seeing the world perfectly, that day I saw my fill of drama. The blurry dreams I had when I set out to teach in the Emirates were becoming clearer. That indomitable spirit of love of life, travel and language connected me to my expatriate colleagues not only in concrete ways but also in intangible ways that are best felt by the heart.

Over the years, that dhow became a symbol of strength. When I feel as if the current is too strong to handle the waves of my sight loss and the undertow threatens my safety, I remember the handcrafted dhow of the Arabian Gulf and how its seaworthiness proved a refuge.

The vessel never stayed tied to its dock. The sea beckoned and it answered. Can I be as strong as the ship, uniquely designed by my Master? I strive to welcome others, reminding them while the waters may be rough, some of life's best moments can be found on the waves.

Our dhow

Dog Days in Uruguay
by Syd Blackwell

BEFORE THE BEGINNING

To tell the story of dog days in Uruguay, we must first go back to Canada, to Revelstoke, British Columbia, where I was an innkeeper. When I opened my inn in May 1995, I had two old dogs. I lost the first one before Christmas and the second two years later. I missed my dogs, and I missed the daily walks. However, life as an innkeeper was certainly easier without dogs.

Three years later, at a Chamber of Commerce social function, I spoke with two women who remarked that my dogs must have passed as they no longer saw me on dog walks. I confirmed their thoughts and added that it was easier to do my work without dogs. They countered with, "so you wouldn't own another dog", and I conceded that perhaps I would, if a small, house-broken dog was in desperate need.

Apparently, one of the local veterinarians was standing behind me.

A few days after the event, I got Simon. He was a shiatzu/terrier cross, nearly two, abused, and unwanted. He was not delivered by the vet's office, but by a surly girl in an old truck. I opened the passenger door and Simon, who actually did not have any name at that time, snarled to let me know he would bite me if I tried to touch him. The girl offered to drag him into my inn if I would accept him. I accepted the dog, declined her assistance, and asked her to pass me his leash. We made an uneasy passage to the inn. We also had a lengthy adjustment time, but Simon became a great inn dog.

However, this is not a story of the inn, or even how I met my wife, Gundy, also an accommodation provider in Revelstoke, or why and how we ended up in Uruguay in 2007. This is a story of our dogs in Uruguay, and Simon was the first.

AND IN THE BEGINNING

Gundy arrived in Uruguay a full seven months ahead of me. Her business had sold easily. Mine was difficult. At the beginning of October, I put Simon into a carrier cage at the airport in Vancouver. It would be an incredibly stressful, twenty-five-hour journey before we would finally get to Montevideo.

After I boarded the flight, I was pleasantly surprised when an air hostess stopped by my seat to assure me Simon had been loaded on the plane for our first leg to Chicago. We were scheduled for a brief stop-over before continuing to Washington, where Simon and I would change planes for South America.

However, we did not leave Chicago as scheduled, sitting for a long time on the runway. No explanation was given. As the time passed, our transfer window shortened. By the time we flew, it was obvious that we would only make the flight to Buenos Aires with some luck and assistance. I called an air hostess, explained my situation, and, as I was seated at the very back of a full plane, asked if there was some way I could deplane before everyone else. She said yes, they would make an announcement.

No announcement ever came. I was one of the last to get off and had no idea what was happening with Simon. I ran to the departure gate for the next flight, but when I arrived, the area was empty. One of the last staff persons left said the plane was loaded and ready to pull out and I was too late. I frantically explained I was travelling with a dog and had no knowledge where the dog was due to the late arrival from Chicago. She called the plane and learned Simon had indeed been transferred to the plane. With this information, the gate was re-opened, and I was allowed to board. I had no idea if my six suitcases had also been successfully transferred, but at least I knew that Simon and I would get to Buenos Aires together.

Things did not get easier in Argentina. Although I learned in-flight my bags had been loaded, I also learned that we would be required to "enter" Argentina to have Simon inspected before we would be allowed to make the short flight to Montevideo. This required passing through customs with six huge suitcases and a dog carrier cage, with stern instructions that the dog must not be allowed from his cage, racing (as best one can do when moving a mountain) to the other end of the airport, standing in line to check-in for the flight to Uruguay, and then having an Argentinian veterinarian inspect Simon.

Well, there never was an inspection. After most passengers had been checked in, a vet finally did show up, but she did not look at Simon or the papers attached to his cage. However, she did collect the US$250 inspection fee and leave me with insufficient time to make the Uruguay flight. An understanding airline employee took care of us, helping us to get around security through an airline personnel gate, and we made our flight.

Of course, I expected more problems as I approached Uruguayan customs control with the six large suitcases and a dog in a cage. The customs officer asked how long I was staying in Uruguay. I answered, forever. He said welcome to Uruguay. Nothing was opened or inspected, not even Simon's papers.

Simon heard Gundy's voice as soon as we came out the doors, and he started barking. We headed straight out the front door and opened the cage. Simon had a very long pee before going crazy with both of us.

A NEW LIFE

I was nearly 61 and Simon was 9. Gundy had worked hard to prepare our home, Casa Inspiración, for our arrival, but it would take some time for Simon and me to settle in. Neither of us had ever lived in a different country.

A month later, I wrote this poem.

BORN IN THE YEAR OF THE DOG

My human life experience
Without the dogs would not make sense;
My first was Pat who guarded me,
In baby buggy 'neath a tree;

A Cocker Spaniel black and white,
Through childhood rarely out of sight;
He shared his life for fifteen years;
His death, my loss, brought teenage tears;

My friends back then had dogs I knew,
Like Sandy, Spot and Skipper too;
Or Boozer who found thinking hard,
And Sparky, a great Saint Bernard;

Two decades through my adulthood,
I owned no dog; nor thought I would;
Shared dogs of colleagues that I met;
Just one stray cat, my only pet;

But when the dog next door had pups,
My life would change, and quite abrupt;
We brought one home to live with us;
Soft fur and wiggles, our Rufus;

He did what all bad puppies do,
He peed, he pooped, found things to chew;
The bad things lessened as he grew,
And Rufus somehow changed to Boo;

All brown and black with golden fleck,
With breeds too many to detect;
He was quite smart, our strong-willed Boo;
He trained us well 'til nearly two;

But circumstance would alter all;
A dog in need; we heard her call;
And Didi now joined with we three;
We were a two-dog family;

She cringed in fear of people's wrath;
Her life before no easy path;
But our love overcame her fears;
It was the start of her good years;

When groomed she was a true beauty;
Australian Shepherd and Collie;
All mottled grey with black and white;
Her eyes now shone from inner light;

Insep'rable were she and Boo;
Shared food, shared walks, and things dogs do;
He was the leader of the pair;
It is dog's way; she did not care;

But sometimes when they were at play,
She showed her teeth and got her way;
Together through ten years up north;
They spent their final years down south;

When they were gone, my wife was too;
A dog-less life I lived anew;
My business consumed all my time;
Without a dog I was just fine;

Or so I thought, until one day
The local vet chanced hear me say,
I might consider one again,
If homeless, small, and housebroken;

A week had passed, I'm sure not more;
A small black dog came to my door;
Abused and needing loving care,
I called him Simon, then and there;

Adjustment to life at my inn,
A battle that I had to win,
Took quite some time; but when I did,
His love suppressed, no longer hid;

I was his daddy; he my son;
My life now bright; he'd brought the sun;
He shared with me all guests who came;
I gave him love; he'd eased my pain;

A lady came into my life;
I did not know she'd be my wife;
But Simon sensed right from the start,
That she belonged; she'd won my heart;

Eventually we became three,
And Simon was as pleased as me;
We walked, we biked, we canoed too;
It was a good life that we knew;

My business changed; old ladies came;
For Simon 'twas a brand-new game;
He won them over with great ease,
To feed him lots of dog cookies;

As always happens, life moves on;
Her business sold, my wife was gone
To Uruguay; to our new home;
We only talked by telephone;

I thought we'd join her in no time,
But months went by before I'd find
Us both on plane to Uruguay;
Our lives to live in a new way;

Now here in Uruguay we sit;
Our house, our pool, all bright sunlit;
As Gundy knits; I write poetry;
And Simon keeps us company;

How many years he's yet to live
Is something only God can give;
But I am sure my life will be,
Ne'er long without a dog with me.

02/11/07

POSTSCRIPT

It has been nearly thirteen years since I wrote that poem. We lost Simon two years later, but we had already acquired Kiya. Kiya was eventually joined in turn by Jordan, Leah, Sofia and Lorena. All were rescue dogs. All five continue to live with us. However, we are not adopting any more dogs, so one day *Dog Days in Uruguay* will be completed. Before that time, perhaps I will have an opportunity to share some more bits from the intervening years. I hope you enjoyed the start. Comments welcomed.

(A later excerpt from *Dog Days in Uruguay*, entitled *Of Rat and Dogs – The Winter Blues* appeared in Robert Fear's *40 Memorable Life Experiences: 2020 Edition*)

Casa Inspiración – 2007

The Kindness of Strangers
by Robyn Boswell

It's a trip I've done hundreds of times over the years. This particular time I'd spent a cold winter's weekend with my friends in Auckland and was heading home to Whangarei, about two and half hours away. Not very far up the road, my car, which was a little old but had always been totally reliable, suddenly began to lose power. I only just managed to pull over onto a wide area on the side of the road as it completely ground to a halt. I tried to restart it; the motor just stubbornly and noisily turned over and over but refused to fire, and I started to panic a little. Mobile phones were still a dream which would be realised in the future, so I was stuck with no means of communication. Since it was a Sunday afternoon and it's a busy road, cars were streaming past, so I lifted the bonnet and stood alongside it, a lone woman, trying to look helpless, feeling sure someone would stop to help me.

I know the area well. The only house anywhere within sight had a huge sign on the gate – "Beware, dogs bite". I'd always thought they must have been on their third or fourth generation of dogs since the sign had been there so long, but there was no way I wanted to test its veracity. I was also very reluctant to leave my car in such an obvious place. Apart from the fact it was full of my belongings, it was old enough to look abandoned. I could imagine coming back to find it stripped of my gear, its wheels and other useful parts.

More and more cars streamed past, yet none stopped as I felt more hopeless and unsure of what to do. Eventually a zappy little red sports car pulled up alongside. The young man who levered himself out of the tiny interior was an Adonis in tight white jeans. He looked the part of the sexy prince riding to the rescue of the desperate princess. I could imagine his portrait splashed across the gaudy cover of a romantic novel. He opened his mouth to speak and his smooth French accent completed the picture. The illusion was shattered when I quickly discovered that his mechanical knowledge was even less than my paltry comprehension of what's under the bonnet of a car. He was a nice guy, though, and did his best to be useful. He was on his way past the little village of Puhoi a few kilometres inland and said he'd call in at the local garage on the way past to see if they were still open at that time on a Sunday. Naively, I thought that meant he would drive the three or four minutes back to let me know. As time went on, it became obvious that he must have found them closed and gone on his way. I was in a further quandary; if I left to try to find help, maybe he would return.

Evening was almost upon me and a slight, cold drizzle began. No one would miss me until work the next morning, because I lived alone. I was facing the unpleasant and scary prospect of a freezing night sitting in my car on the side of the road.

Suddenly two cars pulled up together alongside, making me a little uneasy. A man hopped out of one, followed by a veritable tribe of children. It was a family – with eight children, they needed two cars! The man quickly fiddled around in the engine of my car and soon had the engine running whilst his wife stood and chatted to me. However, he discovered that it was a problem with the starter motor and he couldn't fix it properly without the tools he had at home. He was very reluctant for me to head out on the road again without the proper repairs. These complete strangers, without even consulting each other, invited me to follow them home so he could effect the necessary repairs.

We travelled in convoy, me in the middle, way up into the hills along a road that got narrower and narrower until it was little more than a dirt track with grass growing in the middle. I had never even realised that such rugged hills existed that close to the road that I had driven so many times. Perched high on one of the steep hillsides was a jumble of shipping containers. There was no sign of any houses and I soon realised this was the home we were heading for. There was obviously very little money, but a great deal of love in this family.

The children tumbled out of the cars and within a couple of minutes they and their mother had swept me inside, whilst their Dad started work on the repairs to my car. There was an amazingly large living area, with the walls festooned with colourful woven floor rugs to keep the warmth in. Within a few minutes some of the kids had lit a roaring fire, whilst others helped their Mum to serve a meal of thick homemade soup, with lashings of fresh bread and butter. I felt as though I had known them for years and was just included as part of the family as we laughed and chatted our way through a very hearty, warming meal. The love they had for each other was palpable.

Their Dad had managed to repair the starter and my car was seemingly back to normal. I offered to pay for the work he had done, which would have cost me a considerable amount at a garage, but he wouldn't hear of it. They were worried about me having to drive so far at that time on a cold, wet night with a car that might not be reliable and strongly urged me to stay the night, offering me a warm bed. I very reluctantly had to refuse, as I needed to get to work the next day. They tried to change my mind, then when they realised I just couldn't do it, they sat down and worked out how long it would take me to get to each of the three little towns with a phone box that I would need to drive through on the way home and insisted that I phone them from each place. If they didn't hear from me within a reasonable time, they would get in their car and come searching for me. They were prepared to drive for an hour or more should that be necessary. Their generosity was incredible. Luckily, I made it home, stopping every so often to phone them, with no more drama.

Now every time I pass that stretch of road, I remember a wonderful family who were willing to share the little that they had with a distressed stranger. I will never forget how they made me feel like a long-lost friend, welcomed me into their home without any misgivings, got my car up and running and helped me get safely home.

He aha te mea nui o te ao? He tangata! He tangata! He tangata!

What is the most important thing in the world?
It is people! It is people! It is people!

High Tea in Colonial Williamsburg
by Patricia Steele

I was twenty minutes early for my birthday event with my friend, Barbara, and I was relieved to see no snow on the ground. The anticipation for Christmas was in the air, as only that holiday season can create, like dewdrops on a rose petal at dawn. Walking for the first time on the cobblestone driveway leading into the foyer of the Williamsburg Inn, I was mesmerized by the mystical beauty. I knew a little of the Inn's history: Since opening in 1937, the Inn had reflected the vision of benefactor John D. Rockefeller Jr. to provide the experience of staying at a comfortable Virginia estate with gracious décor that retained the graceful elegance of the period-designed rooms.

The lobby and entrance room invited with colonial luxury. However, the valet's whispered welcome ruptured my preconceived idea that the Williamsburg Inn was only for the rich. With his smile, my misconceptions dissolved. Tall leaded-glass windows sparkled from the sunlight above richly burnished wooden floors. Colonial-period wool carpet greeted me and dulled the loud click of my heels. Oil paintings decorated the walls; portraits of men in historical clothing, each with one hand hidden beneath their vested coats, pierced me with their dark eyes. The eyes, however, could not match the depth and feeling that shone out of the portraits of the women. Stilled, I studied each one closely, and I wondered at the youth and serenity that their faces revealed. The clothing, of course, was Colonial England; their smiles were poignant, and a quiet mystery was reflected in their eyes.

The Christmas tree just inside the foyer nearly touched the ceiling, standing regally in front of the tall, glass windows. The decorations were both exquisite and simple, if that is possible. Sparkling lights wrapped around each limb of the evergreen from tip to stalk, and everything took my breath away. Plopping down in a striped satin chair near a Colonial table, I focused my camera and Christmas joy sang in my soul as I snapped to my heart's content.

While waiting for Barbara to arrive, my eyes flicked around the room to inhale the beauty surrounding me. The watchful eyes in the oil portraits followed me as I walked past the wondrous Christmas tree and into the Inn's gift shop where I found unique and simple decorations of Colonial Williamsburg.

When I walked into the main artery of the Inn, I found the entrance to the tea room, which was still and quiet, almost dark inside. I saw women in long dresses scurrying around with glass-filled trays and Champagne bottles. The white linen-covered tables told me they might expect the Queen any minute. The luscious smells drifted and enticed to add to my anticipation, and my heart sped up.

Where was Barbara? She was never late. I tapped my fingers along the door frame, wondering at her delay. Peeking into the room again, I saw linen napkins at each place setting and empty Champagne glasses waiting to hold the bubbly. I had no idea what the solid silver piece was, placed at the right of the knife. I saw beautiful, white china embossed with green trailing leaves amid red birds flitting around the perimeter and in the centers. I strained to look closer at the slightly oblong dish, about seven by nine inches in length. I was, of course, impatient for our High Tea to begin for my birthday celebration.

I glanced at my watch again. Ten minutes to three. Where was Barbara? Glancing around, I saw a short glass-walled hallway leading into an elegant dining room where several four-foot brass planters stood on the floor snug against the windows. Each moss-filled box held three breathtakingly beautiful Amaryllis in full bloom in various shades of red, white or candy-stripes. They were intertwined amid green ivy that spilled over the sides of their pots. A festive spirit dominated the area; one side of the hallway abutted the Golden Horseshoe Golf Course where my husband had chased balls as a young boy. The other side was a brick-walled, private courtyard with small rocks littering the ground around various, neatly planted shrubs. I paused. I wanted to open the double-glass doors and walk down the stone steps into solitude; to pretend I lived in those Colonial times. But I had a birthday date and could almost taste the bubbles of Champagne on the tip of my tongue.

Five minutes later, Barbara had still not arrived. When I found the ladies' restroom, I was immediately transported backwards in time. I was in the Queen's castle in London. Subtle brass edged the wood framed, wallpapered walls. But what smacked of opulence inside the entrance were the oyster-colored linen napkins tiered across the marble countertop. No paper towels. No blow-dry machines. I moved toward the corridor again and saw a wicker basket waiting for the patron's used linen. When I left the room, its luxury wafted after me.

Three o'clock. And still no Barbara. I returned to the entrance to the tea room and sat on a tufted bench beneath a painting of a young woman with vivid blue eyes. I watched ladies enter the tea room in pairs. Time passed slowly. My nerves began to twitch as I stared at scarlet Poinsettias below a large, ornate mirror on the wall across from me. I glanced at the mirror and nearly jumped when the woman's intense face stared back at me mesmerizingly.

And at that moment, Barbara rushed around the corner in a beautiful Christmas sweater. Her eyes lit up when she saw me, as if she'd found a long-lost friend. She had been waiting near the wondrous Christmas tree in the foyer while I'd loitered in the halls around the tea room. After a good laugh and a bigger hug, we joined other ladies inside the tea room and chose satin, upholstered chairs by a window.

We felt like royalty. All at once, the scent of apples and cinnamon mixed with evergreen struck me. I inhaled the aromas and prepared for the thrill of my first English high tea. Delighted with the elaborate table setting, we raised our eyebrows when our server poured golden, bubbling Champagne into our flutes. As we tapped each other's glasses and sipped, we were offered several tiny tea sandwiches. No crusts, of course. We chose one of each that included cucumbers and ham sandwiched between white and brown bread, white asparagus and salmon pâté. Everything melted in our mouths.

Tea time. I chose Strawberry Green Tea, Barb chose Berry Tea. Ornate china teapots were steaming hot, and I learned the silver tools I'd seen earlier were tea-leaf strainers. I held the tiny, four-inch handle and placed the strainer on top of my China cup before slowly pouring water through it. Then, I replaced it in its silver holder to catch the loose water that might still drip. I felt like a princess. Barb and I couldn't stop smiling. What next?

A large silver tray filled with Colonial sweets was delivered as my empty Champagne glass was whisked away. Oh! What to choose? The server held it aloft and beckoned us to choose. In a heartbeat, I had a strawberry tart sprinkled with shaved chocolate, a chocolate cake roll stuffed with sweet, whipped cream and a sugar-speckled cream puff on my delicate china plate.

The chairs embraced us. The tea warmed us. The sweets made us swoon. And then, a woman in period costume stood beside us.

"Good afternoon, ladies. My name's Maddie." She shook our hands. She began a conversation as if she was living in 1773 during the Boston Tea Party.

"I apologize for intruding. I wish you both a Merry Christmas," she said as she raised her eyebrows and glanced into our tea cups. "I'm very glad to see you fine ladies are drinking Liberty Teas since the new exportation taxes will soon cut the importation of real tea leaves from England. My brother works in Philadelphia, you see, and he has regaled me with the current news on the upcoming protests against the British East India Company."

Barbara and I smiled at her, bemused with her costume, her voice and the conversation.

"It threatens to decimate small shops so there's a revolt just around the corner, you see." Conspiratorially, she whispered, "I hope you learn to enjoy the Liberty Teas since that will probably be all we can drink after March."

"What exactly is Liberty Tea?" I asked.

"Well, milady. They are teas made from Chamomile, Mint, Peppermint, and the like. Not like real tea leaves at all. I fear I will never get used to them, but we must. We must fight this excessive exportation tax and fight we will." Her eyes sparkled with a fervent promise.

Barbara and I nodded serenely. What could we say to that? Reading about the Boston Tea Party in our history books was quite different from hearing a woman discuss it like it was happening any moment. As we lifted our Liberty Tea to our lips, the woman curtsied, nodded goodbye with a smile and headed toward the next table of ladies. We watched the ladies drink from their tea cups with raised pinky fingers and then forking the food on their little plates.

We turned back to our tea. Fresh hot scones! Could I possibly eat any more? We looked at the two gems that sat on top of plates painted with green vines and red birds. Beside them, a server placed a two-part dish between us filled with lemon curd and clotted cream. A pot of fresh raspberry jam nearly spilled over from the center of the table.

We ate everything.

High Tea at the Williamsburg Inn was amazing; a memorable birthday since it was on December 14, my day. I will always remember the beautiful, glittering tree sprinkled with lights and welcoming spirit as I walked into the door. Friendliness at the Inn seemed to be the epitome of Colonial Williamsburg that day. Oh, and by the way, Barbara had been waiting by the Christmas tree while I was wandering, worried... because I had told her I would meet her there. Forgetfulness comes with each birthday, I'm told.

Williamsburg Inn

Elspeth
by Andrew Klein

Sometimes, when we least expect it, the Universe tosses us a glimpse of the destiny we will face. There are things that happen in life that allow us to share experiences with those who we had no idea we would meet. I actually believe that people are here to help each other get through certain trials. I'm not sure if I was helping her, or she was aiding me, but I know that we got past a rough time together and that this story still touches me in ways I can never disremember.

Geno and I had recently returned to Israel from Egypt, and he decided to stay there to be close to his girl, who worked on a kibbutz not far from Tel Aviv. We had spent the last six months traveling together, and this being my first time overseas, I couldn't help but feel a bit apprehensive to split up and go on without him. We said goodbye, and I took a ferry from Haifa to Athens. I had only $60 in my pocket but enjoyed the knowledge that $500 more sat in an account waiting in the Greek capital at the American Express office. The trip was cold, rainy, and somewhat lonely. I took the days to reflect on the past six months and wonder what the near future had in hand for me.

I arrived in Athens on a Sunday morning and took the train into town to book a small room in a pensione just off Omonia Square. Early the next day I set out for the American Express office whistling a tune of happiness, but that tune turned quite gloomy as I found my money had been there over 30 days and so it was sent back to Los Angeles. My mother, knowing I was on my way up north, then shipped the $500 to Oslo, Norway. I was stuck, as the office in Oslo reported that the money would not be available until the following Monday.

Grief-stricken, I wandered off to have a coffee and ponder my next move. I had, in my possession, about $48 and a one-way ticket from London to New York. I knew that a flight was double what I had and found that the train was even more including the ferry over the Channel. I was wary of hitchhiking and thought it might take forever to go the 1600 miles. I visited a bus company that had the trip for $52, and when they heard me moan, they recommended the 'Magic Bus'. The Magic Bus was a budget mode of transportation used by the traveling youth of Europe. I found the place and inquired about the price. It was $45 to Oslo and took four days with many stops. Including food, that would be impossible for me. I settled on a $27 three-day trip to Amsterdam and decided I could hitch the rest of the way in a day or two. I purchased the ticket, went outside, and sat on a bench near a cafe.

As fate would have it, at that very moment, I looked over to see a young girl sitting at a table at the cafe and literally 'crying over spilled milk'. She was frustrated with something and it was affecting her judgment as she poured cream into her coffee. I walked over and gently took the creamer from her and said, 'let me help you' and poured it into the cup. She smiled and looked down, obviously embarrassed not only by her ineptness but also her currently unbalanced mental state, as she wiped away her tears. She was very polite and invited me to sit. She had a lovely British accent, which I incorrectly pegged as Cornish. She was, instead, from a small town near Brighton. Her hair was cut short, and she had a distinctly unkempt look about her. She wore shorts, sandals and a tank top that read, 'Ouzo-12 me-0'. She was braless and I could not help but notice her ample sidewalls. She was not a true beauty, but there was something quite attractive about her.

I ordered a Fanta Blue (non-carbonated) and we began to tell our individual stories. I told her about Geno, and our recent split, and how I was now on my own with very little resources to speak of. I explained that I needed to get to Norway to receive the monies needed to continue my trip and then get me back home. I also told her that I intended to take the cheapest way there, which I understood to be on the Magic Bus (later jokingly called the 'Tragic Bus'), and that's why I was at the travel agent next door. She, on the other hand, was shy at first, nodding in understanding of my travails, and saying very little.

When I finished and took a sip of my drink, she took the opportunity to begin opening up and sharing her own story. She started her trip alone, but quickly met up with some other Brits and headed south to the Riviera. In France, she met a man whom she fell in love with. She stayed in Nice while the others went off to Italy. After a week she found out the man was married and took off for Rimini, on the Italian Adriatic Sea. There, she drowned her grief in Peroni and met a Scottish girl she traveled with, all the way to Crete. In Crete, her friend fell for a local winemaker and she left for a week in Santorini, where she began to run low on money and decided it was time to start home. A ferry strike, which lasted only a week, kept her a bit longer on Mykonos, and she just made it back to Athens with a mere £35 in her fanny pack. We laughed as we realized we were pretty much in the same boat. I paid the bill, and we went next door to get her a seat on the bus with me to Amsterdam, only hers went on to Bruges and included a ferry to England and a bus to Brighton. The problem was it cost £22, and she was now virtually penniless.

She was staying at a cheap place off Syntagma Square, and it was decided that I would fetch my things and move to her location. The owner of the pensione was really nice and gave us a deal to stay on the roof. We dined that night on tomato and feta sandwiches and afterward walked up to the Acropolis. It was quite lovely, all lit up that evening. As we walked back through Plaka, we came across a 'busker' playing songs on his guitar and singing. He was quite good, and we stayed to listen for a while. We went back to our rooftop and laid out our sleeping bags. We talked for hours, and I realized why I was so strangely attracted to her. She told me she loved sports, travel, academics and dreamed of one day having a family. As she went on, I concluded that she was a lot like me. We finally fell asleep, feeling safe and content in our friendship.

The next day we shopped for our trip north. We were leaving at 9 a.m. the following morning. We bought pita bread, tomatoes, water and fruit. We were nearly broke, but somehow happy. That night we stayed on the roof eating giant spanikopita and washing them down with cokes. I had purchased a bottle of ouzo for the trip, but it never made it that far, as the stars were so bright, and we so excited, it seemed only natural that we should celebrate our last night in Athens.

The next morning, we climbed aboard the Magic Bus North and took two seats in the back. The bus filled up quickly and by 9:15 we pulled away. I thought of Geno, my friends in Norway, and our current situation. I held just $19 in my pocket. I watched as Elspeth stared out the window. We were so much alike that I knew she was thinking similar things, only she had but £2 to her name. Still, we turned and smiled at each other, happy to be on our way. At lunch, we ate from our supplies, and dinner we bought at an overpriced roadside joint. Some of the travelers complained that the places the driver stopped at were too expensive. We were sure the driver got a kickback from the restaurant owners. That night we talked with others on the bus and had drinks with our seat neighbors. We slept a few hours and awoke in Yugoslavia.

The Adriatic coastline is rugged but beautiful. The rocks and cliffs form a sharp contrast to the blue of the sea. By the time we got to northern Italy, we were nearly out of food. We drove slowly through the mountains and by evening, were in Switzerland. It was so expensive there, and I commented that we should have bought more food in Greece where it was cheaper. Elspeth used her last money to buy water, and I got us a sandwich to share. Late that night, the bus stopped for a break just outside of Bern. We went into the rest stop just to stretch our legs. We looked at the menu prices and they were outrageous. $4 for a coffee, it made us laugh. We sat down on a bench to wait for the others to eat. We were hungry and Elspeth said she could go for a nice cup of Swiss hot chocolate and a biscuit. We sat there dreaming of food when I looked over to see a strange man walking by. The moment I saw him all time seemed to slow. I could hear his shoes clicking on the floor, and Elspeth breathing a sigh. He wore a wide-brimmed dark hat, sunglasses at night, a full length, black Aussie Dry-as-a-bone drover and carried a cane. He glanced over at us and glided by without a word. As he passed, he dropped a piece of paper. No, it was money! I watched as it slowly fell to earth, like a feather. It moved through the air, back and forth, effortlessly, until it settled softly on the ground nearby.

Time switched back to normal. I grabbed the bill and looked up to see no sign of the strange man in the drover. I looked all over for him but could not find him. He had disappeared, vanished, poof, gone. I returned to Elspeth and showed her the note. It was ten Swiss francs, enough to buy her a hot cocoa and a box of cookies. On the bus, as we traveled on, we joked that the man was an angel, or maybe a member of some secret society who helps broke travelers. In any case, we were content sharing our lucky bonanza. Elspeth happily fell asleep on my shoulder as we passed into France.

In the morning we stopped for coffee and finished our cookies. We drove on to Belgium and by noon we were at the docks near Bruges. The bus stopped to let Elspeth off. She acted as if it was no big deal. A peck on my cheek, and off she went. I had slipped a couple of dollars into her pocket the night before, and as she walked away, I knew she would make it home. She never did look back as the bus pulled away. Later that afternoon, I arrived in Amsterdam. How I got to Oslo, retrieved my money, saw my friends, and made it back home is a story for another day, but I will never forget Elspeth, my kindred spirit.

Still the English Teacher
by Patty Sisco

Before I became a school counselor, I was an English teacher for ninth through twelfth grade. When I graduated high school in the 60s, career choices were limited for daughters of working-class parents: I could be a nurse (I hated the sight of blood); a secretary (boring – and those typewriter keys ruined my nails); or a teacher (OK, I had some good teachers. I liked school. That sounded good). Having few options was both good and bad. I didn't have to slog through a lot of research exploring all the marvelous opportunities the world offered me, because the world didn't offer me much. It's no coincidence that many of my girlfriends also went to college and became teachers. Consequently, our country's schools have burst at the seams with female Boomer teachers for decades, and I was happy to be among them. Unfortunately, though, a subsequent teacher shortage has ensued, as most college grads today would rather drive a nail through their big toes than face a classroom overloaded with teens whose undeveloped frontal lobes, unrelenting hormones, and devotion to electronic devices supersede even the slightest inclination to read *Moby Dick* for fun.

I cruised along at North Texas State University, majoring in English with teacher certification, and in three and a half years I was a fully certified secondary instructor of English and French in the state of Texas. That's right... French. I minored in French in Texas, where Spanish is overtaking English at warp speed. Fortunately, though, nobody ever asked me to teach French. Trying to communicate with Parisians when I traveled there a few years after graduation convinced me that I could probably teach Calculus just as expertly, even though I barely got through Algebra 2.

Imparting knowledge to 130 or so teens a day is NEVER boring, so, as one who has never tolerated the humdrum, I took to teaching like a rat to a nibble of cheddar. I ate it up. I loved thinking of unique ways to lure my unwitting students into the delicious web of literature and writing. However, teen scholars in my 70s classrooms were in many ways very different from those I encountered in the late 80s, when I went back to teaching English following a stint as a junior high counselor, and then a stay-at-home mom. In the 70s, a call home got quick results if a student even thought about misbehaving, so discipline wasn't a huge issue for me then, though I was only five years older than my students when I started teaching. In 1985, when I returned to the classroom, I was shocked at the change in my students' attitudes over the next five and a half years. I taught juniors and seniors, some in advanced English, who differed dramatically from my former students. They seemed to be less interested in school, less interested in reading, and more interested in MTV and voicing their opinions openly. Or was I the one who had changed? Whatever it was, my knack for running a disciplined and orderly classroom had completely exited my toolbox, taking with it my punctilious bookkeeping skills.

Part of the reason, I'm sure, for my rather frazzled approach was that this time around I had three kids at home, and advanced high school English was so demanding, it was all I could do to stay a step ahead of my students, who now had cable TV and video games in their repertoire of entertainment options, rendering Wordsworth irrelevant. Aside from working harder to create engaging, stimulating lessons, I took home mounds of essays and tests to grade. Focusing on the need to produce writers who could compose a coherent paragraph, I made my job ten times harder for myself by requiring my students to keep a daily journal that I always graded shortly before the end of each grading period. I would post a usually mundane topic on the board every day for students to expound upon while I took care of a few housekeeping chores at the beginning of the class period. Most of the students dawdled and groaned about putting their thoughts on paper, but a few were really into it. Every six weeks I carried those bulky spiral notebooks home in gigantic containers, terror and dread accompanying me as I eyeballed the looming grading deadline that still haunts me. Even today I have occasional dreams that I have postponed all my grading, my dining room table collapsing under mounds of papers and notebooks, when I suddenly realize that grades are due in an hour, and I haven't entered a single grade in my gradebook.

I had a love-hate relationship with those journals. They had taken on a life of their own. I wanted to read and comment on everything my students wrote, but there simply weren't enough hours in a day to do that. Most wrote about typical teen concerns – boyfriends, sports, after-school jobs, parents' lack of understanding or outright stupidity, friendships, extracurricular activities, and so on. Most of the students wrote pretty mundane stuff, considering their journals a chore. It was easy to skim over their narratives. Some of them, though, were so surprisingly forthright and emotional that the counselor in me was drawn to the compelling stories that were filled with anger, fear, sadness, elation, sincerity.

I was sad for Allison, a slightly overweight introvert, who wrote pages and pages filled with loneliness and longing for a boy I knew she'd never even talk to; proud for David, an immigrant whose work ethic and desire to go to college were paying off in scholarship offers; and I laughed out loud at Bert's hilariously clever quips, even though I knew his parents' recent divorce was gnawing at him. But I was worried sick about Jeff. I gathered from his journal hints that his mother was alcoholic and usually absent, and indeed his sporadic attendance reflected a lack of parental supervision. What I gradually learned about him, through his very nebulous narrative, was that he was meeting well-to-do older men who were using him for sex for a short period of time and then tossing him aside. He would meet them in parks and other popular gathering places, having no idea who they were, frequently going home with them. Occasionally, he would miss a few days of school and write later that he had accompanied an older man on a luxurious vacation where he had consumed so much alcohol and/or cocaine, he had crashed for a few days afterward till he had sobered up. This was at the height of the AIDS epidemic, and I was terrified for him. He was dreadfully conflicted. He knew his behavior was extremely risky, but the draw of money and excitement continued to pull him in.

At first, his journal entries had been vague, dropping clues he hoped I would put together. His accounts became explicit, though, after I wrote in his journal, "Jeff, I am worried about you. I'm here if you want to talk." Obviously, he needed someone to confide in, but I felt so out of my league, I was frustrated that I didn't know how to help. This was a time when gay teachers were afraid to come out of the closet, and even though I knew some of my colleagues were gay, there was no way I would have approached them for advice. Then one day, I asked him to stay after school to talk about his abysmal English grade, not because he wasn't smart, but because he was seldom in class. I told him I was worried about these encounters with strangers, that I wanted him to know that I cared, and I asked if there was anything I could do to stop him on this path to destruction. He made it clear that his mother had no idea of his activities, and that even if she had known, she wouldn't have cared. He assured me that he was very careful, and that he wanted to stop, but these men paid attention to him and made him feel important. And then, not long afterward, he simply quit going to school. A few years later, to my surprise, he called me at school, wanting me to know he had finally realized how risky his behavior was and had gotten his GED, had a good job, was attending college classes, and that he had been living with a partner near his own age, in a stable relationship, for over a year.

"And (I hesitated) you're healthy?"

"Yes, I'm fine. I get tested regularly, but I feel confident I'll be ok. I just wanted to tell you that your words stayed with me and turned me around. I knew you were disappointed when I quit, and I just felt obligated to tell you how much you influenced me. During that time, you were the only person who cared. You saved me." I was stunned. I had felt so helpless with Jeff – so unable to express the empathic words he needed. It was then I realized that all those hours spent on those damnable journals was time well-spent.

Another one of my students was Steven, a blonde, blue-eyed, rosy-cheeked senior whose cherubic appearance totally belied his unpleasant attitude of unearned entitlement. He was the son of a very well-known local physician, and his indolent demeanor annoyed me no end. He usually slept in class, was absent more than present, and when he did choose to grace the chair with his privileged derriere, he chose to ignore my questions, or when pushed, answered with a smirk and a shrug. He spent the entire school year on the precipice of failure, and his lackadaisical attitude toward passing my English class, a required step to earning his diploma, combined with his snarky, condescending attitude, made me secretly hope that he would take a misstep and learn that being rich didn't necessarily equal success. The daily journal was a major test grade each grading period, given the fact that the students had to write in it every day, and Steven usually chose not to write in it or submit it to me at all, even though it was a relatively easy way to earn an "A".

At the end of the school year, teaching Senior English is a beating. Parents and students who haven't seemed to care the previous eight months, suddenly become acutely invested in every single assignment that makes up the final grade for that required credit. It's stressful, to say the least, knowing the grade you assign could mean the difference between an elated student graduating in May with his classmates or sullenly slinking into summer school registration having learned the lesson of a lifetime. To be honest, very few of my students put in so little effort that they didn't graduate, and I was always willing to offer those hanging on by their fingertips the opportunity to bring up their grades. But they had to ask for clemency, and Steven never did. I wasn't surprised, a few days short of graduation, as I churned through those massive piles of spirals I had fetched from the plastic tub in the back of my Chevy Suburban, to discover that, once again, Steven had not submitted his journal, even though he had a failing grade. When I brought this to his attention the next day, he innocently claimed he had turned one in, but going through all 125 of them, one by one, that night, the phantom journal was not to be found. He subsequently did well enough on his final exam (the kid wasn't dumb) to bring his final grade up to 68, 2 points shy of the 70 needed to pass, and therein my dilemma took shape. Teachers were discouraged by administration from allowing a student to fail for the year with a 68 or 69. I even talked to his Vice Principal about it, and his advice was, "If he's going to fail, you should lower that grade to 67, because in all likelihood, a 68 will result in his parents visiting the Superintendent, and we'll all end up having to eat crow." So, gritting my teeth, my brain screaming at me that I was just enabling his egregiously irresponsible behavior, I raised his final exam grade enough to boost his yearly grade to 70.

A few months later, graduation forgotten and summer vacation refueling my tank, I was driving my kids to their summer activities when my 8-year-old daughter, sitting in the rarely occupied third seat of the Suburban, said, "Mommy, what is this book?"

"What book, Adrienne?"

"This book that has some writing in it. It has a name on it. Steven somebody."

I almost veered off the road. It was Steven's journal that had slipped beneath the seat. He had indeed turned it in. You know those old cartoons of the angel on one shoulder and the devil on the other, both telling you what you should and shouldn't do? Thank God the angel won, and I got to keep my job. I guarantee that if I had lowered Steven's grade, causing him not to graduate, I would have burned that journal that very day and never mouthed a word to a soul about it. Shortly thereafter, I came to the conclusion that teaching English had worn me down to an exhausted nub. I applied for a counseling job that summer and never taught English again.

I was invited recently to my ex-students' 30-year reunion and was amazed at how many told me they had actually enjoyed my English class. Obviously, they had been drinking. To my further surprise, one of them, now a psychologist whom I embarrassingly didn't remember, approached me with tears in her eyes. She told me I had started her on a journey she still traveled – keeping a journal every day. Astoundingly, she had kept all her high school journals as well. I was shocked. Where do you put that many spiral notebooks? But I was also honored that she credited me with a lifelong habit that had played a vital role in the self-actualized woman she had become. I told her, "Those journals are treasure. Read back through them, and you'll see you have a book on your hands. Write it!" Still the English teacher after all these years.

Flock of '88

My Year of Nothingness
by Susan Mellsopp

It arrived again, without warning, not long after Christmas. The blackness overwhelmed me in an instant and I woke from my unconscious state several minutes later. Lying on the carpet with my head bleeding profusely, I realised I had hit it on the heavy metal framing of my ranch slider as I fell. Drowsy and confused, I staggered to my feet, turned on the shower, and knew I needed help urgently.

Unwilling to spend another day being 'observed' at the hospital, I visited my doctor who had me watched for a period of time then sent me home to 'rest'. I soon learnt I should have been referred that day for professional help to deal with the severity of my concussion.

Once again, my brain was damaged. I was about to revisit the fight for normality. Battered and bruised, I felt as though someone had hit me over the head with a heavy metal bar. The insidious blankness, thick fog, and loss of awareness I remembered so well filled me with increasing dread. I was unaware this was to become a year of nothingness.

Eventually support for my bruised brain arrived. A plethora of professionals used to rehabilitating the concussed began to tour my muddled grey matter. Some weeks there were five exhausting appointments. As I struggled to stay awake, my brain swirled, protested, and retreated into its curves and folds. It demanded frequent sleep and destroyed my joy. I existed in five-minute energy sapping periods of time. Living was cancelled.

The experts insisted my brain would love a walk, twice daily. My body drunkenly swayed and swerved as I navigated the local footpaths, fearful of stopping in case I could not start moving again. Mentally unable to discern the abandonment of balance, I crashed into walls at home and frequently became dizzy. A visit to the supermarket exhausted me for the whole day. I could not tolerate noise, bright lights, and people talking. Told I should frequently stand up and sit down to help with balance issues, I didn't have the heart to tell the physiotherapist I already did this a multitude of times daily letting my dog in and out of the house. My lovely brain which I admired so much was a separate entity disconnected from who I really am.

My biggest love, language, turned into my enemy. A week after my head injury, I gave a speech for International Women's Day. I have no idea if it made sense, but it took my muddled self several weeks to recover from the effort. Time passed slowly, my spoken and written language remained stilted, muddled, misunderstood and echoing. Swirls of letters were nauseating, words were jumbled, dyslexic. Books were abandoned, my computer left in solitude, emails unread. A month of concerted mind-numbing effort to accumulate travel claim documents saw my brain collapse in a puddle on my spinal cord. A gnawing fear that I might fail to recover my precious language abilities made me spiral into a vacuum. Like a thief, depression crept up with its own insidious agenda. Slowly, I sank into a black mire of jumbled neurons and synapses. I fought to help every knot and tangle of my battered head.

Summer dissolved into autumn, then winter. I struggled incessantly with my missing intellect, damaged body, and loneliness. Anger, grief, frustration, and rudeness permeated every cell of my being. I raged at myself, at the loss of my hard-won freedoms and dreams. Concussion ruled; not the brief passing event assumed by many. Six months I was told, then nine, now perhaps twelve. Disbelief exploded all around me. The reality meant few visited, some sympathised, and my brain detached itself into solitary confinement. I now wonder if it's misfiring and sludgy responses drove my private world away. My only solace was canine. I wrapped myself in the loving presence of my golden retriever where I found unconditional acceptance in my difference. He allowed my brain to relax.

Months shifted, weeks dissolved, days melted. Tests and more tests occurred as neuropsychologists and neurologists trawled my aching lobes. Music became my soothing friend. Initially unable to listen to any sound which scratched and tormented my mind, strangely I began to devour opera, entranced by great Russian singers I had never encountered. I listened from daybreak to nightfall, and my neural circuits started to thank me for the stimulation. I began to rejoice in short spurts of reading, just five minutes, before the overwhelming tiredness won. Talking to people submerged me in an echoing sea in which I drowned. All I wanted was to sleep and sleep.

My pulpy brain fooled me into doing many strange things. I have put my clothes in the rubbish bin instead of the washing machine, left food out of the fridge, forgotten to feed my beloved dog, or fed him twice, and rung someone I had just spoken to. I also forgot if I had showered and cleaned my teeth too frequently. I made two separate diaries, one written and one electronic, my grey folds often failed to discern where I was supposed to be. Lists were a lifeline. Builders hammering next door for long dreary months drove me to despair.

Today my brain and I are reluctant friends. Journeying together to overcome the vestiges of the head injury which has broken this year apart, we have a truce. I have taught it to interpret the uninterpretable. I force it to stop and analyse every situation, however ridiculous. It complains and rejects my pushing and encouragement, yet I continue. Its loving response is to return my intelligence, innate curiosity, and ability to write. Creativity fills my days as I use language to reconnect.

Yet my brain begs to differ and still reacts accordingly. Silent cognitive issues rule. Decisions I make are forgotten in an instant. Conversations disappear into a mist. They can stop mid-sentence as I unexpectedly disengage and fall into a deep white hole where wires are disconnected or wrongly welded. My brain ceases working, and thoughts freeze in a Siberian tundra. I lose words as soon as I think of them and have to urgently write them down. Strangely, I can now read properly and retain content. But I can suddenly forget a pin number or password, a friend's name, or simple directions. It is difficult to remember bus timetables. Sometimes I cannot use simple gadgets such as a row counter when knitting or decide which buttons to press on my stove or washing machine. Occasionally I still sway all over the footpath when out walking and fear being asked by a policeman to walk a straight line. This rabbit hole is layered in ridges over normal forgetfulness. Impatience and anger bubble to the surface unexpectedly. The insidious damage of concussion on my jumbled grey cells retracts and revolves around who I was. My lobes do seem grateful to no longer live in another dimension, removed and distant from the living.

Christmas now hovers near and the New Year beckons. I tolerate the new revised me, one with still healing neural circuits. Each challenge diminishes that deep white hole where thoughts disappear, and words are dead on the lips. When Christmas trees sparkle with baubles and tinsel, carols fill the airwaves, people shop frantically and my guide dog jumps with joy at the sight of Santa, I will express gratitude for my year of frustration, defiance, protest and loss, for the presence of my wonderful brain.

Prick of Conscience
by Ronald Mackay

Kathleen raised a plump hand. "Miss? How is it wrong to copy from your neighbour when you don't know the right answer?"

Like most of us in Scotland, then, Kathleen used *"How?"* to ask *"Why?"*

Some pupils giggled at her challenge to conventional wisdom.

"Your conscience, Kathleen! Your conscience tells you it's wrong!" Miss Goodfellow was kind to the quick and the slow alike.

"Listen to me, class!" Dutifully, we straightened backs and clasped hands on desktops to signal our attention. "Inside here," our primary school teacher tapped her head, "is your conscience and inside your conscience there's a wee spiked marble."

Eyes widened.

"When you are tempted to transgress, these tiny spikes prick your conscience. The discomfort tells you that what you are about to do is wrong."

Kathleen frowned. Miss Goodfellow continued.

"If you ignore the pain once, if you make a habit of ignoring it, these tiny spikes wear out." She paused to make eye contact with the most wayward. "Eventually the marble is worn smooth. Then there's no spikes to tell you right from wrong."

The pupils seated at the back nodded obediently. Those in front shifted uneasily. The middle rows nodded, hoping to win approval.

I shared Kathleen's perplexity. If my conscience could prick me into doing the right thing, what was stopping it from telling me why the alternative was wrong? Wouldn't it be easier to spell out the principle that makes an action wrong so I could apply a simple rule the next time I might be tempted? Less discomfort than having a prickly ball rattling around in my head!

The exasperation on Kathleen's face reflected the complicated world we pre-adolescents were expected to thrive in.

* * *

"What are we going to do?"

Sandy and I had taken half an hour to bicycle from Dundee to Barnhill on the north bank of the estuary of the River Tay. Barnhill was home to the great 19th century mansions built by bold entrepreneurs who had risked all to make fortunes shipping jute from the Ganges Delta and lumber from Archangel.

That Sandy looked to me for leadership was perhaps why we had been friends and cycling companions since we'd acquired bikes. He was no blind follower, however, and I no despot. If either of us came up with a proposal that strained our moral boundaries, one of us would object, then we'd discuss it and arrive at a solution guaranteed to protect our level of comfort.

"We're going to scrump apples!" That preposterous proclamation was out of my mouth even before my brain had formulated the intention.

The previous day, I'd learned the verb *'to scrump'*. It meant to steal apples from others' trees. Although we'd occasionally gathered pocketsful of windfalls from farm orchards, we'd never given that act of boyish bravado such a deliciously wicked name. The sonorous *"Scrump!"* raised a mere mischief to the stature of plundering the Spanish Main.

"What does *'scrump'* mean?" Sandy's ignorance justified my superior command. A middling student, he had left school at 15 two years previously, as the less academically gifted did, and had articled as a management apprentice with the Eagle Jute Mills. Given my higher academic performance, I had opted to stay on at school for another three years with the expectation of *'doing better'*. His ignorance of the term *'scrump'* and my ability to explain it seemed to confirm the fitness of the divergent paths directed by the educational system we shared.

"*'Scrump'* means to climb over the wall of a mansion and steal apples from the orchard." I offered the explanation with as much bravado as I could muster, entirely confident of Sandy's opposition to such villainy.

The great mansions of Barnhill attracted us every autumn, but all we dared to do was to stand below the high walls surrounding secluded grounds and wait for ripe chestnuts to fall, splitting in shiny splendour on the quiet road. We'd pounce on the biggest, thread a dozen on a string, and take turns at attempting to smash each other's *'conquers'* as we called them. Each success added a score of one to the winner. As our remaining conquers dried and hardened, we'd increasingly prize the one that had destroyed the greatest number of opponents. Modern-day jousting, it was, *sans* horse, *sans* lance, *sans* physical injury and, most importantly, in frugal Scotland's post-War days, *sans* expense.

"We'll do it. We'll scrump apples!" Sandy's enthusiastic approval took me by surprise.

We were the kind of boys who did not climb mansion walls to raid orchards. Other than pocketing a few rotting windfalls from a farm-yard – which didn't really count as pilfering because of the danger of being stung by wasps – we were well-behaved. Now, I was in a predicament. Here was Sandy, a bank-manager's son, suggesting we should breach the sacred security of the walled estates of the Barnhill mansions to engage in plunder!

"You have the best ideas, Ron!" Sandy beamed approval, worsening my quandary.

His words reminded me that the suggestion was mine alone; that he was merely responding to *my* initiative, following *my* leadership. Worse, he was praising me for suggesting an enterprise that was already beginning to prick my conscience.

How was I to handle this dilemma? I could retract my suggestion thereby admitting my foolhardiness or I could accept Sandy's support and together, ride boldly into action. My moral predicament was all the more serious since he, by opting out of school at 15, had admitted academic defeat whereas I had shown myself equal to the challenge of performing better.

My reckless words and our contrasting circumstances had deposited onto my shoulders a leadership that I neither wanted nor warranted. Our relationship had suddenly become perilously lopsided. Sandy had formally acknowledged that I was now the leader, he merely the follower.

"You really want to?" I asked, hoping that his laughing: *"Of course not!"* would give me an honourable way out.

"Scrump apples? Sure, I want to!" Sandy had been seduced by the sonorous word, just as I had.

The wee spiked ball inside my conscience was rattling about uncontrollably, causing me unbearable discomfort.

* * *

"This is a good place." We rested our bicycles against the 10-foot outer stone wall of the mansion we knew as Ravenscraig, beneath a chestnut tree that had loyally supplied us with *conquers* for years.

"Och, the wall's far too high!" Was this a way out?

"Here, I'll give you a hoisty-up." Sandy stood with his back against the wall, his hands clasped together.

So, what could I do but step from his cupped hands onto his shoulders and then onto his head so that I could just reach the top? I pulled myself onto the cope-stone.

"What do you see?" Sandy's enthusiasm was making him impatient.

I had somehow anticipated the beauty that awaited me. Almost two years after the War ended, I had lost the spiritual comfort of my grandmother's stone-built Homebank in the village of Coupar Angus when my father was demobbed and we moved away into the city of Dundee. As soon as I could, I had acquired a bicycle and had become, by the age of seven or eight, free to roam at will. I cycled in pursuit of the contentment that I had known in Homebank, and from time to time found consolation behind the protection of stately deciduous trees, in walled gardens whose potting-sheds smelled of warm moist soil and peat moss and in the contemplation of sun-warmed houses built from Arbroath's smooth red sandstone or dappled yellow blocks from the quarries at Scone.

I was not, however, entirely prepared for the beauty before me. The mansion stood at the highest end of the secluded, six-acre property. Mature chestnut trees, oaks and sycamores protected the periphery. Visible from where I sat, down worn paths lined with autumn flowers, lay a fragrant orchard, branches heavy with apples and pears. Wasps tunnelled into sweet windfalls. Beyond the orchard, a striped lawn. Beyond the lawn and the flower gardens, the house. No, not merely a *house*; it had to be a much-loved *home*. It spoke of the standards of an age in decline, but not quite over. It offered the peace I sought, the security of a time when elegance and authority embraced unashamedly. Someone had made a home of warm stone, mossy paths, rose-mantled arches, scented orchards and the soothing autumn colours of mature trees.

The scene conveyed a reassuring order still protected by love while much of the world was being torn asunder by the War and its aftermath. The mansion in its grounds offered the abiding dignity of serene confidence.

"What do you see?" Sandy's impatient voice.

A thin spire of blue smoke arose from a pile of leaves that the gardener had burned before leaving. The scent choked me with memories of Homebank, more modest, but our childhood sanctuary against the mystifying uncertainties of lives during war. The ground on the inside was no more than five feet below the top of the wall. I could have easily hopped down and into the orchard. But the spiked marble of my conscience was pricking.

What do you see?

"Not too much. A bonfire." I knew Sandy could smell the scent.

"Apple trees?"

I obfuscated. "I can just make out a few, but I think the gardener's probably raking leaves to burn."

"Can you get the apples without him seeing you?"

"How would I get back up onto the wall again all by myself?" I left it to Sandy to imagine that the drop into the garden was as deep as it was on the outside.

"Better not risk it then!"

With guilty relief, I took a last longing look at the changing leaves, the autumn flowers, the ripening fruit and the great home. I breathed in the scent of smouldering leaves. Then, turning away, I hung from my fingertips, let go, and dropped onto the roadside at Sandy's feet.

"Let's find another place. We might have better luck." Sandy wasn't going to let go his grip on apple-scrumping nor free me from my unsought role as Prince of Thieves.

We cycled into the road that would take us past the entrance to Ravenscraig and those of several others.

"Look!" Sandy pointed as we passed the widely spaced stone pillars that guarded Ravenscraig.

Just inside the gates, two beautiful, espaliered apple trees stretched in trained parallel lines against the stone wall alongside the drive. The series of lateral branches offered leafy supports for eye-catching bright red-and-green fruit.

We pedalled past slowly, assessing the situation. It was one thing climbing over a wall to get to an isolated orchard, it was quite another to walk through a family's gate, up their gravel drive and violate an obviously cared-for espalier.

"You could do it, Ron! Easy-peasy!"

I was busy wishing, wishing that I'd never learned the seductive verb 'to scrump'; that Sandy had not, irrevocably now it seemed, ceded leadership to me; that Miss Goodfellow had never embedded the image of the prickly ball on my pained conscience.

Although there was no traffic in this exclusive part of Barnhill, we didn't want to draw attention to ourselves by lingering.

"Let's go round again." I was playing for time.

* * *

Once more we approached the entrance to Ravenscraig. This time, two elderly ladies were standing comfortably between the pillars.

Sandy and I automatically prepared to increase our speed and give the impression we had another destination in mind. As we drew abreast of the gravel driveway where the two beautiful espaliers clung to the wall, one of the ladies stepped forward.

"Are you looking for apples?"

Alarmed, Sandy sped off. Surprised at her unaccountable ability to mind-read, my foot slipped, and I hopped to a halt in front of the lady who had spoken. She and the timid one behind were similar in dress and looks suggesting they were sisters. The bolder one accepted my pause as encouragement.

"I'm asking, you see, because these espaliers," she gestured past her sister to the identical, manicured trees that spread neat parallel branches against the warm stone, "are a late variety and although they *look* ripe, they have a few weeks to go."

I knew from experience that apple varieties ripened at different times. She made perfect sense. But it was how she had uttered her words that disarmed me. They were not formulated as an accusation, more as a fact that might be of interest to a respected fellow-gardener.

"What school do you attend?" Her tone was even, honestly curious, as if I were worthy of her interest.

I looked from her to her sister. Identical woollen twin-sets, brooches pinned to silk scarves, tweed skirts, worn brown lacing shoes, hair drawn into neat buns. They might have been my grandmother's better-to-do neighbours in Coupar Angus. The ones she conversed with in Standard English, not in everyday Scots. I especially enjoyed my grandmother's conversations with such neighbours because they were somehow conducted on a more significant level and dealt with deeper matters than the price of eggs.

"What school?"

Our 'Rector' as we called our school principal, could punish us for a misdemeanour no matter where committed if he deemed it brought the Morgan Academy into disrepute. Common civility demanded I answer the lady's question; the need for honesty demanded the truth.

"I'm in the fifth year at the Morgan." Unaccountably, I was confident that she wouldn't use that information to my detriment.

"Ah! Peter's school!" She turned to her sister. "This nice young man is a pupil at Peter's school."

The timid sister smiled. Peter Robertson was our Rector. I'd never imagined anybody calling him by any other name than 'Sir' let alone in a tone that suggested anything but fear.

"Let me show you and your friend the espaliers you were admiring." By ignoring Sandy's flight, she was refusing to countenance our intention to steal.

Reassured, I leaned my bicycle against the entrance pillar and accompanied her to examine the green fruit flushed with orange.

"Cambusnethan Pippin. A dessert apple with a nutty taste." She was offering me the gift of knowledge.

"We grafted them ourselves." Timid sister said with pride. "Cuttings from our brother's orchard in Stirling."

"Twenty years ago."

"Our 50th birthday gift one to the other."

The twins regarded each other and their matching espaliers with love and pride. Together, we stood in admiring silence.

"We have Golden Pippins picked from the orchard." Timid sister made the statement sound like a suggestion.

"So why don't you bring some to this young man and his friend." Bolder sister approved, keeping up the fiction of Sandy's presence.

Timid twin disappeared and returned with a brown paper bag full of apples.

"For you both to share." I strapped it carefully into my saddlebag.

"Come back early next month. We can let you have one Cambusnethan each."

They had generously overlooked our original intention. Now we were being invited back to share.

* * *

Sandy was waiting for me outside his small house in the temporary post-War prefab development. He was relieved to see me return with a smile, an uplifting story to tell, and a bag of apples.

"I can't take them!" Sandy was adamant. "My Mum'll think I stole them!"

"I'll tell her how we came by them,"

"She'll never believe it."

* * *

When I arrived home with a bag full of Golden Pippins, I told my mother the story – the whole story including Miss Goodfellow's answer to Kathleen's question about how we know what is wrong. I admitted that I thought Kathleen's question had some merit.

"How *do* we know?"

Pearl paused. Then she said:

"I've sometimes wondered myself how we manage to get through life without an unending list of imperatives: *Do this! Don't do that!* And after all this time, all I can tell you is what my mother told *me* when I asked her the same question at about the age you are now. Pearl closed her eyes and repeated the words of her mother, words that had guided her.

"Pearl, my lass," she said, "the important thing in life is to do what *feels* right and keep from doing what *feels* wrong. Each one of us knows a right and a wrong that goes beyond what we are able to explain in words."

I understood then that that some of the real truths in life, those that guide us as truly as the North Star, are not accessible to mere explanation. Miss Goodfellow's metaphor was sound just as Kathleen's amazement, or my own, in the face of this mystery was inevitable.

I understood too, that when we're on the verge of giving in, others, like a wise parent or those shrewd twins standing erect at the entrance to their home can anticipate the frailty in us and with a nudge guide us onto the better path.

The term the *Prick of Conscience* was first used as the title of a popular English 14th century poem. The poet's intention was to encourage the reader to attend to that internal voice we all possess where heart, mind and memory intersect and, together, guide us towards a virtuous life.

A Scottish house not unlike Ravenscraig

In the Library
by Mary Mae Lewis

Shielding her eyes from the summer sun, Marjory looked up at the imposing, Edwardian, three-story, redbrick building in awe. Creeping up the granite steps, hauling a big bag, she reached the main entrance to the library, a little out of breath. She paused before struggling to push the heavy oak door, with its polished brass handles, open.

The cool air inside stunned her like a dunk in a cold bath. She scuttled across the painted terracotta Minton tiles, her tiny footsteps echoing around the great hallway, then dissipating into nothing up the broad, winding staircase. She stopped again at the next set of double doors and prayed for courage.

To her right, in the reading-room, cloth-capped working-class men and waist-coated middle-class men stood silently at opposite sides of the chamber. One group perusing the broadsheets, propped up on dark wood contraptions, the others the tabloids.

The four-foot-eight girl, savouring a moment of solitude, looked up to admire the stained-glass door panels, behind which was the library reception; she cringed with fear and inferiority. This was the home of the mighty intellectuals.

Taking a deep breath, she pushed hard, propelled herself forward and finally entered the lofty space with floor to ceiling rows of books. With fortitude, she hauled the well-worn leatherette bag, onto the check-in counter. The thud caused a few heads to swivel and beady eyes to register disapproval, but no one spoke and the eight-year-old was left to wait. The polished mahogany surface, on which the bag stood, was level with her nose. Her body rigid, and arms hanging limply by her sides, she turned her head slowly; her eyes scanned from left to right like a searchlight.

A middle-aged librarian was straining at the top of a ladder to replace a book on the top shelf. The black lines of her nylon stockings ran perfectly straight up her legs from her Achilles heals to disappear under her neat grey pencil skirt, the hem of which sat one inch below her knees. A man in a trilby, and belted up Mackintosh, stood watching her. His moustache twitched every time the woman stretched up and revealed more of her legs. Marjory felt sick; her blood rebelled as she recognised the face; *Mr Rhede!* Her cheeks reddening, and her neck tingling, she remembered how he had lured her to his house and sat her on his knee, in his parlour, in return for a tube of Smarties. She recalled the man's cold thin white hand touching her thigh and felt her feet weld to the floor in anger and humiliation. She heaved at the thought of his long, lean fingers and unblemished nails.

"He's nowt but a poncy pen-pusher. Stay clear of 'im and the likes of 'im," Marjory's father warned after she had confided in her mother, who, of course, had told her husband.

But Marjory hadn't revealed all. The secret inside poisoned her reasoning, crippled her self-esteem and, in her own mind, had condemned her to the gutter. Her heart thumped and swirled around inside her chest like a wild bird trying to escape from a cage. She dribbled in her pants, then clenched her buttocks and crossed her legs to stop the flow.

Only when she sneezed did she attract attention.

"Yes?" An older librarian asked, thrusting her ample bosom over the counter, and shoving her wrinkly face into Marjory's.

Marjory leaned back to regain some personal space and indicated to the bag of books, thinking, *I wouldn't trust her with my guinea pig!*

Miss Ugly Sister, (Marjory's name for her) lifted the six library books out of the bag one at a time as if she were removing dead rats from a baby's cot. As she placed each one on the counter the wire-haired woman winced and wiped her hands on her pleated plaid skirt before extracting the next one. Finally, she took the bag, turned it upside down and shook the remaining contents over the wastepaper basket. Marjory blushed again, as bits of soil, carrot and cauliflower, remnants of the previous day's greengrocery shopping, she had done, for her family, at the market across the road, fell into the rubbish bin. Her heart froze. Riveted to the spot, she felt like a pillar of salt, struck dumb like Lotte in the Bible.

Her thoughts were in turmoil, struggling in her head as wildly as a turtle tangled up in a fisherman's net and fighting for its life; she didn't move, not until ten-year-old Melinda Cartwright swept past and landed her a punch in the middle of her back, sending a sharp pain up her spine.

"You smell!" this girl, from Marjory's primary school, hissed.

Marjory lifted her arms to her face as the blonde bright-eyed girl, pigtails swinging provocatively down her back, slipped into the children's room of the library, to the right.

I don't smell, Marjory spoke the words quietly to herself; she wondered if Mr Rhede had taken advantage of Melinda.

Marjory sniffed her skin again to reassure herself she was not dirty; the scent of Life Buoy toilet soap, used that morning was clearly evident. But then she thought of her clothes and the fact she had just wet her knickers. She only had three sets of garments: one on, one in the wash and one ready for use. Today was Saturday, her clean set of clothes wouldn't be issued till Sunday morning, for Sunday school and the start of the school week. She'd have to dry her pants out, somehow, and manage till then. Marjory looked down at herself and recoiled yet again, embarrassed that her flimsy cardigan was so old the wool had bobbled. Two buttons out of five were missing, and she had had it so long it was much too small for her now. How she envied Melinda with her polished soft leather shoes, hand crochets boleros, velvet dresses and pink ribbons. She was teachers' pet. She rang the school bell and was 'well read'. She won all the school competitions for writing, poetry, and short stories. *A woman in the making, to be sure. She'll go far,* they said. *She'll fetch ducks of water.* Marjory writhed inside with self-pity, but she didn't show it.

"Yes," the librarian asked again, slapping her hand on the counter to regain Marjory's attention.

"Two Romance, two Historical novels and two Romance," Marjory said, adding, "For my mother." It was one of the girl's errands to go to Library, once every three weeks, to fetch her mum's reading material.

My mum definitely doesn't smell, the child thought as the Librarian was busy choosing six books as requested. Marjory envisaged her mother dabbing herself behind her ears with *June Perfume* from a tiny bottle about two inches square. It was so precious you had to unscrew a spherical, pea green top and peel back a black rubber stopper to get at it! Mother gave Marjory a dab on Sundays before Church and on special occasions like birthdays and Christmas. Nelly also used Imperial Leather talcum powder and Pears soap.

Marjory concentrated on the books being stamped brutally by the curmudgeonly library assistant, and cringed, but choked back a tear when finally, the paperbacks were shoved carelessly into the scruffy bag.

"There you are." The harridan snapped as she pushed the bag towards Marjory over the counter. The pungent smell of the unkind woman's body odour, a musty smell mixed with sweat, made Marjory wretch. She grabbed the bag, and with a hand over her mouth, she shot back through the two sets of doors, into the waiting fresh air as if she was getting out of a building on fire!

She raced along The Boulevard, turned left, passed Little Park and headed home. Anxious to get her reward for the week's chores, she ran as fast as she could up her street and only stopped when she reached the back gate of her home.

Singing *Oh What a Beautiful Morning,* she let herself into the Victorian workers' terraced house and put the bag on the kitchen table, then waited for her mother to come downstairs with her purse and dig out a sixpence.

If mother was quick, she would still have time to go to the pictures, *Chums' Club*, at Barber's Palace cinema, or if not she would go swimming the next day, with her cousins, at the Public Baths, big decisions for a little girl in the 1950s from Tunstall, Stoke-on-Trent.

Marjory's phobia for the library stopped her from ever enjoying the delights of the books in the children's section for herself but she made do with reading what books she had access to at school, comics handed down to her from cousins and second-hand books from her father's employer's daughters. As she grew older, she read the local daily paper, *The Sentinel* and the Sunday newspaper, *News of the World,* her mother bought, but she never went to the town's library again once she was 13, when she got a Saturday job stacking shelves in a supermarket. She didn't need the money from her mother for doing errands, anymore. However, her acute dislike of that library impacted on her when she went to the grammar school and she avoided the school library too, as best she could. The feelings even persisted when she went to teacher training college, but somehow, she got by; she bought the books she needed or asked others to go and get books out for her.

It was a great moment when computers came into common use and anything anyone wanted to know was there at the click of a button; Marjory never stopped reading. When she got a kindle, she thought she was in heaven.

Marjory hasn't lived in Tunstall for over fifty years, but she's heard that the library is being moved to the Town Hall. What will become of the old one? Well, no one knows yet, but whatever it may become, it doesn't matter to Marjory. She's finally got over her fears and has even installed a library in her own house!

The American smugglers in Cuba
by Denis Dextraze

After my arrival in May 1998, I spent the first few days in Marina Hemingway meeting the dock's neighbors, who to my great surprise were mostly Americans. Where was the embargo? During the second term of the Bill Clinton's administration, the rules about visiting Cuba had not changed but were seemingly more relaxed. Actually, many American boaters coming to Cuba never reported their visit when they came back home. Some had a very good reason. They were smugglers.

The outgoing trade was mainly limited to Cuban cigars, illegal in the U.S., and escaping people. However, just like the Spaniards using Carrara marble as ballast for their Caravelles on their way down to the Americas and gold and precious wood as ballast on their way home, the real professional smugglers traded both ways. The most popular goods to smuggle into Cuba in those days were items which were illegal for Cubans to own like notebook computers and VHS VCRs for the general population and very useful instruments like walkie-talkies, portable VHF telephones and GPS for *balceros*, people planning to escape Cuba on makeshift crafts, floating trucks and cars. Yes, I said, floating trucks and cars!

Once, a floating 1949 Chevy pick-up truck loaded with Cubans was stopped by the U.S. Coast Guard off the coast of Florida. This unlucky and resourceful group were not to set foot on American soil and claim refugee status by invoking the "Wet foot, Dry foot" law in effect since 1966. As per an arrangement previously made with Cuba, the U.S. Coast Guard brought the sad escapees back to Mariel, a large bay thirty miles east of Havana, and sank the floating invention because it was a hazard to navigation. The next day, this event made the news in Key West and there was an uproar of protests against the Coast Guard not so much for bringing the *balceros* back but mainly for sinking the running vintage truck, a collector's item.

Back in those days, to renew their tourist visas, Canadians had to go out every two months just like other foreigners. I could take short flights to Nassau or Cancun, but the least expensive and more adventurous way was to sail across the straight to Key West, only ninety nautical miles away. Therefore, two or three boat owners with the same need to renew their visas would get together and share the cost of the fuel for the round trip. I did that with different boats, but Jerry's Hot Potato was my favorite ride.

Jerry was not in the smuggling business. He did not need the money. However, he routinely brought a few boxes of cigars to impress his American political friends like Bill Clinton with a very exclusive, rare, and illegal gift.

Jerry always entered the Key West Channel at night. He then would call the U.S. Coast Guard on the VHF and inform them that he was coming in from Cuba and was going to a specific marina. He would be instructed to call again when he was at the pier and stay on the boat until an official representative would come. As soon as the boat was tied down, he would dump the bag containing his precious illegal cigars in the closest trash can. I did this trip with him maybe five or six times and it was always the same routine. The same elderly gentleman from the Department of Agriculture would show up, review your papers, check the refrigerator, and ask you if you had any fruits or fresh meat. He would call the Coast Guard on his portable VHF, transmit the ID information, and get a clearing number. He then would tell us that if nobody from Customs showed up within the next three hours, we should go downtown the next day to the Immigration office to have our passports stamped. Nobody ever showed up to check on us, probably because they had a limited number of custom officers working at night. This is what smart Jerry always counted on. He never lost a box of precious cigars!

The next day, we would show up downtown at the Federal building and report to the Immigration office. We then would be confronted by "the bitch", the nickname given to the head of Immigration in Key West by all the American boaters checking in after an illegal visit to Cuba. The story is that she was married to a Cuban American whose family had lost everything when they left Cuba after the revolution. The first time we met "the bitch", she asked Jerry, the U.S. registered boat owner, if he had spent any money in Cuba. The reason for this crucial question came from the wording of the American embargo with Cuba, which did not prevent American citizens from visiting Cuba but forbade them from spending any money on the island. When cool Jerry said no, she inquired how he had paid for his docking fees. He said that a Canadian friend of his who loved sport fishing had paid for all his personal and boat's expenses in exchange for using the boat for fishing outings. When she asked who and where this generous soul was, he turned around and pointed at me. From there on, probably because we both were in the Immigration computer's central data bank, Jerry had no problem checking back in the U.S. when returning from Cuba. I was his official Canadian legal benefactor.

Bob, a greyish long-haired Marine veteran, still kept the shape for his age regardless of his excess smoking and drinking. As a good storyteller, he had a knack for making you believe that all his exaggerated tales of smuggling were true. That was particularly effective with Cuban women who were hypnotized by his blue eyes. He used to joke about the fact that his old forty-foot power boat might not make it to harbor on his next cigar run. The reason he evoked for this planned lack of maintenance was that the money he would spend fixing her would not be recuperated in the sale. Indeed, he planned to sell the boat and move to Cambodia, where he would invest the money on a "friendly house & bar". Like half of his stories, we did not believe that he was serious about this dangerous venture. One day, someone coming back from Key West, where he had run across Bob, informed us that he had indeed sold his old junk and was making plans to leave for Cambodia. Nobody ever heard from him again.

Some of the "professional smugglers" made a good living from this two-way trade and did the U.S./Cuba round trips regularly. They had constructed inventive caches inside their boat to hide away their illegal goods from the Cuban Coast Guard and Customs inspectors. I know of a smuggler who had built a double ceiling through the length of his boat. The cache was about four inches high, high enough to hide a full-size VHS VCR or two stacked boxes of large cigars like *Robustos* or *Esplendidos*. Some smugglers were openly bragging about their illegal trade, but I am sure that there were many others who were very secretive and smartly kept their business to themselves. The best example of that discretion was the case of Swamp Charlie.

Swamp Charlie was a small, unpretentious, mustachioed man in his fifties. He came from the lowlands of Louisiana near New Orleans where he got his nick name. He lived with his minuscule dog in a small and old twenty-eight-foot wooden power boat. He was a chain smoker and a good drinker judging from the number of dead bottles and full ashtrays lying around his totally disarrayed single cabin. He had a younger Cuban girlfriend with two kids living in the next town, *Yamanitas*. She was taller and bigger than he. Rumors had it that she was beating him occasionally, probably when he was too drunk to put up a fight.

Swamp Charlie kept to himself. I did not particularly befriend him, but I was there to give a hand when help was needed. Since I had a car, a gold Mercedes 300SD equal to one of Fidel's car, which I had temporarily imported from Canada, I drove him a few times to downtown Havana to find parts. By way of thanking me, he would buy me a few Buccanero beers in one of the sleazy downtown bars. He did not really socialize with his neighbors except when someone threw a party for a special occasion and invited everybody to bring a chair and join the group sprawled on the grass next to the channel. He went back and forth to the U.S. for a period of fifteen to eighteen months and then stopped coming. What had happened to Swamp Charlie?

I was to find out two years later after I had sailed Aventura to Key West. I met Swamp Charlie by coincidence at my favorite watering hole, the Hogfish Bar and Grill in Safe Harbour. He immediately offered me a Cuban cigar. Because he was not going back to Cuba anymore, he confided in me an incredible story, the kind that you can see only in movies. He said that during his stay on the island, he had made many round trips trading both ways i.e. cigars for the U.S. and VCRs for the Cubans. He had found an American that went after the illegal Cuban cigar trade in a big way. He had bought so many boxes of various size cigars that it took him four trips to deliver the total order.

His boat was now in dry dock in a neighboring Marina. So, he invited me for a visit the next day to see his caches, which the authorities both American and Cuban had never found. It was ingenious. The small boat had two very large fuel tanks. Both had a see-through section on the side where you could visually inspect the level of the fuel. Swamp Charlie had baffled both tanks so that the fuel only occupied a small portion of the space. One of the spaces was so big that he smuggled the teenager son of his Cuban girlfriend past the Cuban Coast Guard and let him loose once on U.S. soil to claim refugee status using the "Wet foot, Dry foot" law. He was in the process of taking the baffles out. Now that he did not need them, he did not want the suspicious caches to be discovered.

His smuggling days were over. He was bringing his old boat back to the swamps of Louisiana to sell her. He felt that he had made enough money to last for a long while. This uneducated, discrete, and unpretentious redneck was the smartest of all smugglers for not being too ambitious and quitting while he was ahead. His judgement was right on. I could imagine Swamp Charlie drinking rum, chain-smoking cigarettes, and occasionally leftover smuggled Cuban cigars in the shack he had swapped for his old boat. He was enjoying his retirement from smuggling.

Although smuggling cigars was the predominant trade, smuggling people was much more lucrative. There were many ways that Cubans could be taken off the island by outsiders, but for boaters living in Marina Hemingway there were only a few options. If you owned a large boat, you could build a hiding place that hopefully the Cuban Coast Guard would not find; you could plan your exit for a time where a "friendly" inspector would turn his head for a good tip which did not represent much since a one hundred-dollar bill represented five months salary. Another option was to pick up the escapees at sea.

That ultimate option was much more complicated, but much more lucrative since you could transport many people at the same time. The whole process depended on timing and organization. First, you would provide the "aspiring escapees" with a portable VHF phone, a portable GPS, and with only one walkie-talkie and keep one of the pair for yourself. Then, you had to give them precise GPS coordinates of latitude and longitude and a precise time for meeting them at sea. Then, the Cubans had to find a fisherman with a boat that would take the risk of taking them illegally to open sea at night by either sneaking past the Cuban Coast Guard check point or simply bribing them. The smuggling foreign boat would try to time the complicated and lengthy exit procedure from the Marina so that he would be on time for his rendezvous at sea. He would sail out of the Marina on a straight course until his running lights were out of the line of sight. He would then turn off all his lights and locate the fishing boat, preferably using the walkie-talkies which had a shorter range and were not listened to by the port authorities. Once the small fishing boat was spotted, he would quickly take the precious human cargo on board and get out of the twelve-mile coastal zone at full throttle.

If he were a smart and cool captain, he would not take a direct course for the U.S. Rather, he might take a course as if he was going south west. Then, when he was in the middle of the Gulf Stream, he would turn to starboard and let the Stream increase his speed by an additional five knots, as if he was part of the heavy maritime traffic going north from South America. By doing it that way, his odds of being picked by the American Coast Guard patrolling the area were greatly reduced because they could not stop every boat. There was simply too much traffic.

I personally know of only a few cases where smugglers staying in Marina Hemingway got into the human cargo business. It was probably too complicated and too risky. However, while I was in Cuba, I personally witnessed two famous cases of escapes from Cuba that made the headlines on American news. Of course, these exploits were never reported on Cuban media. It could have given new ideas to the herd of eleven million poor souls left behind...

Not every Cuban wanting to escape had to hide in foreign boats or as *bolseros* taking life-threatening risks at sea on flimsy crafts. Some did it in plain sight of the Cuban Coast Guard. While in Key West, I read one morning in the Key West Citizen, the local newspaper, an interesting story about two junior Cuban coast guards having escaped Cuba in their small Cuban Coast Guard craft. To prevent this type of escape from Cuba, the two operators of these small boats were never allocated fuel for more than a two or three-hour run at low speed. These kids had planned their escape by hiding fuel in small containers. When they got to a public pier in Key West, they tied their craft, abandoned their AK47 at the bottom of the boat and started walking downtown in their olive-green fatigues. They were hoping that, just like in Cuba where citizens have to take turns at night watching each street for unusual activities, they would be spotted and reported, or they would run into local police officers. At four o'clock in the morning, there wasn't a soul in town. They wandered around this strange dead town until they finally found a police station and turned themselves in, evoking the "Wet foot, Dry foot" law. When interviewed by law enforcement officers and the press, one of the defectors summarized in just one sentence the reason for his escape from Communist Cuba. He said this: "I have been a coast guard for almost ten years and I never had enough money to buy myself just a radio". This incident became the talk of the town. Local citizens complained about harbor safety. Where were the Homeland Security people?

I was in my "Office", the beach bar across the street from my house, on a nice Sunday afternoon when the beach in front is always swamped with people. All of a sudden, we heard a commotion outside with people all running in the same direction. We rushed outside to witness a cigarette power boat heading at full speed towards the damaged and abandoned concrete pier about half a mile away. Five or six Cubans with backpacks got out from under the shrubs where they had been hiding and rushed to the pier. They all jumped on the boat which never really stopped completely. Before you knew, the cigarette boat had turned around and was heading out at full speed while the beach runners were shouting "Yo tambien, Yo tambien, Yo tambien", Spanish for "Me too, Me Too, Me too".

I am sure that there were many of those quick pickup and delivery runs dearly paid for in Miami which I never heard about, but this one was special to me because it happened in front of my eyes and the event also made the U.S. News. I guess that the captain of this boat did not have a Coast Guard Captain's license. Indeed, he had miscalculated the distance and strong currents and had not figured out the consumption of the two huge gas-guzzling engines. He ran out of gas on his way back. The expensive cigarette boat was found drifting in the Gulf Stream and seized by the U.S. Coast Guard. The illegal passengers were sadly returned to Cuba.

After I was gone from Marina Hemingway and during the two years of my absence, the new George Bush administration put a clamp on American boaters visiting Cuba and the Cuban authorities cleaned up the smuggling. Fines were given, boats were seized, and owners were jailed, It was the end of the golden years for American smugglers.

Running wake

Maywood
by Tina Wagner Mattern

I wish I could go back in time to that day my adopted parents took the gamble of a lifetime and brought a terrified 7-year-old child into their home and hearts. I would sit them down, look into their eyes and tell them, "I'm sorry for everything I'm going to put you through. It's just going to take me awhile to learn that you love me and that no matter what I do, you'll never send me away."

Today, if a couple were planning to adopt a child from a troubled background like mine, the first thing they would do would be to get her into counseling. But back in the early 1950s, this wasn't something that was done. My new parents had no idea what they were getting themselves into.

And if I could go back in time and talk to the little girl I was back then, I would hug her and tell her, "It'll be okay, you'll see. These are wonderful people who are going to love you like you've never been loved before. You have a forever home now."

* * *

It's been 63 years since the day I stepped off the plane that had carried me from Delaware to Portland, Oregon; from my birth mother's arms to the airport terminal where the man and woman who were to be my new parents waited anxiously for my arrival.

I walked into the terminal on shaking legs. The other passengers were laughing and talking above me; down below them, I felt so small I could almost hide inside my suitcase. Then, when we reached the big glass doors of the terminal, I felt even smaller; there were so many people everywhere, shouting, calling to one another, jostling, moving in a stream to the left and right of me. People were hugging, crying, calling to one another. I didn't know what the people looked like who were supposed to come get me. My eyes were filling up with tears so fast my blinks couldn't keep up when I heard my name. "Tina!"

I looked up over the heads of all the people and saw a very tall man towering over everybody. "Tina!" he called out again, with a big smile. He patted the lady beside him and pointed at me. All I could see of her was from her shoulders up; she had dark red hair and glasses. She was very short compared to the man and would have had to stand on her tiptoes to see me, which she did, I guess. She was smiling too, waving her hand up in the air. They rushed towards me, moving people out of their way.

Overwhelmed with sheer terror, I closed my eyes.

When I opened my eyes again, I was looking at a pair of trouser legs. I followed them up and up and up until I was looking into a pair of gentle blue eyes. Dropping down to his knees beside me, the man said softly, "Don't be afraid, honey. We're here now. You're not alone anymore." The lady with him reached out and touched my arm. "That was a long flight; you must be so tired."

I pulled my suitcase up against my chest and wrapped my arms around it in case they tried to hug me. They seemed kind of surprised, but they just smiled and told me their names. The woman called Mary said, "We're so happy you're here. And we're going to take good care of you." The man, whose name was Eddie, patted my shoulder and said, "I'll bet you're tired *and* hungry."

I was still trying my best not to cry, so I just nodded. I was tired. I just wanted to lay down right there on the floor and sleep forever.

"Let's go home," Mary said. "I'll make you some lunch and then you can take a nap, if you want." Eddie stood up and laid his hand on my arm, nudging me gently towards the exit. "Come on with us, sweetheart."

I moved to follow them, but my suitcase suddenly seemed so heavy that it slipped from my fingers and I just didn't have the strength to pick it back up. Instead, I started to cry.

The man bent down to whisper, "I'm going to give you a ride, okay?" Without waiting for an answer, he scooped me up in his arms and wiped my tears with his handkerchief, and for the first time in a long time, I felt almost safe.

Outside, in the parking lot, Eddie carried me along and after walking past several rows of cars, we all stopped in front of a big, shiny blue Oldsmobile, though of course I didn't know that's what it was. To me, it looked like something Elvis would drive. I was so blown away that for a minute, I forgot to be scared, and asked, "Are you guys rich?"

They laughed and Mary said, "Not by a longshot, honey." Eddie set me down and opened the trunk to put my suitcase in, then opened the passenger door. Mary stood waiting for me to get in, but there was no way I wanted to be trapped there in the front seat between them. I opened the back door, jumped in and scooted over to the far side of the seat. They looked at each other and then Eddie smiled and said, "Too crowded up front, huh?"

I just shrugged and pretended to be looking for something in my purse.

My new parents drove me to a lovely, though unpretentious ranch-style home on a street in N.E. Portland, called Maywood Place, or as everyone living there called it, simply "Maywood". It was, I would soon discover, one of those quintessentially perfect neighborhoods to grow up in; a place where children were as welcome (and safe) in a neighbor's home as they were in their own. Where the people who lived next door, down the street and across the way, were more than neighbors, they were extended family. Any loneliness I might have anticipated by being essentially an only child, (since my new sibling, Richard, was an adult by the time I came) would soon be soothed by the realization that I was surrounded by surrogate brothers and sisters.

God had brought me to a place of peace, to a new beginning with two people who would love and nurture me. It would take some time, but I would heal here.

* * *

"This is your bedroom," they told me.

Awed, I stood in the doorway, looking in at the pretty room with yellow-flowered wallpaper. It looked to me like a princess's chamber. The bedroom I shared with my sister, Sharon in Delaware had been plain and nothing special to look at.

A large window with lace sheers shone sunlight down on the white chenille covered double bed. Against one wall was an old steamer trunk covered with an amazing assortment of stuffed animals and dolls, obviously new. My heart was immediately won by a large stuffed pony wearing a cloth bridle and saddle. I knew he'd be sleeping with me from then on.

Against the other wall stood a tall dresser with 6 drawers. Mary walked over to it and pulled one open for me to look in... it was full of brand-new undershirts and panties. The other drawers she opened contained shorts, sunsuits, pedal pushers, and a variety of kid-colorful shirts. Next, she went to the big closet and slid the doors open; it too was filled with clothing: dresses, blouses, jackets, hats... and on the floor, a shoe rack held at least 6 pairs of shoes.

I was speechless. All of this for me? I couldn't get my head around it.

Eddie patted me on the shoulder. "Hungry?" he asked.

Suddenly, I realized I was, so I nodded my head.

"Well, come on then," Mary said. "I'll make you some breakfast." While I sat at the kitchen table with Eddie, she fried me an egg, buttered me some toast and set down a glass of ice-cold milk. I dug in. Two more eggs, another piece of toast and some fruit cocktail later, I was finally full.

When my eyelids started to droop and my head got too heavy to hold up, I laid it down on the table. Eddie laughed and scooped me up in his arms. "I think this little one needs a nap, what do you think, Mom?"

"I'll go turn down the bed," she said.

I was asleep as soon as my head hit the pillow.

* * *

Truthfully, I don't remember a lot of those first few weeks and months with my new parents, only a few particular memories come to mind. I'm sure the anxiety of finding myself, once again, at the mercy of people I didn't know, was enough to send me into the protective anesthetized-feeling zone that had gotten me through a myriad of emotional crises in the past. But the patience and understanding of my tender-hearted parents, not to mention the perfect neighborhood, would eventually win me over.

When I woke up a few hours later, I didn't know where I was for a few minutes. It felt like I was still lost in a dream. But then, as I looked around the room, it all came back. There was the darling stuffed horse that I was already calling "Trigger" in my mind, since it was the only famous horse name I could think of. I laid there for a few more minutes, listening, wondering where Mary and Eddie were, when suddenly I had a panicked thought and sat bolt upright in the bed. I lifted the covers, scooting to one side to check under my butt. Whew—no wet sheets! I scrambled out of bed and ran to the door, peeked left and right for anybody watching, and then went across the hall to the bathroom. Locking the door, I plunked myself down on the toilet. A few minutes later, someone knocked and tried the door, and I was glad I had thought to lock it.

"Are you okay in there?" Mary called.

I wiped, then stood, flushed, and pulled up my undies.

"Do you need any help, honey?" Mary asked. "Could you unlock the door, please?"

What kind of help would a kid need to pee? I wondered. But I unlocked and opened the door to tell her, no, I could pee all by myself.

"How about a quick snack?" Mary said, "And then I'll take you next door to meet the neighbors. This is a wonderful place to live with plenty of kids for you to play with. I know you're going to love it here."

My new mother was right; I did fall in love with Maywood. In spite of all the emotional chaos I went through during those first weeks and months of my new life in Oregon, one adjustment was simple to make: the reclaiming of my childhood. Falling in love with Maywood was so easy; I was suddenly surrounded by happy, well-adjusted kids in loving families, who accepted me into their lives and play with no questions asked. When I think back on my life there, I'm overwhelmed with sweet memories.

I can close my eyes and let my mind drift backwards and in a moment, I am back there; 7 years old again….

"I love Maywood! See that pink, two-story English Tudor house over there? That's where our neighbors, the Gray's, live. They have 4 kids: Lesley, Lori, Layne and Robbie. Mrs. Gray's name is Maxine, and she's the most beautiful lady I ever saw in person. She is tall and has very pretty legs, which are obvious because whenever the weather is sunny, she wears shorts to show them off. I think she does this because she used to be a fashion model before she got married, had kids and got old. I didn't believe she was really a model until Lesley, the daughter 3 years older than me, showed me her mother's scrapbook one day. There Mrs. Gray was in a real magazine picture, dressed in a red bathing suit, all shiny-lipped and smiling, just like Marilyn Monroe! I asked her for her autograph after seeing that, but she just laughed and told us kids to go outside and play.

Later on, I told Lesley that I thought her mom could have been a movie star if she hadn't gotten fat. But Lesley said, "She's not fat, you dip; she's gonna have a baby!" And sure enough, one day when I went over there to play, there Mrs. Gray was with a flat stomach again and a tiny baby on her lap. "This is Robbie," she said.

I couldn't get over it! She's not only nice, and beautiful like nobody's business, but she can have a baby out of her stomach, just like a magician pulling a rabbit out of a hat!

Mr. Gray's name is Mr. Gray, as far as I'm concerned. I've heard Mrs. Gray call him Bob, but he doesn't seem like a Bob to me. He's nice, I guess, but kind of stern and he sells insurance. When he's home, all us kids have to be quiet while he drinks his Martini and eats his olives, which we all like but can't have because the whole bottle is his. And it is "Off Limits" on the top shelf of the second cupboard to the left of the stove—the one where the door sticks a little.

The Gray girls are the first friends I've ever had, aside from the sheep on the farm (but they weren't human, so I don't think they really count). I love hanging out at their house and while I'm there, I like to pretend that I'm one of the family. When I get to sleep over, Mrs. Gray always kisses me goodnight, just like her own kids, so I kinda feel like I am.

Besides the girls and Robbie, the Grays also have the cutest dog. His name is Twinkletoes. He has some bad habits though, that my mother says she would shoot him for (but I don't think she really would). See, our kitchen table window looks right across the driveway to the Gray's kitchen table window, and when they aren't home, Twinkletoes walks around on the table and eats the butter in the butter dish. I always have my bread without butter when I eat dinner over there because I can't tell if there are Twinkle-tongue prints on it or not.

Another small problem with Twinkle is that he loves me. He seems to love me more than anybody else because every time I go over there and I pet him, he gets so excited he pees all over the floor. Usually on my shoes. He doesn't do this for anybody else but me. So now, when I come in the house, everybody yells, "DON'T PET THE DOG!" I hate to hurt his feelings, but my sneakers keep shrinking in the washing machine. So now I just say, "Hi Twinkle" and keep my hands to myself.

Across from the Gray's house is the Amato's house. Dr. and Mrs. Amato are very nice, and I am just amazed to have someone who can save a person's life living right across the street from me! They have 3 kids; David and Susan are a few years older than me, and Sally is a little younger. Susan is very pretty and is really smart. It's Sally, however, who is my favorite. She's smart too and has a wonderful face that's shaped like a Siamese cat's and a ponytail that's as big around as the handlebars on my bike. This is something I envy so much that it takes up to 10 minutes of my night prayers, asking for my hair to get thicker and longer so it'll be like hers. So far though, nothing's happened; my hair is still short and frizzy. It's a good thing Sally and I are such good friends, otherwise her hair would be a big problem in our relationship.

On the other side of the Gray's house are the Christensen's. Mr. and Mrs. Christensen are very tall, friendly, and laugh a lot. They make me laugh too when I'm over there. They have 2 kids, David, who's a teenager, and Betty, who's the same age as Lesley Gray and Susan Amato. Betty is a funny, warm-fuzzy person. I liked her the first time I met her.

Betty, Lesley and Susan all treat me like a little sister. I love that. And I like to pretend I'm a big sister to all the younger kids.

My life before was sad and awful. Now I have a new life, and new parents who love me, and I get to live in a perfect place called Maywood. I am a lucky girl.

* * *

As I look back over my life, I know now more than ever how blessed I was to have had a birth mother who, knowing she was incapable of being a good parent to me had the courage and faith to give me up to people she had never met.

And as I look back, a deep, abiding gratitude rises up in me, that my childhood begun in trauma became an idyllic childhood of peace and joy beyond measure.

While the Roses Still Bloom
by Malcolm D. Welshman

Roses have always been associated with romance. Certainly, for me, they are a symbol of love. So, when Valentine's Day comes round, I'm there, roses in hand, ready to present them to my wife, Maxeen. A token of my enduring love for her these past 43 years. It's not a bouquet of traditional red blooms, but an array of pink buds similar to the ones that surrounded us when we kissed in my Gran's garden many moons ago.

Maxeen and I had met in London just after I'd qualified as a vet and we'd gone down to Bournemouth for a weekend to visit my parents and to see Gran in her thatched cottage, nestling on the edge of the New Forest.

It had been mid-June, a hot, blazing day, and Gran's garden was a mass of roses in full bloom, shimmering in the heat haze. The air filled with their heady scent. A perfect setting for a romantic kiss. And I obliged, despite the fact I was aware of Gran peering down on us from the upstairs bedroom of her cottage, agog as to what was going on.

Gran was a keen gardener and throughout the year there was always something in her cottage garden to be admired; from the tiny heads of purple and white crocuses that emerged in the early spring to the towering, flamboyant pink trusses of Japanese anemones in the autumn. But roses were the true love of her life as evidenced by the cascades of blooms in June, the creamy-white heads of *Moonlight,* the heavy fragrance of *Old Pink Moss*, and the rich clove scent of *Blush Noisette* with its delicate clusters of small lilac-pink flowers. I could remember as a lad in my early teens, lying on the sun-scorched lawn of her garden on a hot mid-summer's day, eyes closed to the bleached-blue sky, ears filled with the hum of bees, and breathe deep of the heady scents that surrounded me. Even today, fifty years on, I only have to bury my nose in a fragrant rose and breathe deep of its perfume to be sent spinning back to my memories of Gran's garden and those abundant blooms.

Perfume apart, there's something about roses that I hold dear to my heart. In my more fanciful moods, I often wonder if it's linked to my babyhood. Part of my upbringing. My mother was a great believer in the benefits of rose hip syrup. It seems I was plied with daily spoonfuls of it, my mother declaring it an excellent and natural way to boost my vitamin C levels and ensure I bounced with health. Looking at grainy colour photos from back then, I do seem to have been a bonny baby if the full, rosy cheeks are anything to go by. So, maybe Mother was right, and all that rose hip syrup made me positively bloom.

My affinity with roses was further enhanced by Gran's potpourri. She was a dab hand at making it. Rose petals would be carefully collected and then blended with lavender before being packed to small cream muslin bags tied with blue ribbon. These would be liberally deposited in every cupboard, wardrobe and chest of drawers possible. In her house and ours. One bag of crushed petals found their way into the crutch of Grandpa's long Johns – only discovered when he'd put them on and winced when he sat down.

I'm not sure whether Gran had the apothecary's rose – *Rosa gallica var. officinalis* – growing amongst the many varieties that flourished in her garden. Nevertheless, she did have a tried and tested recipe for making rosewater, which she'd make in abundance. In late June, her kitchen would suddenly become a steamy scent-filled den with several black cauldrons simmering on her range. I'd be commandeered to help and would find myself perched on a stool, leaning over the range to stir each stew of petals with a long wooden ladle. Occasionally, the contents of a pot would spill over with a hiss and a spit, a bubble of perfume bursting into the air. Gran would dart between the range and a bleached wooden table cluttered with bottles, rustling to and fro in a floor-length pinafore dress, pouring out amber liquids, sieving them through muslin, adding a pinch of this, a dash of that, whispering words I could never quite catch. She only needed a broomstick propped up in one corner and a black cat on the windowsill to complete the bewitching picture she conjured up.

And her garden was certainly magic. Since those days, I've tried to emulate that garden and attempted, on many occasions, to cultivate roses of my own. But sadly, I seem to be devoid of Gran's magic touch. Green fingers have not been my forte.

Many a rain sodden June, I've stared glumly at my dripping rose gazebo, the wrought–iron pillars covered in a thin layer of leaves; the leaves covered in a thick layer of Blackspot. The buds of my soaked *Malmaison* roses have failed to open and look like sodden cream tennis balls rotting on their stems.

I realise that's not quite what Napoleon's wife, the later Empress Josephine, had envisaged when her rose garden was created in 1799 at the Palace of Malmaison in Paris.

They say 'roses grow on you' but not on me they don't. Over the years, I've ramblers that fail to ramble; climbers that fail to climb despite being shown the way – carefully trained to trellis-work yet failing to grasp it. My floribundas too have flopped. And my China roses always look as if they're on a slow boat back to where they came from.

I bet Gertrude Jekyll didn't have such a problem. She recognised the full potential of roses and combined them with other plants while giving them architectural roles on buildings and garden statuary.

I've tried her approach. We've a grey, concrete aggregate statue of a well-endowed lady holding a bunch of grapes above her left ear. She was a reduced item at the Garden Centre as her breasts were chipped. I named her Gloria. In Jekyll mode, my intention was to smother Gloria with a mass of *Golden Showers*, picturing the sprays of canary yellow blooms cascading over her shoulders to cover her nicked nipples. Alas, no. My *Golden Showers* turned into a drizzle of blooms that hung limply round her feet.

Not to be outdone, I decided that if I couldn't grow roses, I could at least try painting them. So, one autumn, I joined an evening class in water-colouring for beginners. I felt I was following in the footsteps of some very illustrious painters of roses. Joseph Redoute, for instance. He created some beautiful compositions in the 18th century with water-colour on vellum. His artistry was matched by the exquisite illustrations painted by Alfred Parsons for the 1914 book *Genus Rosa* by Mrs Ellen Willmott. I doubted whether attendance at evening classes would ever draw such mastery from me; but in my quest to become a budding artist – rose buds in particular – I persisted. The result was one paltry painting of the variety *Iceberg* frozen in time on a sheet of A4 paper and which now hangs behind the loo in the downstairs cloakroom.

However, even if I'm unsuccessful in growing my own roses, there's always the memory of Gran's garden to fall back on. It was there, on a tranquil summer's evening, the sun just having set in a molten halo of orange, fingers of warm air sifting through the roses, their fragrance heavy in the air, that I went down on bended knee and asked Maxeen to be my wife.

That's why roses are so symbolic to me. A bouquet – given to Maxeen each year on St Valentine's Day – expresses the love that blossomed that day in my Gran's arbour of blooms.

Okay. Maybe I'm making it seem more romantic than it actually was. But what's the harm in seeing those far-off halcyon days of my youth through glasses that just happen to be 'rose-tinted'?

Fragrant rose

A Lamb, a Dog and a Haircut
by Irene Pylypec

My definition of paradise is a childhood spent on a farm on the vast Canadian prairie of Saskatchewan. Our small quarter section of land was my playground. Here I was free to roam, to explore, to lie on my back while looking at the ever-changing cumulus clouds forming animals, castles and whatever else my imagination imagined. And, of course, dream of... well, whatever is a young girls' dream.

It was a mixed farm. Because much of the land had not been cleared for growing crops, and what was cleared was rather rocky, my parents chose to raise a true menagerie of animals instead. There were cows. There were pigs. There were chickens. There were horses, sheep, ducks, geese, dogs and cats.

The farm was also self-sustaining. Besides being one of the family's main sources of income, honey collected from our bees provided us with a year-round supply. Wool, shorn from the sheep, was not only another major source of income, but also gave us comfy comforters and sweaters knitted by my mom. Goose down and chicken feathers were used to stuff quilts and pillows. On the flip side, our horses were primarily work horses (yes, we were poor) but we also rode them for fun.

As far as food sustenance goes, a huge vegetable garden (fertilized with manure) and some of the animals satisfied our nutritional needs. A fresh-water spring nearby provided us with refreshing, cool, potable water in summer. In winter, we melted snow. And we had a continual supply of milk, cream, home-churned butter, cottage cheese and eggs.

To my recollection, the main consumer products we ever purchased were baking ingredients and clothing. And the clothing was mostly limited to new school clothes because both my mother and I sewed.

To me, it was an idyllic existence. Springtime was especially exciting because it meant the birth of baby animals. I loved to cuddle baby chicks and ducks and to feel their down tickling my skin. I loved to watch baby calves trying to get their footing on wobbly legs. And I loved to watch the lambs frolicking about in their races and games of tag.

They say sheep are silly. Unfortunately, some also don't appear to possess a maternal instinct. It seemed that every spring at least one mother would abandon its young. But that just meant my parents would bring the baby lamb inside the house to warm up behind the wood stove. And we got to bottle-feed it! As it grew, it became our pet and followed us wherever we went. Now you know the backstory to *Mary Had a Little Lamb*...

Our other pets were cats and dogs. We had two pet dogs named Blacky and Brownie. Hey, don't blame me for the lame names. One of my brothers named them. He's the sibling with no imagination.

Blacky was a mutt, or as we called him, a Heinz 57, named after the sauce. He was beautiful, what with his long, mostly black fur, white throat and paws. Heinz 57 or not, he had an innate herding sense. All our farm animals knew they were "barn" animals; they slept in the barn and lived in the barnyard. Except the chickens. They thought the entire property belonged to them – not just the chicken coop. Blacky knew different. Whenever the chickens got too close to the house and the flower beds, he immediately rounded them up and chased them back into the barnyard. The chickens probably wondered how THE DOG got special privileges of remaining near the house, because they would consistently challenge his authority. Silly chickens. They got chased away every time.

But let's talk about those woolly mammals otherwise known as sheep. Sheep are pretty useless without a shepherd and on our farm, tending these balls of wool on four legs was one of my chores. To be honest, it didn't feel like a *chore* to me at all. To me, it was an awesome opportunity to stick my nose in a book to instantaneously and effortlessly be transported into another world.

The sheep, meanwhile, saw my distraction as an opportunity to escape into the alfalfa patch or into the neighbour's wheat field. Not good. Unlike the more intelligent animals such as cows, sheep don't know when to stop grazing at the forbidden alfalfa patch. As a result, they can become bloated and even die if they aren't stopped in time. Besides being gluttonous creatures, sheep can also be very obstinate. The minute I would chase one sheep out of the alfalfa patch, a second would take its place. Then, when I chased the second one out, the first came back. It was an impossible task. That is, until Blacky stepped into the picture.

One day, I decided to take Blacky with me when shepherding. It didn't take me long to find a pleasant spot to plunk myself down in the grassy meadow and commence to read. I looked up just in time to see a cloud of dust in the distance. It was the entire flock of sheep making a mad dash towards the neighbour's field. But then, I spied a black streak encircling them, stopping them in their tracks. Blacky to the rescue! I watched in awe as he contained every single one of the woolly bunch within a tight circle. This had never happened before. No one ever taught our mutt to herd sheep. He just knew what to do!

After my able assistant and I directed all the sheep back into their pen in the barnyard, I couldn't wait to tell my parents what had transpired earlier that day.

My mother acknowledged the feat but seemed to have something else on her mind.

"How would you like to cut dad's hair?" she asks.

"Uh, well... but I don't know how!"

"We'll teach you. It's not that difficult."

My mother momentarily disappeared into the house and returned with a chair, towel, fine-tooth comb and scissors. Mom sat down in the chair and wrapped the towel around her neck. Dad lovingly combed out a strand of mom's long hair. Then he demonstrated how to trim while simultaneously moving the comb. It looked complicated.

"That looks hard," I say.

"Blacky, *thweet* come here, boy!" my dad whistles.

Blacky dutifully trots over to us, tail wagging. Poor, trusting soul.

"You can practise on Blacky!"

I lovingly comb out a section of Blacky's beautiful, long fur and start trimming, all the while getting encouraging tips from both my parents. My mother seemed satisfied with my efforts. Or maybe she just didn't want me to completely ruin Blacky's coat.

"OK, dad! You're next!" she announces.

My dad takes his place in the chair, and I, encouraged by my haircutting lesson, begin trimming his hair. It's going swimmingly, and I'm growing more and more confident by the minute. But then the comb catches on a knot in dad's hair. The comb just stays there. And I've just created a big bald patch at the back of dad's head.

Sensing that something is wrong, my dad asks, "What happened? Did you cut too much?"

"Oh no," my mom chimes in. "It looks great!" Sometimes, parents can be such convincing liars.

"It'll grow back," she whispers to me out of the corner of her mouth.

Well, the bald spot on dad's head and the one on Blacky's back did eventually grow back. And you probably think that after receiving this training, I left home to begin a professional career as a hairstylist. It was not to be. But I was given license to be the family barber from that day forward. And my parents' resourcefulness has been an inspiration to me to this very day.

Irene on the farm

Raining Cowboys and Injuns
by Mike Cavanagh

When we were kids, my older and larger brother, Pete, and I spent most of the time goading, prodding, dobbing in (me on him) or just outright whacking (him on me, hence see 'dobbing in') each other, interspersed by occasional bouts of sibling harmony, bordering on true affection in rare times indeed. Apart from sibling mayhem, most of my earlier memories of the house we lived in at Burling Avenue are full of sunshine and running around like mad things. Pete was a sun and beach boy from day one, but I always loved the colder, grey, wet days, feeling snug inside, sitting near the window panes and watching the rain spatter on the glass. The smaller water droplets coalescing in their slightly manic zig-zagging, growing in size and picking up speed as they pulled in other droplets until they careened down the glass, leaving a thin trail of liquid silver that gradually broke up into droplets again. They seemed alive, and the whole process some miracle I was privileged to observe. It was my brother however, who bestowed upon me what still seems a miraculous precipitatory experience.

It was one of those days that just couldn't make up its mind as to whether or not it was a rainy one or a sunny one, alternating between moods for much of the morning. Pete was ten and I was eight and we'd just come inside out of yet another shower of rain that had interrupted our 'cowboys and injuns' on the front lawn. We'd used the large sandstone fishpond as 'The Old Lone Star Ranch Dam' or some such where me and my 'injuns' were camped waiting in ambush for the brave blue coats of the 45th Cavalry to trot into all unawares, unsuspecting and stuff like that.

"Better keep a look out boys. Reckon it's a might too quiet 'round here," had opined the devilishly prescient blue coat Captain.

I mean, how in heaven's name could he suspect anything with we injuns well-hidden on the other side of the ole dam? Yes, OK, we were in full view only three metres away, but you know, story continuity and all that.

"Wampa-a-pampa-pa. Wamapa-pamp-a," we injuns intoned as we danced around our fire.

Strangely it seemed to be night-time in injun territory and daylight where the blue coats were… oh well, can happen.

The massacre (of the injuns – it was always the injuns) of Old Lone Star Ranch Dam was just about to ensue as the brazen blue coats rounded 'Rattlesnake Gulch' (Dad had left the garden hose in the fishpond after last filling it) when a shower of rain hit, sending brave blue coats and injuns alike scampering up Stoney Creek Falls (the tiled, concrete front steps) and onto the High Chaparral (the verandah) to get out of the rain. Good thing too, as we heard Mum's voice from inside the house,

"Peter, Michael! The Toll House cookies are out!"

Toll House cookies – chocolate chip cookies that I had developed a far from healthy appetite for. Pretend massacres gave instant way to real life push, shove, scrimmage, and the screen door slamming in my face as Pete beat me through as we bolted Toll House cookie-ward. I paused for the merest, fleetest second, pondering whether to scream blue murder and dob my brother in, but in a most rare moment of logic, decided that would only delay my arrival in cookie-dom, so I reefed open the door and bolted to the kitchen, oblivious to my mother's cut off entreaty,

"Don't slam the …"

Bang!

"… door. *Sigh.*"

Ah, Toll House cookies – one of the few things that I can remember my mother cooking consistently to perfection. Couldn't get enough of 'em.

Having come in out of the rain and settled into my fourth Toll House cookie, I was oblivious to the change in weather, again, and that the sun was now shining. Pete noticed though and grabbing a fistful of cookies called over to me as he ran back outside,

"Come on, it's sunny again!"

I forwent immediate response as I concentrated on sucking the last morsel of chocolate chip from between my front teeth whilst simultaneously stuffing another cookie in. Within seeming seconds, Pete came banging back in through the front door, grabbed me by the arm and fair dragged me outside.

"Come out here, it's amazing!"

"Mmmph, flumpph, gaffgawg…" was the best I could manage as I was man-handled back out to the High Chaparral, then down the Stoney Creek Falls. Heck, can't an injun even eat a hearty meal before he's massacred?

On the lawn in the sunshine the sky was mostly blue above us apart from one large grey cloud and there was no rain falling. Pete let go of me and ran two metres to our left, towards the back gate, laughing like a maniac. What the blazes was he…? Then my eyes opened wide and my mouth opened. I think I made a small sound of wonderment and glee, like,

"Eeeek!" and I ran over to where he was.

And we stood there waving our arms about for three seconds, still in bright sunshine but now within a shower of sun gilded rain. Then we both ran back to where we'd been and hopped around shaking off the raindrops for three seconds in the sunshine but with not a drop falling on us. We ran in and out of the rain for about ten seconds more before the edge of the sun shower moved on across the house and away, to leave us giggling and laughing, bespeckled with raindrops glinting in the sun. For those brief moments, my brother and I had literally run in and out of the rain, something I've never experienced since. A small wonderment had befallen us, and though of no importance in the great scheme of things, it's still a thing for which I consider myself blessed and forever thankful to my brother.

Mind you, only a short time later the injuns were still massacred, but at least with far less complaint than was the norm.

It came from above
by Alison Alderton

The wild river tumbled and fell over the rocks at Höljerud sending up a fine mist to refresh the towering spires of purple lupin blooms bordering the banks. The dippers dipped, flew a short distance before settling to bob and dip again whilst an iridescent turquoise coloured kingfisher darted by, fast and low to the water. The scene was never still, totally different to the lateral canal cut overlooking the river where we had spent the night on our barge *Lily*. Here things were quiet and still, there was only the slightest sound of water over rapids to be heard. Now, it was early morning and we somewhat reluctantly prepared to leave the nature reserve and all the beauty it had bestowed upon us. Beagle Maksi, having already enjoyed a walk, had his lifejacket on and was sitting in *Lily's* wheelhouse eager to see where we were heading next.

We met the lock keeper as previously arranged. He had the lock gates open for us so Roger guided *Lily* into the chamber with its jagged walls, the result of being blasted through a rocky outcrop, and timber uprights which to me resembled giant toothpicks. With *Lily* safely roped in, we were soon passing the time of day with the lock keeper.

Being at the bow and directly in front of the leaking lock gates I was unable to hear the conversation so once we started gently and slowly rising, I found myself becoming engrossed in the tiny maidenhair ferns protruding from the lock wall and trying my best not to let the ropes rub on them. The various species of ferns which make lock walls their home never cease to amaze me. They not only endure a vertical existence in frequent submersion of cold river water but thrive on it. Suddenly, there were raised voices. I looked up to see the lock keeper pointing towards the front of the lock. Concerned the rope I was controlling had become snagged, I checked but could not see a problem. Looking back, Roger had climbed onto the rails surrounding *Lily's* back deck and was also pointing, but I could not see anything, only the uneven lock wall and the sky above me.

It was obvious that something was wrong. Hoping to gain a better view, I took a few steps along the deck then gazed up, my eyesight following the hand pointing that everyone was earnestly making and, as I did so, a huge beaver leapt off the side of the lock! The silhouette of its body temporarily blocked out the light, and I found myself plunged into darkness as it brushed by my head and landed with an enormous thud on *Lily's* roof. The noise was unbelievable; the whole boat seemed to shudder, lurch downwards and tip to port then quickly righted itself, but the drama did not stop there.

The beaver had landed partly on the gangplank stored on the roof. This acted as a springboard catapulting the beaver's rear end into a somersault, over the roof edge causing the poor creature to thud down onto the side deck which was just wide enough to accommodate its chunky body. Maksi, with his grandstand view, had gone into overdrive, squeaking hysterically at the extraordinary scene being played out in front of him. I was afraid Maksi would try to leap out of the open window, but before I could think of going to him, the beaver began scrabbling its way towards me. I quickly backed up, jumped onto the gas locker, the rope holding *Lily* safely against the lock chamber wall still taught in my grasp. The poor beaver was terrified and must have hurt himself but did not seem to want any human intervention, only an escape route. Stopping near me, the beaver somehow managed to turn in the tight space and run back down the deck with its large, flat, tail slapping against the steelwork of *Lily's* deck. This caused Maksi to erupt into a fit of barking and in fear, the beaver launched itself over the side and splashed into the water.

I could not believe what I had witnessed, but these thoughts soon turned to concern for the beaver. It was swimming around the boat as the lock filled obviously hurt or at the very least, well and truly shaken. Eventually, the beaver settled alongside *Lily* huddled tightly between her steelwork and the lock wall, but I was fearful that the poor creature would get squashed. It looked as if the beaver had damaged a front claw, I could see it hanging back at an awkward angle and silently prayed it was not a broken toe, foot or worse.

Suddenly the beaver disappeared. "I can't see him," I yelled to whoever was listening. By now the lock was full. "I think we will haul *Lily* out just in case the beaver has dived down and is sitting on her skeg." The skeg is a rearward extension of the keel intended to protect the propeller and support the rudder. On *Lily*, this is a substantial plate plenty large enough for our beaver to sit on, but not a good place with a churning propeller! Roger was peering into the water, just as concerned as I.

"Don't worry, I'll keep an eye on him," said the lock keeper, but that was not good enough for us. We wanted to check that the beaver was not badly hurt and whether there was anything we could do to help.

Roger and I slowly bow hauled *Lily's* heavy mass through the open lock gates and moored her at the landing stage. By now, Maksi had calmed down,

111

but he remained in the wheelhouse as we checked all around *Lily*. The water was clear yet retained its orange tint from the high iron content found in this area of Dalsland, making the flat platform that formed the skeg easy to make out. It did not look as if Mr Beaver had taken up residence as feared, so we walked back to the lock where the keeper was peering into the depths. "I've seen them sit on the rocks behind the upright timbers," I told him, and sure enough, after a few moments of searching these areas, we found the beaver, sitting just below the water surface on a protruding rock. He gazed up at us with his large black reflective eyes. He looked quite calm but of course, none of us could tell if he was badly hurt.

As there was no more we could do, we somewhat reluctantly continued our journey. Beavers are large mammals, and there is no way we could have retrieved him from the lock to check on his well-being without endangering ourselves. The lock keeper assured us he would leave the gates open so the beaver could swim out and, in the meantime, keep checking on him. He, like us, was completely astounded by what had happened, had never seen anything like it before and we were all sure that none of us would ever again witness such a close encounter of the furred kind!

Maksi in the wheelhouse

O'er the Bridge that Spans the River
by Ronald Mackay

"Je pense qu'il reviendra." Dr Hutchison's eyes searched for the inattentive. "Mackay!"

The sound of my name shattered a daydream.

"Mackay!" His voice was edged with impatience.

* * *

Spring 1959. Dundee. An unusually warm Friday afternoon, for Scotland. Final class. Higher French. Revision before the final exams. *Verbs of hope that require the subjunctive in the negative when there is little likelihood that the action will occur.* The monotonous rattle of a pneumatic drill removing cobblestones had enticed me elsewhere.

* * *

Dr Hutchison served also as Deputy Rector of the Morgan Academy. Like all our teachers, he'd been christened with a nickname. *Bunny.* No, not from any animal resemblance but from an association that went: *Hutchison. Hutch. Domestic rabbits live in a hutch. Bunny is another word for rabbit. Bunny-hutch.* By such crooked, schoolboy logic, Dr Hutchison became *Bunny.* Behind his back, that is.

* * *

The limp slouch of pupils suggested unaccustomed inattention. Bunny was much respected and more greatly feared. We seventeen-year-olds were just beginning to acquire the wisdom to distinguish between fear and respect.

Rumour had it that Bunny had played a major role in Italy during the War as an officer in military intelligence. Like all our teachers who had served, and they were many, Bunny never talked about the War in other than oblique terms.

Nevertheless, it was whispered that his pursuit of intelligence had driven him ahead of the allies advancing through Italy. One sunny day, he entered a village church to admire its frescoes and came face-to-face with a group of Wehrmacht officers sheltering from the heat. Bringing himself to attention, his Webley inaccessible in its awkward holster, Bunny had smiled ruefully at the astounded officers, hands spread. Then in perfect German:

"In the King's name, I declare you my prisoners. You are surrounded by my armed patrol. To respect the sanctity of this chapel, I will not draw my revolver, but you must lay yours down."

Cucumber cool, Bunny had marched the disarmed officers out of that cool, holy place, handed them over to his driver whose Tommy-gun with its hundred rounds in the drum encouraged their cooperation, and radioed headquarters to report that he had taken five valuable prisoners. Before being escorted off for interrogation, the senior officer had stood to attention, saluted Bunny and in perfect English announced:

"Sir, I congratulate you on your presence of mind, which is a credit to your rank, your regiment, your King and to the unequalled British sense of humour."

* * *

I struggled to recall the rule and the subjunctive form of the verb.

"Tell him, Macgregor!"

Macgregor smirked. "Je ne pense pas qu'il revienne."

"Mackay, can you repeat the correct answer *exactly* as offered?" Bunny waited.

* * *

Bunny's questions could mean different things at different times. Woe betide any pupil who, out of innocence or an unseemly sense of humour, failed a *Bunny-question*.

Had I dared to offer a Macgregor-like smirk before repeating the correct answer, I'd have been guilty of insolence and justly punished. We learned to interpret Bunny's tone of voice, give due weight to his facial expression, and always take context into consideration, before daring to reply.

Experience had honed the skills that allowed us to know what his questions meant and to respond appropriately. Failure to do so constituted *insolence* and, in even the slightest degree *insolence* was not tolerated at the Morgan Academy. It was punishable by *six-of-the-best* delivered on each hand by the teacher disrespected. Punishment was administered by a *Lochgelly*, a thick leather strap twenty-four inches long and an inch wide. The end that struck your outstretched hand was split like a serpent's tongue to intensify the pain. Adroitly administered, *six-of-the-best* brought tears to the eyes of the bravest. The Lochgelly encouraged diligence and effort by discouraging repetition of the same offence.

* * *

"Je ne pense pas qu'il revienne." I repeated the answer without the smirk. Bunny nodded, satisfied that my pronunciation was closer to the French than MacGregor's. My determined improvement cancelled out MacGregor's earlier triumph.

However, the moment had triggered something in Bunny. Some intuition that demanded he teach us a lesson, one that he knew we must learn before we *almost-adults*, finally and forever, and in the words of our school song, passed:

> *O'er the Bridge that spans the River,*
> *Soon we pass away alone,*
> *Leaving comrades keen and clever,*
> *For the lure of the unknown.*
> *But, though much or mean our treasure,*
> *Though our fame be great or ill,*
> *We shall still recall with pleasure,*
> *Our dear "Morgan" on the hill.*

"Listen!" Theatrically, Bunny cupped his ear exaggerating the gesture perhaps to admit, after all those years of unremitting discipline and before we passed from his guardianship, that like us he too, was human.

With that simple gesture, Bunny assisted us across an invisible threshold to a place where the customary differences that separate teacher from pupil were intentionally blurred.

The class rallied to his call, conscious of the incandescence of the moment but uncertain of where it might lead.

"What do you hear?" He paused. We knew it was a question he himself would answer. "Repairing the tramlines. Men with shovels, wheelbarrows, a pneumatic drill. They earn a decent living. You can join them. Any of you." He scanned the eyes of each pupil and, it seemed to me, held mine a fraction longer.

"You can join them as a common labourer right now, if you want. They're crying out for you. Crying out!" He let his repetition sink in.

"Why are you in here and not out there with a shovel?"

His eyes drilled into me. I decided that this was a real question.

"I must complete my school education, Sir."

Without altering his expression, he focused on another pupil and then another. Answers came fast.

"My dad's a labourer so my mum wants more for me and my brother, Sir."

"It's better to be educated, Sir."

"I'm here so I can get a good job when I leave, Sir and be better paid."

"Education." Bunny let the word sink in. "What does it mean to become educated?" His eyes roved over the class. We were triggered now, on a treasure-hunt that could lead anywhere.

"With an education, Sir, we'll pass our final exams."

"Sir, an education means to get good marks on all our subjects."

"If we're educated, we can be professionals, Sir. Lawyers, surveyors, accountants."

"So we can apply to study medicine at St Andrews, Sir." Mahaddy's mother, a jute-mill worker, was ambitious for her son to become a doctor.

"Sir, so we can join the Civil Service, work as a reporter for D.C. Thompsons, join the Merchant Navy, be a nurse, a teacher…"

Our answers came thick and fast, even though none of us had pondered the matter deeply. We repeated the hopes, beliefs, aspirations, commands and dreams of our parents. Most working or lower-middle-class, all parents wanted *"more"* for their sons and daughters though what that *"more"* consisted of was hard to pin down.

Bunny relaxed. His expression suggested that none of our answers was adequate; that his mission was to enlighten us.

"Educate… what's the origin of the word?" We were expected to answer.

"Latin, Sir. *Educare. To rear.*"

"*Educere*, Sir. Latin for *to bring forth.*"

Bunny nodded. "The education we offer you here or in any school, is a set of tools that you can use to cultivate your minds, so you can grapple with the best that mankind has produced." He paused. "What's another word for the best that mankind has produced?"

We could see from his eyes this was not a question we were supposed to answer.

"Culture. Culture represents the best that mankind has produced. And culture comes from the *'rearing'* of *educare* and the *'bringing forth'* of *educere*. Acquiring culture depends on being educated. The job of every teacher here is to encourage your growth, to prepare your minds so that you can strive to become cultured citizens of this country."

116

Bunny was silent. Then:

"Why are you here, here at the Morgan?"

We could tell he was going to enlighten us.

"You're here because you've shown yourselves capable of learning. You passed your qualifying exams. You're in the upper quartile."

We didn't know what or where the upper quartile was, but *upper*, we guessed, had to be better than *lower*.

"You've got what it takes. All of you. Your years in school instead of wielding a shovel is not time wasted. What you learn elevates your spirits, increases your knowledge, adds to your experience and understanding of art and literature, physics and chemistry, biology and history, and languages including your own. Education isn't wasted. It fulfils you."

Bunny looked at each of us.

"To receive an education ensures that you learn what's worth learning – but it implies more than just learning." Bunny paused. "It necessarily involves your taking responsibility for pursuing that learning for the good of mankind. So you can stand with your back straight, eye-to-eye with the world and help fix it when it goes wrong. And believe me," he paused and looked into a place far, far from our classroom, before coming back:

"Believe me, a lot can go wrong with our world. I've seen it with my very own eyes."

Our attention quickened. We were used to being told that to *take responsibility* was our moral duty. We weren't used to being told by a teacher that the world could go wrong, and when it did, we would have the responsibility of setting it aright.

"Here at the Morgan we offer each one of you – if you want it – a sense of duty, a moral code, a sense of the importance religion and tradition play in tying us together as a community. And to guarantee that binding holds, we bear the responsibility for being always on the lookout for social improvement." He paused. "Improvement that everyone can enjoy, not just you or your family group. It's up to all of you to rise to this challenge."

"Do we have a choice, Sir?" A lone voice cut into Bunny's message.

Without permission being first granted, questions were frowned upon at the Morgan.

"Who spoke? Stand up!"

David Littlejohn stood. Had it been anyone less-deserving than David, the question might have been heard as an impertinence demanding six-of-the-best. But David was the best among us. Bright, thoughtful, always respectful, and serious beyond his years.

We held our collective breath.

"Do we have a choice?" Bunny repeated the words slowly. "Good question, Littlejohn."

He removed his spectacles and massaged his forehead.

"Not everybody has the ability to imagine a world beyond themselves, beyond their own puny lives. So, pursuing an education, striving to acquire culture, is not so much a choice as the consequence of a gift. All of you possess that gift. You have proved it. But lots of men and women out there who went to work in manual jobs at fifteen possess that gift too."

He replaced his spectacles.

"And more's the pity, you can abandon your gift. Some of you will become professionals but will let that gift wither, the gift that allows you to look beyond your own limited perspective. You'll let your world shrink to merely servicing your own wants and ignoring the broader needs of your community, of our society."

"So, education is a continuous conscious choice." David's face was serious. "We're never off the hook."

"That's right, David. You always have to struggle for education and the culture that it allows you to access. You must be prepared to strive your whole life, never give up and never, ever let your guard down."

I knew I was witnessing, consciously for the first time, pupil and teacher in conversation, talking on the same level, man to man. I knew that David Littlejohn was growing up and that the rest of us must follow his example. To seriously listen, to think deeply, and to question *Why*?

"Do you understand?" Bunny uttered the words as an appeal to our deepest care, not as a teacher but as a fellow human being.

We nodded, conscious that we were being led on an impromptu rite of passage, one of greater importance than our final exams. Bunny, a veteran in the fight for what it meant to be educated and cultured, was offering us a lesson for life, a truth that placed an awesome responsibility on our shoulders. We were conscious in that moment that to shrug off that burden would not only deny our deepest nature but would place us in unfathomable peril. Perhaps drag our families, our country, and our very world into the pit.

Hail "The Morgan" stately, splendid,
Hail the teachers, every one!
Cheer we every goal defended
Every hit and every run!
We would strive with every lesson,
As we strive when at our play,
Learn with every passing session,
"Who would rule, must first obey."

Vivian (sister) and Ronald (brother and author)
visiting the Morgan Academy in 1998

The Cuddle
by Elizabeth Moore

I'm sitting with my baby grandson in the last of the summer sun. I've sought refuge at my daughter's home during such unchartered times. I need family to be the touchstone by which I pace my existence in these, the oddest of days.

I am bald, chemotherapy has seen to that. I'm not working while I have my treatment and feel adrift from my ordered world; the one I lived in before the biopsies and surgeries and drugs. I am tired and have marked my recent existence in days. The day for chemical intervention, the days of not being me with a low grade buzzing of side effects and the days of beginning to feel the world returning to a bearable tilt; my respite measured in yet more days before the cycle begins again. I create my version of approach/avoidance theory, a remnant of Psych 101. I don't want treatment, but I know it has been ordered for my survival, my recovery.

He stirs a little and I shift to make him more comfortable. Dark eyelashes curl down soft cheeks and his little body shudders quietly as he takes in tiny, stuttering breaths and then relaxes again. I have time to marvel at the beauty of new life; the perfection of every inch of him and the tiny stork-beak mark behind his ear. I have time to wonder where he was before he entered this world and I have time to reflect on how quickly he has filled my heart, making room for more love.

He has made this journey with me. He was five weeks and the size of an apple seed at my diagnosis. I was afraid to tell my daughter in case my illness affected her pregnancy, and I shared my fears with the kind doctor who supervised my day of tests. She comforted and assured, and I turned towards the window as tears blurred my view of the basketball court on the roof of the inner-city school beneath me. Students, unaware that the world had just shifted perceptibly for me, called, jumped, passed, and blocked the ball. They should not be happy while I was bewildered, lost, and scared.

He grew and kicked as my world shrank by degrees; each time they pumped the poison and whispered encouragement. His ultrasound showed a tiny, raised hand, waving from his quiet, warm comfort to the world awaiting him. I cradled this as an acknowledgement of my travails, a nod from his safe haven to my current rotation of weeks.

My life was now shaded differently, more greys and shadows than the sharp colours of a normal, uncluttered life. My scalp prickled and itched as hair fell in clumps before being overruled by exacting shaver blades. I tried wigs and scarves, but my cancer had appeared at the beginning of a hot summer and I chose comfort over appearance. My nails were painted black to stop them falling off during the indiscriminate surge of drugs through my system. I lived the Gothic days of a timetable unfamiliar to me.

My careful stock-take of treatment hit a wall. There would be no oncology visit between Christmas and New Year, when my final purge was due. I shrugged off the mantle of stoicism and controlled emotions, donned to comfort those around me; those who loved unconditionally and tried to walk with me. I sobbed bitter tears and railed against the unfairness of the calendar. It was a personal rebuke of all my efforts to scrape through the days and weeks without crumbling.

My last confrontation with the cannula and four hours of infusion was almost an anti-climax. I still had to recover from this final healing assault, and the linear accelerator at the city hospital now had me on a rigid schedule with little respite. To miss a day was the equivalent of darkening the headmistress's study to ask for time away from the school routine.

When he was born, I was allowed a day off to visit my new grandson; three weeks early with time in Special Care. His helpless little form in the plastic crib, the tubes, and monitors; the unconscious surrender to treatment and care mirrored my own. He had no control of the world around him; he just was. I quietly sobbed in sympathy but smiled as I comforted my anxious daughter. He will be fine.

Now my weekly prison still pins me, motionless, beneath the beam of a linear accelerator to the crooning of Johnny Mathis. Today it's Sunday, with time off for good behavior and a cuddle. Tomorrow I will return to the queue of backless gowns for another barrage of high-energy x-rays.

A stretch, a gentle sigh, and two big eyes open. I wonder what I look like to this new life; a tired, bald Nanna in glasses? And there it is, a beaming toothless grin; an eyes-crinkled-shut smile. No bias, no judgment, just love, and it's Monday tomorrow.

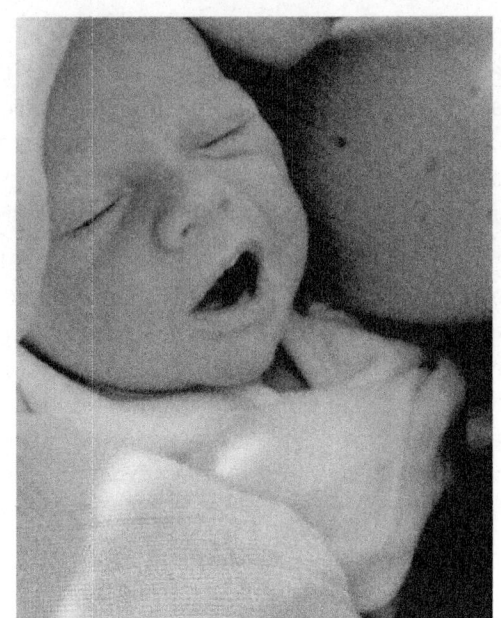

Declan

Going Batty
by Frank Kusy

11th April 2020

Three weeks into lockdown and while a large part of the UK is going batty, we're doing quite well.

Madge is doing particularly well: 'Up till now, and this may sound selfish or smug, but I haven't found this difficult at all. The weather's been fantastic, I'm getting a lot more sleep, and I don't have to get on a bus six times a week to go to work.'

'It's a cinch, isn't it?' I gave a short nod. 'We spend all day long playing cards, reading books, and taking long walks in the park. Not to mention cooking healthy home-made meals, hosting Zoom film quizzes, playing online bridge, and standing in sunlit supermarket queues.'

'And the birds are so loud!'

'Yes, with no traffic around, you can really hear them! They're tweeting their little socks off!'

'But Sparky is upset,' Madge referenced our nervous little cat. 'That scarecrow you made is really frightening him.'

'You made it,' I accused her. 'You cut up that square of aluminium foil and made it into a frilly wig. All I did was plonk it on a garden fork and stick it on the lawn.'

'Well, you didn't want those fat pigeons eating all that lawn feed you laid down, did you?'

I shot my wife a dangerous look. 'How did I know it wouldn't rain for a week? It said, "Fast Grow" on the packet and it hasn't grown at all.'

'Sparky hates your scarecrow,' Madge laughed in reply. 'He thinks it's Satan on a stick or an alien from another planet. It took him a whole day to walk past it, casting it furtive sideways glances as he went!'

To be honest, I feel like I'm on another planet myself. No gym, no cinema, no bridge club, no Buddhist meetings, and no frothy cappuccinos. The whole of Kingston upon Thames, where I live, is shut down. It took me two weeks to adapt to this, and during all that time I had the worst flu in eight years. It may have been the virus, I don't know, but I was coughing, running a fever, and sleeping so badly I didn't know if it was day or night. I was also smoking and drinking a lot more, which, when I come to think about it, means that I was just in 'adaptive shock'. All the routines of my life had been snatched away and my body had reacted as if suddenly plunged into solitary confinement.

The worst thing was, as a writer, there was so much going on that I didn't know where to start. 'There's nothing dramatic to have as a starting point,' had been my lament to Madge. And she had come back with: 'There's nothing more dramatic than a global virus. It's dramatic enough to write about the change of the whole lifestyle – what they call the 'new normal'. You have to completely rethink your life. You can't meet any friends, you can't catch a train or a plane, you even put your life at risk by getting on a bus.'

She was right. With social distancing replacing the earlier UK policy of herd immunity (leaving all the bars and clubs open so that everybody got sick at once), people were now crossing the road to avoid each other. It reminded me of a childhood game called British Bulldog, where you dashed to the other side of the playground to avoid being tagged as 'It'.

The most prominent casualty of herd immunity, of course, had been our Prime Minister, Boris Johnson. Having gallantly shaken hands with lots of Covid-19 victims, he had come down with the virus himself. But not before telling us all to wash our hands thoroughly while singing 'Happy Birthday to You'. Twice.

'My friend Rosemary sent me a funny video about that,' Madge said today. 'Boris Johnson is on the telephone to the Queen. He says: "Your Majesty. I have contracted the virus. What shall I do?" And the Queen says: "Go forth and embrace Donald Trump."'

12th April 2020

Boris Johnson came out of hospital today. He thanked all the people of the NHS for saving his life. 'It could have gone either way,' he said. What he did not say was that the doctors who were most responsible for his survival – who are putting their own lives on the line every day – would be rewarded in terms of increased status and remuneration. No, they would remain the lowest of the low, along with carers, teachers, nurses, and all those who contribute the most to society. The new norm needs to get a whole lot more 'normal' before government will take heed.

Not long ago, we all went out on the street to clap for our doctors and nurses. Then we went out to clap for our carers. But it is not claps they need. They need PPE (personal protection equipment) when they are in face-to-face contact with virus contractors. They also need more pay. In short, less claps, more cash.

Someone else who deserves more cash is Madge. She gets paid a ridiculous £120 a week, minus 20% tax, for six hours teaching at an adult education college in Richmond. What she does not get paid for is the twenty or thirty hours (by my estimation) preparation for these classes, which are now taught 'virtually' – i.e. by Zoom. 'Why do you do it?' I quizzed her, and she said: 'The students have paid already. What else can I do?'

Not that she, or I, should be complaining. We're both retired, I just got my first pension check, we own a large 3-bedroom house, we have no dependents (apart from a cat), and we're both in good health. Madge enjoys teaching, despite being grossly underpaid, and I enjoy cooking (on just one hob since the oven packed up 9 years ago) and preparing film quizzes for the class Madge taught last term on European cinema. It's a whole new world and we have the time and the inclination to tune in with it.

By way of light relief, we plugged into the *Now Show* on Radio 4. 'When you've spent a whole month going no further than your own house,' opined one presenter, 'holiday plans don't have to be so exotic. So, I asked someone, "where do you think you'll be going this year?" And they replied, "Well, we were looking at East Croydon. It'll be great to have a break from West Croydon."'

Gertrudinous
by Robyn Boswell

No matter how much you travel or how many exciting and exotic places you visit, nothing can ever match the feeling of the first time you step on a plane and head to another country across the ocean. That very first trip inspired me to travel the world.

In 1969, I took my first tenuous steps into the big, wide world, moving 100 miles away from home to Auckland to go to Teacher's College, where I made friendships that have endured to this day. In our last year, we daringly left the hostel that had been our home for two years and five of us rented a big old house together. During late nights sitting around chatting, we discovered that we all had a dream of exploring the world. The 'Big OE' (overseas experience) was almost a rite of passage for young New Zealanders so we made a plan to meet up at the end of our first year of teaching to spend our summer holidays in Australia – a terribly big adventure in those days.

Five of us set out on an Air France flight from Auckland to Sydney on Boxing Day. We were wearing our very best dresses and our families, who had all come to see us off on our journey across the Tasman Sea, bought us corsages of fresh flowers which we proudly – and naively – pinned on our bosoms and felt like sophisticated world travellers. The flight itself smacked of old-time travelling luxury with a three-course meal that included caviar, although none of us knew what those strange little glistening balls of fish-tasting stuff were. A tarmac glistening with water greeted us as we landed in Sydney. It was bucketing down with rain, so we got our raincoats out of our hand luggage and suited up, much to the amusement of many of our fellow passengers. In 1973, the only way off a plane in New Zealand was to walk across the tarmac. What an embarrassing surprise to find that Sydney was a bit more classy than Auckland and we walked off through a bone dry jetway, still wearing our raincoats.

Customs quickly disabused us of the wisdom of wearing fresh flowers when visiting another country. Then Immigration almost sent us back home on the next plane when we could only give them the address of the hotel we were staying in for the first night in Melbourne. Fortunately, I had the address of a friend of a friend of a friend who we didn't even know, but that satisfied them. Our education in the ways of the world had begun.

Sydney's incredibly humid summer heat was something we were totally unprepared for, so at the first opportunity we raced into the restroom and removed our panti-hose. We were sweltering! So much for sophistication. A porter at the airport told us to take a taxi into the city and quoted us the price. The taxi driver charged us four times the amount and in our naivety we paid up without comment. Nowadays when I get in a taxi in a foreign country, I pretend that I've been there before and know where I'm going. We managed to cram a bit of sightseeing into the day, but, coming from a country where trains were almost unknown, we were a bit challenged by the rail system. On a train to Central Station the guard called "All change" and we just kept sitting where we were. Eventually the guard had to come along and tell us that train wasn't going any further.

By that evening we were on the overnight train to Melbourne since that was the cheapest way to travel, an important criterion that would underline our travels together over the next few years. Sitting up all night on extremely hard, sparsely upholstered seats was a bit of a come-down from caviar and corsages, especially as we had to queue in the dining car for ages and dinner turned out to be tea and toast. At some ungodly hour just around dawn, the train lurched to a stop, and we discovered we had hit a couple of horses on the line, so were delayed for some time – that was also a portent for our further adventures together.

My neighbour's daughter's boyfriend was a used car salesman in Melbourne, and we had arranged to buy a used car from him. The morning was spent making a series of calls to Denise. In later years I have had my suspicions that she hadn't actually made any arrangements about the car before we arrived, but eventually she and her boyfriend turned up at our accommodation – the inappropriately named 'People's Palace' – with a car for us. I had never met Denise or her boyfriend before and he was the epitome of a slick, smooth car salesman in a shiny suit who didn't inspire the confidence that he was no doubt hoping to portray. In fact, after we met him, had someone said, "Would you buy a used car from this person?" I would have said an unequivocal, "No!" There was just something about him. I should maybe have listened to my inner voice, but we really had no choice as he had a car lined up for us for $285, so we paid our money and were the proud owners of a somewhat ancient, blue and white Holden station wagon. We very quickly named her Gertrudinous. Despite our apprehension and her rather noticeable flaws, we became quite fond of her over the few weeks we owned her.

The oily salesman had offered to fly to Sydney – at our expense – at the end of our trip, collect the car from the airport, drive it back to Melbourne, resell it and send us the money. We didn't hear from him for months. Then he spun us a tale about how he'd tried to drive the car back to Melbourne, but the engine had blown up half-way through his trip. We didn't believe him for one minute, and he probably had a great weekend in Sydney at our expense. We never saw a cent of our money, but oh well, it hadn't really cost us anything much for several weeks of fun.

With some trepidation, we set off on our first drive – around the block – to find a parking place. Linda and Pauline didn't drive, Teresa and Helen had only had their licenses for a few weeks, and I had mine for a year. Guess who got the job of driving first? We made a very slow and stately trip with me driving and the others adding lots of encouragement.

Having never been in a city that size, it was terrifying, but we survived. The next day I even managed to drive to the caravan park on the outskirts of Melbourne where we'd be staying for a few nights.

A couple of days later, once we had all gained a bit of confidence by driving out into the beautiful Dandenong Ranges and down to the beach, I plucked up courage to drive us back into the city for the day. I still wasn't confident to drive much above snail's pace and was taken aback when we were pulled over by a couple of young cops. They said they were doing a license check, but I'm pretty sure it had a lot more to do with a car load of young, attractive women. They didn't seem particularly interested in my license, but they did suggest I might like to drive a little faster. They treated it as a huge joke – we nearly had heart failure!

Teresa opted to drive home after dinner in the city. We were quite lost and crawling along a dark, deserted street trying to find the way out when poor Gertrudinous, our new pride and joy, failed to stop at a red light because the brakes had suddenly given up. Fortunately, we drifted to a halt right opposite a petrol station where the proprietor took pity on the five naïve Kiwi girls. He couldn't find anything wrong and rang the RACV to have Gertrudinous towed to a garage that could repair it in the morning. Luckily – although we hadn't thought so at the time – we had to pay to join the RACV so we could get insurance on the car. We all piled into the tow truck for the trip to the garage, then had a very hairy taxi ride back to our caravan park. The kind guys at the garage checked the car over, fixed the leaking brake fluid and put on a new radiator hose. Sadly, though, they apparently didn't discover the lack of a handbrake, so we had to learn to live with foot brakes only. That caused great hilarity when we went to a drive-in theatre for the first time ever and kept rolling back on the slope, so someone had to sit in the driver's seat for the whole movie with their foot on the brake. Driving off with the speaker attached to the car was another story.

We wended our way from Melbourne to Adelaide along the stunning Great Ocean Road, enjoying the sights and spending most evenings enjoying meals and fun in various pubs along the way. Unfortunately, Victoria was having its hottest weather in 71 years and Gertrudinous, being a rather old 1963 lady, didn't have aircon. With the temperature hitting 43C, we drove with all the windows open, which only led to a searing hot current of air flowing over us.

I've always loved exploring back roads and byways. Down one particularly rough country road we came across a dead snake in the middle of the road. That just had to be explored, so we hopped out and were suddenly pursued by two very fierce dogs who were far more terrifying than the snake. A little further down the same bumpy road, the muffler fell apart. The nearest place we could get help was 50 miles away so there was nothing for it but to carry on, sounding like a 747 taking off and scaring every living beastie for miles. We roared past one old lady on the side of the road and nearly frightened her into the ditch. Eventually we came across a garage where a laconic young mechanic hoisted the car into the air and unenthusiastically banged on the exhaust pipe with a hammer, somehow hoping to push it back into the muffler. A few days later it dropped off again, so that night Linda scrambled under the car with an unravelled wire coat hanger and wired it all together. We had no further problems with the muffler for the rest of the trip.

About the same time, the speedo broke, which was very disconcerting to say the least. We tried to get it fixed without luck so had to drive on a bit of a wing and a prayer until we could get it fixed in Adelaide.

It was in Adelaide that I learned that getting lost when you travel is one of the most distressing things that can happen. I had taken note of the fact that we were parked in a square somewhere, but that was it. Somehow, I got separated from the others and suddenly realised I had absolutely no idea where I was or where the car was. Wandering around looking didn't help at all, so panic started to set in. I couldn't even remember where we were staying for the night. After walking fruitlessly for what seemed miles, I eventually hopped in a taxi, told the driver my dilemma and that the car was in 'the square' – he looked at me and said, "There are nine squares in Adelaide." I just said, "Well, take me to all of them." I sat there shaking with fear and trying to figure out where I would find my friends. Fortunately, the very first square we came to I spotted dear old Gertrudinous just pulling out of the carpark. They had waited over an hour and a half, also in a state of panic, so had finally decided to go to the police. Relief doesn't even begin to describe how I felt.

The next week or so we rambled through the Barossa Valley, availing ourselves of the products from the various world-class wineries, and along the Murray River, taking every opportunity we could to jump into the cool river waters to escape from the oppressive heat. We spent one night at a drive-in movie in a sandstorm which made for interesting movie viewing.

Gertrudinous behaved very well until we went to take off one morning and discovered we had a puncture. Fortunately, we were in a town and not way out in the wilds and we managed to get a new tyre from a wrecker's yard. He shook his head in disgust when he discovered we didn't have a spare – not one of us had actually noticed that – and gave us a second tyre for free to use as a spare.

The cooler air of the Snowy Mountains was a great relief. Although the mountains were nothing like our mountains at home, there were some very steep stretches of road. It was here that poor old Gertrudinous began to show her age. Several times we had to stop while trying to get up a hill and give her time to take a breath – and cool down. It was all a bit too much for our poor old pride and joy.

In Canberra we stayed in a Youth Hostel run by a very imposing older woman, who brought back unwanted memories of the overbearing matron from our teacher's college hostel. This one somehow thought she would look after the five Kiwi girls who were on her doorstep for a few days. We sure didn't appreciate being given the job of cleaning the loos! She warned us against going out at night because there was a large black snake that lived in the carpark. I've never been sure if that was true or if she just thought she was protecting our virtue.

As we got closer to Sydney, the heat was accompanied by fierce humidity, which was even more uncomfortable. In Bundanoon, while we waited for the Youth Hostel to open at 5 pm, we were told there was a swimming hole in an old mine in a park on the edge of town. It was only a 'short walk'. After an exceedingly steep walk through clouds of flies, we eventually came to the edge of a cliff – way below was a small, green pool. Linda was the only one of us brave enough to climb down to it and had a dip, although she did admit it was rather slimy. The walk back up the hill was horrific and made all the worse when I actually swallowed a fly.

Sadly, our few days in Sydney were marred by a petrol strike so we had to park Gertrudinous up and explore where we could by train and ferry.

At the airport we bid a very sad farewell to our erstwhile travelling companion. Despite her temperamental hiccups, Gertrudinous had become one of our gang and it hurt to leave her standing all alone in the vast carpark. We phoned the slippery salesman, and he promised he would be up the next week to collect her. If only that was true.

We had learned many lessons, amongst them that you don't need to dress up for a flight. However, Helen and Teresa had bought some very spectacular (think 1970s!) false eyelashes and were determined to wear them on the flight home to show everyone how trendy they had become. Due to the petrol strike, our flight was delayed, then rerouted via Brisbane for the plane to refuel. By the time we arrived home at 1:30 in the morning, our families had been waiting for many hours and were very happy to see us. No one noticed the false eyelashes!

Gertrudinous certainly set the pattern for all of my future travels – every long trip I have done since has been highlighted by breakdowns and technical failures, including one engine failing whilst flying out of LA and having an emergency landing, our ship delayed by a week when a generator blew up, nine weeks on a shaky bus in Europe, and a 4WD drive that caused us many anxious moments in three months in the Australian outback. All of those just add to the adventure. That first trip was the one that showed me how much fun it can be to set off and explore our wonderful world.

Gertrudinous

Espressivo
by Vernon Lacey

'You must be Vernon,' Mr Voigt said, from his workshop doorway. Blue eyes radiating welcome.

He invited me in and led the way to the test area. Guitars at different stages of manufacture, face up on benches, hanging on pegs, bound with twine as glue dried, spoke of artisanship, and the tonewoods stacked neatly on shelves, waiting to be born of their forest origins.

'Japanese,' Mr Voigt said, seeing I took a particular interest in a set of chisels, neatly lined up on a bench. 'Superb.' There was not a single power tool in the place.

I'd wanted to buy a new guitar for over a year and a new guitar had meant one thing, one country: Spain. Spain of the Felipe Conde guitars played by Paco de Lucia. Of the Ramirez guitars played by Segovia. And in recent times, the Marin guitar played by Isabella Martinez. Each one of these guitars has a unique tone. Design. And each captures some strand of the unmistakable magic and mystery, the passion and the pathos of Spain.

But then a chance conversation with another guitarist brought me closer to home, to Germany, where I live. I spent weeks reading. Learning. The Hauser Luthiers in Bavaria who made an instrument for Segovia in the 1930s and who declared it the greatest guitar of the era. The Fritz Ober guitars prized by the German virtuoso Johannes Kreusch. And the famed Matthias Dammann guitar, played by the Scottish guitarist David Russell. They were pinnacles of German *Technik,* and the more I read about them, the more I wanted to learn.

Soon there was a catch. The Hauser guitars could cost €30,000 or more. And even the cheapest of the other German guitars would cost €15,000. And so, with my modest budget, I started to look elsewhere.

In the studio of Voigt Luthiers, I sat under a framed black and white poster of Paco de Lucia. Mr Voigt handed me the guitar. The Conservatorio model, he explained. 'Cedar top, only finished a few weeks ago.'

It was light. Had a deep brown sheen. And the first note set it apart immediately from my ageing, low-end Raimundo Spanish guitar.

'Coffee?' Mr Voigt said.

I nodded approvingly, and for the next five minutes I was left to try out the guitar.

'The sound will improve,' Mr Voigt said, returning with a Bodum coffee canister. 'The sound is still dry.'

The aroma of coffee filled the air, compelling the delicate smells of cedar and spruce to withdraw. Sunlight streamed through the window and the workshop was transformed. The face of a newly polished guitar glistened. Gold tuning heads sparkled. And the rosewood body of another was no longer dark brown, but a spectrum of auburn, ebony, and tan.

A lingering church bell rang out the half-hour. Clear and singular. Strange coincidence, I thought.

'Call me Claus,' the luthier said as we swapped my coffee cup for guitar. 'Tell me, Vernon. Do you have a goal with your new guitar? Where do you see yourself – say in two, three years?'

'Well, I'm not him,' I said, pointing behind me at Paco de Lucia. 'But a guitar – well – it's always been therapeutic. It gives me hours of pleasure. Helps me to switch off – disconnect. Like you do when you go walking in the mountains.'

'Do you listen to your guitar?' Claus asked.

'Listen?'

'Yes – does it communicate to you, and you with it?'

Silence. Birdsong. Church-like calm.

'That piece you were playing –?'

'*Canto de Septiembre*? By Cabrera – the Cuban piece.'

'Yes – the slow one. Now play it again – only on another guitar.'

Mr Voigt picked a guitar from a rack.

'The Espressivo,' he said. 'I believe this might be better for you – you can play well. It will help you grow.'

I took the guitar by the neck. Raised it up and down in my hand. It felt no heavier than a book. Could it project? I thought loud guitars needed solid, sturdy bodies.

'It has a cello shaped back. Convex. To give it strength – and to allow me to miss out the struts. Saves weight.'

Unusually, the guitar had an additional sound hole in the side, a *Zargenmonitor*, Claus said, facing upwards. I peered inside the apple-size aperture.

'To create a direct connection with the player,' he said. 'You will see – especially if you ever play ensemble.'

I played the first five notes of *Canto de Septiembre*. They spanned the whole string range and the separation between the notes was crystal clear. It was a guitar in a different class than the Conservatorio.

Mr Voigt sipped his coffee. He bore the look of quiet confidence. The *Meister* with nothing to prove. Only observe. Listen. Accept. The guitar was a unique Voigt creation. It bore the name of his son – Marc-Julian Voigt. The sum total of over three-hundred years of family tradition and expertise. I continued to play the Cuban piece.

I was nervous. I pressed too hard and my fingers stumbled. Accustomed to a beginner's guitar, I was a novice. In my hands for the first time was a guitar of exquisite quality, sound and playability. I restarted the piece. Easing off the pressure. Finding the notes with a mixture of caution and growing confidence. Claus sat back in the armchair. A discernible smile emerged. It felt like fatherly approval. The resonating basses and contrasting trebles floated on the air, amidst the birdsong and the milky light.

'2017,' Mr Voigt said. 'That's the year the guitar was made. Here in this very workshop. We used the best of everything. It was a development on the former Espressivo. It's only ever been here. A showroom guitar.'

'It sounds sublime,' I said.

'Look. Vernon – you have a budget of €2500?' Mr Voigt said. 'Normally the Espressivo sells for nearly €8000. Let me offer you something to help. If you want. You give me the €2500 and pay a remaining €2500 whenever you get the money.'

'€5000?' I said, astonished. 'Such a reduction?'

'Yes – it's time to make another one for the showroom.'

'But – I'm on paternity leave. It could be a year, even two, before I get the money.'

'Pay me when you can,' he said. 'Let's say... within three years. I'll always help a musician when I can.'

'But I have no passport with me. No ID. How can we formalise the credit?'

'You'll return. I know you will.'

I looked at the guitar. French polished to perfection. Not a blemish. It had been played but kept pristine. In a world of data checks, automated payments, Amazon records, it seemed improbable I could leave with such a guitar on the basis of a verbal agreement to return with the final payment. Like an agreement done in ancient times. 'To be as good as one's word' as it was, in the old ways.

Claus got up. 'Try them both,' he said. 'I'll leave you for a while. Take more coffee if you want.' He left the test room and, visible through big interior partition windows, took up position at a wooden bench.

I played an Irish piece called *O Carolan's Concierto* on both guitars. Quick and lively. Then an air, *Blind Mary*. From there I played *And I Love Her*, for solo guitar. Bach's *Allemande* with its cascading notes and clear ringing of open strings. Each time the Espressivo was streets ahead. It had unparalleled sustain – every note ringing like a bell, pure and true. The strings went down with minimal effort. Here was a guitar of exquisite detail and comfort. The expression of generations of Voigt that had wrought a masterpiece.

I was still nervous. Hesitant about the financial commitment, but inside I knew this was my guitar. It somehow called.

I glanced out of the window, towards the Alps. Between here and there lay dozens of forests and countless trees. It seemed on that balmy spring day some ancient music, the music of nature, whispered, encouraging me to take the guitar whose wood had come from such forests, forests where the wind plays on branches and birds warble original melodies. Here in the workshop was nature transformed by human hand. The Espressivo. As though the songs of nature were captured inside, waiting to awake by the hand of a skilled caller.

I felt humbled. Like a novice about to set out anew.

'You'll grow with the guitar,' said Claus, bringing with him the smells of wood. 'Come back some day. And play it again for me.'

'I will – I'll learn my favourite piece – *Mallorca* by Albéniz. One day I'll come and play.'

The Espressivo

Summer Faith
by Tina Wagner Mattern

It was one of those miserable cold and rainy days in February that Portland, Oregon is famous for, and I was in a mood. Some people like rain. I am not one of those people. I had already gotten drenched once that day; taking my three-year-old daughter, Summer to her Christian preschool, so the last thing I wanted to do was to go out in it again. But it was 2 o'clock, and she needed to be picked up by two-thirty.

The traffic was terrible—when I finally arrived at the school; it was quarter-to-three and since the staff couldn't go home until all the children were safely in their parent's care—I knew Summer's teacher was not going to be happy.

Parking, I pulled my coat collar tight and buttoned it, reaching for my umbrella, which *wasn't* under the front seat where it should have been.

Someone (it couldn't have been me, of course) had left it in the garage that morning. I muttered a couple of words that likely made my Guardian Angel cringe and hurried through the lake forming in the parking lot.

Inside, Teacher Jennifer lifted an eyebrow at me in what I considered to be a very un-Christian like manner and pointed down the hallway. Summer was bent over a table, working to finish a painting.

"Hi Mommy," she chirped.

"Come on, honey," I called. "We're late. Teacher Jennifer wants to go home!

She held up her artwork. "Look! I drawed it for you!"

I took the paper and squinted impatiently at it. "Uh-huh. Good." I nodded and handed her coat to her. She put the picture down and folded her arms.

Arggghhh! I knew that stance.

"You hurt my feewins," she told me.

She wasn't going anywhere until I apologized—and it better be believable.

"It's wonderful!" I gushed. "Best one you ever did!"

She narrowed her eyes suspiciously.

"Really! Now please, can we go?"

She finally nodded and obediently held out her arms for her jacket. Outside, the rain was now a freezing, nearly sideways sheet. Both of us were soaked by the time we got to the car.

"It's wainin," Summer observed from her car seat behind me.

"No kidding," I said, drying my dripping hair with a handful of Kleenex before starting the car. I was just pulling out when Summer yelled, "WAIT! We gotta go back!"

Slamming on the brakes, I turned around. "What are you talking about? Go back outside? Are you crazy?"

"My Care Bears mitten," she cried, waving a lonely right-hand Care Bear at me. "My mitten's gone. I musta leaved it in school."

"Oh, for heavens..." Wait a minute, I muttered, backing the car back to the curb. Parking, I turned around to lean over the seat and undo her seat belt. "Okay, look in your pockets," I told her.

"I did!" she wailed. "It's not there!" She turned both pockets inside out to demonstrate their mittenless-ness to me.

"Get up," I sighed. "Maybe you're sitting on it." She climbed out. No mitten. We checked around and under the seat and on the floorboards. No mitten.

"See!" Summer cried. "We hata go back!"

"No! Maybe it's outside, next to the curb." I opened the door and stuck my head out—Niagara Falls poured over what was left of my hairstyle. No mitten.

"That's it!" I pronounced with finality. "You have three pairs of mittens at home, for crying out loud. Now, get back in your seat so I can buckle you in."

"I want my bestest Care Bear mitten!"

"Well, I want a week in Jamaica," I said.

Thinking on that kept her quiet for a moment or two, allowing me to get the car headed for home. But five minutes later:

"I want my MITTEN!"

Looking at her fuming countenance in the rear-view mirror, I said, "You've made that perfectly clear. Now give it a rest. Please!"

Eyes narrowed, frown lines deep as canyons, she muttered something under her breath.

"What did you say?"

"I say," she said, "I ask Jesus! Jesus will get me my mitten!"

Rolling my eyes, I said, "Jesus is NOT going to get you your mitten. He's BUSY!"

"He will too," she stated firmly.

I groaned. "Whatever. Now, not another word until we get home."

A rather loud raspberry sounded from the back seat.

Once we finally got home and into the house, I told Summer, "I've got a lot to do before I get dinner ready. Go play in your room."

"I don't wanna."

Shaking my head, I muttered, "Fine. Don't play, but no more about that mitten."

No comment.

I hung up our coats in the laundry room and headed to the kitchen to deal with the dishes in the sink when I remembered the mail had to be brought in—from outside—in the rain. Groaning, I put my coat back on and stomped down the hallway to the front door. Summer followed on my heels.

Opening the door, I looked hopefully up through the rain for any sign of blue sky. A clap of thunder echoed somewhere in the distance. "Oh, shut up!" I muttered and prepared to sprint to the mailbox.

Before I could take a step though, Summer squealed.

"What now?" I cried, spinning around.

"I tode you!"

"Tode me what?"

She pointed out the door, grinning. I turned, and following her finger with my eyes, looked down at the doorstep.

There, on the welcome mat, was a Care Bear mitten. A left hand, Care Bear mitten.

I blinked in disbelief, my mind scrambling to make sense of what I was seeing.

What? How? My common sense tried to say, well... she must have dropped it on her way out this morning. But no—we hadn't been anywhere near the front porch—we'd gone out through the garage. We had, in fact, not been out the front door in more than a week.

Stunned, I turned to look into Summer's shining face.

"I TODE you Jesus would get it for me!" she said, beaming.

Gathering her into my arms, I whispered, "Yes, you did, little girl. You really did."

Holding her tightly, I was overwhelmed with awe at our God who would perform such a miracle for a little child, simply because she stood steadfast in her faith.

After a minute, Summer pulled away to say, "Thank you, Jesus!" picked up her mitten and skipped off to her room.

I looked up to heaven and whispered, "Amen to that, Lord. Amen to that!"

Rambo, the ex-U.S. Marine in Cuba
by Denis Dextraze

Todd liked to be called Rambo. He was an ageing New Yorker vet wearing a bandana to hide his balding head. He had long ago forgotten his boot camp training, judging from his beer belly and his unshaven face. Sometimes, he might exceptionally shave that face by showing off his marine field shaving technique of using his razor-sharp twelve-inch combat knife that he always wore on his belt. He was a tough SOB who forgot that he was getting old. When he was not on what he called his first mistress, *Fantasma*, his fifty-three-foot Cheoy Lee ketch, he divided his time between his real Cuban wife and sons and his younger *mulata* girlfriend, his second mistress after *Fantasea*. In Cuba, any man of stature has to have mistresses. "*Noblesse oublige*". Didn't Fidel have dozens?

One day, Rambo asked me to accompany him for a crossing to Puerto Plata, Dominican Republic. He would assume all travel expenses including food, entry and exit cost and a ticket back to Cuba. He knew that, as an experienced blue water sailor, I had navigated the Bahama channel many times and negotiated the tricky entrance to the small Puerto Plata harbor twice, the first time on a moonless night. He also knew that both the currents and the prevailing winds were against us. He wanted to bring *Fantasma* to D.R. to close the sale to an American resident who had already inspected her. My interest was not so much the discomfort of spending four or five days beating the prevalent easterly wind against the current in his old disorganized and smelly boat, but I wanted to bring my Yamaha Virago motorcycle into D.R. to sell it. Indeed, the Customs authorities in Havana would not renew my temporary import permit, and I was not allowed to sell the motorcycle in Cuba.

I knew that hot-tempered Rambo maintained tense relations with the authorities, especially the Marina authorities. I once witnessed an altercation he had, in his poor Spanish, with the security guards, and finally, the coast guards on duty that came to the rescue. In some kind of premonition of events to come, I decided to get a reference from the Canadian Ambassador who lived in the Canadian mansion in Siboney, Playa District, only ten blocks away. This beautiful and large estate, just a mile away from the immense estate where Fidel Castro's family passed most of its time, was Canadian owned land in Cuba with its own pre-revolution titles.

The Canadian Ambassador's residence bought in 1945 had never been expropriated after the revolution because Canada never broke diplomatic relations with Cuba. I had easy access to the Ambassador because I was a member of the Canadian Club, a businessmen's group chaired by the Commercial Attaché. Since her agenda was full at the Embassy's office that day, she invited me to the mansion early in the morning and over a quick coffee gave me two business cards which she back signed after a short introduction. It started with something like "To Cuban authorities..." and ended with "give him the utmost considerations". That was enough. It justified the hundreds of dollars I had spent for two years contributing to the Canadian Club and encouraging the Canadian charity fundraising events like the Terry Fox cancer fundraiser, which had become an International Canadian Embassy annual event and was promoted by the Ambassador in person.

Our sail for the first day of this memorable journey was acceptable because although we were against the current which was not yet too strong and against the prevailing easterly wind, we had enough room at sea to manoeuvre and change tack every now and then. Once we passed Varadero, the channel got narrower and narrower and the current stronger and stronger as I had experienced before. Therefore, considering that the wind direction had not changed, we had to start the engine and bring all sails down except the mizzen which I like to keep for stability. Keeping some canvas up reduces the rolling action. We went on motoring all night, making slow headway. This undersized engine could not propel us forward against the bottom at more than two or three knots against a three or four-knot current. Fortunately, it only gave up huffing and puffing the next morning after we had passed the narrowest stretch of the Bahama Channel.

So, while Rambo was down in the bilge cursing as if that would help in fixing the engine, I put all sails out and started sailing closed hauled in an east-northerly direction towards the Bahamas. That big cow was a lost cause if you tried to sail close to the wind. So, sailing by depth meter only, I would get as close to the shallower bottom as possible and tack back south towards Cuba. Rambo never could fix the engine and we found ourselves tacking back and forth until we thought that we could make a run for the entrance of *Puerto Naranjo* in the lee of the *Guardalavaca* peninsula. Regardless of the fact that I had my hands clawed to the helm and my mouth shut grinding my teeth, the sails ran out of wind about half a nautical mile from the entrance. Since we started drifting towards shore, we had to drop anchor. Through the binoculars, we could see the Coast Guard shack on our starboard side just ahead of us, but our repeated calls on the VHF were never returned. That was probably normal because it was around 13:00 hours. Siesta time!

We sat there for a while waving at the few small pleasure crafts like Seadoos rented by tourists going in and out until one larger official boat with a portable VHF noticed us and out of curiosity came by. We told them of our predicament and after a call to the port authorities, they accepted to tow us into the marina. That is when we had the welcome red-carpet treatment! The port authorities, the coast guards armed with AK-47s, and some other kids wearing olive-green uniforms were there to grab our mooring lines at the pier. Their "investigation" lasted the remainder of the day. Our papers were checked. We were individually interviewed. The boat was meticulously searched. Divers went underneath to check if we weren't carrying torpedoes or what? An electronic "expert" checked our radar and GPS for our sailing history. We were the actors reliving a 1960 spy movie, but it was forty years late!

Finally, because of my less aggressive stance than Rambo and my better command of the Spanish language, they accepted our story that we came in for repairs and we would be on our way as soon as the engine could be fixed. It was explained to us, like the situation that I had experienced a year before when coming into the port of Baracoa, that this facility was not a port of entry and that we had to stay on the boat. We were given the privilege to access the terrible cafeteria up the hill. It took three days before a mechanic showed up and got the engine started again. Then late afternoon, we did not waste time and were out of that hole without looking back until... the engine quit again, never restarting.

We tried sailing, but the wind was very mild and coming from the east as usual. While wasting time at the pier, Rambo had rigged a steel outboard motor mount on the side of *Fantasma* as an emergency propulsion system in case the engine quit again. So, while still protected from the current by the *Guardalavaca* peninsula, we busted our backs lowering the very heavy 35 HP outboard on the side motor mount. After nightfall, when we got into open sea, the current just swung the twenty-ton ketch around and took control. We spent all night trying to get back into the protection of the peninsula and finally into the harbor entrance. This time our VHF call was received, and the same impressive welcoming committee was there waiting for us upon our arrival at the pier. Before I went to sleep from exhaustion, I remember the technician watching the radar history on screen and witnessing a bunch of circles which was our previous night's route. Funny!

The next day, Rambo and I agreed after a short meeting that *Fantasma* was not going anywhere unless she got a new engine. So, wearing my four bars Captain's uniform with my name on the I.D. plate like any military officer, I surprised the harbour master in his sleep. My desire to leave the boat with my motorcycle was met with strong resistance from both the harbour master and the Coast Guard officer. Their argument was that we originally had come into the marina illegally without stopping at the coast guard station. My answer was that the Coast Guards never answered our numerous calls, and that they failed in their obligation to render assistance to a boat in danger which, as a licensed captain, I know is the law of the sea. I told them to call Marina Hemingway, to confirm that I owned a boat, called *Aventura*, moored in the Marina. I also I told them that I was not an American but Canadian and that I had embarked on this journey as a second mate to come back to Cuba once *Fantasma* was delivered. Finally, I handed them out one of the cards that the Ambassador had given me and told them that if both Immigration and Customs officers did not show up that morning to legally clear me into Cuba again, I would create a diplomatic incident because I was being held under house arrest for no reason at all. I don't know what worked the arguments, the uniform or the business card, but by 11:00 a.m. I met an Immigration officer who stamped my passport and a customs officer who wrote a temporary import permit for the motorcycle. I was free again, but I was still in Cuba. I would never make it to the D.R. but I no longer needed to as I now had a new import permit issued by Cuban customs from the next town, Holguin. I had no more need to sell the motorcycle.

So, on a Friday afternoon, I found myself on a fast run to Holguin to find a *Registro de vehiculo,* Spanish for vehicle registration office that could issue me a temporary plate to make my Yamaha Virago legal to ride in Cuba. Of course, when I finally found that office, there was as a line-up of the kind that would not be eliminated until the next Monday even if the office was opened all weekend. The long line-up was a nuisance that every Cuban had lived with all their life and gotten used to. It was inspired by the Russian system where I had seen people lined up in Moscow at 7:00 a.m. in the cold and snow waiting to storm the store when it opened at 9:00 a.m. to buy shoes which were rumored to have finally been made available. Somehow, the officer in charge spotted me not for my good looks but my foreign looks, which is understandable since I was wearing a black leather motorcycle jacket, Durango riding boots and a black Harley Davidson T-shirt. It only took about thirty minutes and the equivalent of a ten dollars *propina,* Spanish for tip or more appropriately bribe, to complete the formalities. Now, not only was I free, but I was also legally riding again in Cuba.

After spending the weekend on R & R in Holguin, I headed out east towards Bayamo. Once past the Holguin airport, the Virago died suddenly as if you had turned the current off. I found myself in the middle of nowhere in front of a few shacks bordering the street on the left-hand side. As I pushed the motorcycle through an entrance, I could feel eyes bearing on me and watching my every move. My efforts to use my cellular phone proved useless since there was no service in that area. The owners standing on the porch told me that there was no phone in this neighborhood but invited me to come in and bring the bike inside the house out of view of any curious passersby. In reality, it was against the law to let a stranger come into your house without informing the authorities, but I guess that this family's curiosity was bigger than their fears. I tried to do a few basic checks on the bike, but it was clear the there was no more electrical current feeding the spark plugs. Jorge, the head of the house, went to get a friend who fixed the local old motorbikes. When that mechanic saw my shining new wheels, he threw his hand up in the air in an emotional mixture of awe and incapacity and admitted that he did not have any experience whatsoever at servicing these "beasts". I needed to call Luis Enrique, my friend in Havana, who was an expert about the modern Yamaha Virago motorcycles. He was the official mechanic for the state police who were using the exact same model. There were only two privately owned black Virago in the whole country. To confuse the local police in their car when they saw me coming at top speed, I had bought a windshield of exactly the same model as used by the *Cavallitos*, the Spanish for "Small cowboys", the local motorcycle police.

Jorge informed me that the only available phone in the area was a public phone located two miles away inside the pharmacy in the next town, called Cacocum. In lieu of public transportation, a friendly and generous neighbor let me borrow an old trail horse, which I rode proudly without saddle to town. I finally reached Luis Enrique in Havana, but he told me that he could not come to Holguin for personal reasons. Because I knew Luis Enrique well, I knew what the personal reasons were. Luis Enrique was a known womanizer, and his new wife would never let him out of her sight to go to Holguin, the Cuban city renowned for having the most beautiful women in Cuba. Instead, Luis Enrique told me to call him the next day. He knew Roberto, the mechanic in Holguin who was fixing the police's Virago motorcycles in that area. So, loaded with a "Care Package" which contained two bottles of rum, a chicken, detergent, soap, a few soft drinks and some candies, I jumped on the old horse and hip-hoped my way "home". We spent the night eating the chicken, playing dominos, and drinking rum with the neighbors. I had been Cubanized!

Jorge's small wooden house had luxury like electricity but no running water. There was a well, an outhouse and a shower stall in the back. The plank floor was worn out from being scrubbed and the bedrooms had no doors, just curtains. Although the accommodation was minimal, to say the least, I enjoyed my three-day stay with that family who welcomed me with open arms but surely with some concerns about the Cuban authorities. Every day, I hip-hoped to town on the old horse to make phone calls, buy food and drinks, and every night we would have a noisy domino competition, sometimes interrupted by some woman wanting to teach me salsa.

On the second day, Roberto showed up and quickly diagnosed the problem, the mysterious black box which is the small computer controlling everything. Of course, this part was not easily available in Cuba, especially in Holguin, but Robert was a true Cuban. He knew how to "invent" which as I mentioned before is a Cuban term used for "stealing" from the State. He told me that he knew of a Virago that had been completely wrecked and still sitting in the police garage. He would have the black boxes substituted and nobody would know any better. The third day, he showed up with the part, installed it, and the Virago started immediately. If I recall, the service cost me the equivalent of U.S. $100, which was one-third of what the part alone cost in the U.S.

So, regretfully, I saluted my new family after leaving a bit of money on the table for their hospitality. I made a promise to come back, which I must admit I never could keep because I never came back to this area of Cuba. Based on my experience of driving a modern motorcycle in the "deep country", I was now reluctant to ride out of the Havana area unless I was driving a Chevrolet '53 which everybody can fix anywhere in Cuba and which I ended up buying later. I rode to the Cacocum's train station, took the saddlebags off the Virago, checked it into a cargo rail car and spent the next twenty-four hours enduring this terrible ride to Havana. I was back home on *Aventura* again without ever having been in the Dominican Republic as planned!

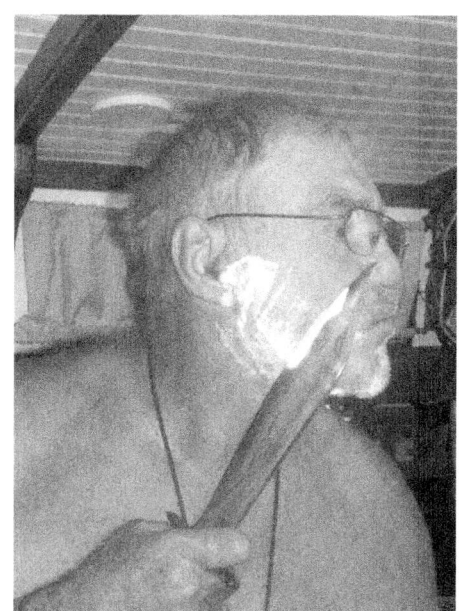

Rambo

My Silvery Friend
by Susan Mellsopp

I have a new friend. She is tiny, slim, and a silvery ball of energy. Her name is unusual, Acalia. We have become very close in a short time. Her positive attitude makes me feel really special as she constantly checks that I am well, happy and content.

We met one cold morning in early September last year. I quickly began to admire her wiry nature, ability to always be switched on and aware of everything around her, yet she was quite unusual in her opinions and actions. Initially, I found Acalia's constant attention quite difficult and overwhelming, if not rather painful. I was used to being totally independent, not having someone else moderate and watch me continually.

The first few weeks of our relationship were taken quietly. I have always believed that a restrained introduction to a new connection is essential. A few days after meeting her, I asked Acalia to accompany me to an important yet very stressful meeting. Although supportive, it was probably not a good idea as Jay tugged on her incessantly and strained our fledgling friendship. After the hiccup with Jay we left him at home sometimes, other days we took him out just on a lead. Acalia and I began to attend concerts together where we swayed in unison to the beautiful rhythms, went shopping for new clothes, shoes, and tried the menus at trendy cafes with other close friends. We became hot chocolate connoisseurs.

As we got to know each other we were extremely surprised how much we had in common. She loved books and reading as much as I did, enjoyed spending time in the garden, and we began to plan an overseas holiday together. Acalia's personality quirks matched mine, though she seemed to have more energy than I did, always pushing me to try harder or go further. I began to relax when realising this was a friend for life, someone who would look after my best interests and help me when I was stressed, or times became difficult. Her constant presence seldom worried me.

Occasionally we did have a difference of opinion and she really hurt me. I would wake in the night and toss and turn, unable to get comfortable as I felt compromised by her proximity to my wildly beating heart strings. My mind wavered between friendship and modifying my soul response. In the depths of the night I listened to quiet music, a book, meditated, and soon slipped into thankful oblivion.

I tried to explain to Acalia that I was not quite who I normally was. I had experienced two bad concussions when my heart rhythm had stuttered and stopped causing me to black out. Recovering from the second concussion was still a focus of my life. I had cancelled a long dreamed of trip and my whole lifestyle was still on hold. She seemed to understand and offered to help with my recovery and overarching disappointment. Assuring me that I would not black out again, she vowed that concussion would be a thing of the past. Acalia promised she would keep me on an even keel, something no friend had offered to do for me before.

As the days, weeks then months passed we became increasingly comfortable in each other's presence. I began to sparkle again. I was wired for fun. One or two of my older friends became concerned at her role in my life, reassurances failed to abate their worries. Several still don't believe my thin, energetic silvery friend will be there for me when I need her the most.

Acalia and I began to take longer and longer walks together, arriving home hot but refreshed. Jay began to realise she gave me more vitality, so slowly accepted this interloper into his life. She had taken a little of his place in my heart. He bounced and bounded around us both and begged for attention. His love for Acalia grew despite his own failing health and subsequent retirement.

In February, I made the decision to travel with Acalia on holiday. We needed a life affirming break from the realities of daily life. Exploring Christchurch, we walked miles, got soaked in a downpour, grieved for the loss at the mosque, became very lost in Hagley Park, travelled on the trams, and punted on the Avon. Life was good.

As concerns about our close rapport abated, I was aware when Acalia hugged me close to her it made my chest ache. On a visit to the hospital for a check-up I explained how this exclusiveness was impacting on my life, how my feelings were changed, how uncomfortable I still was in her company. Told to accept it, nothing could be done about it, I gave in and decided to adjust.

Acalia is a great companion. She is my Accolade Medtronic pacemaker, my life saver, heart regulator, my lover and responsive best friend. She keeps me alive.

The 'Keeper wi the Lauch
by Ronald Mackay

(That's in my native Scots. In English it is: The Gamekeeper with the Laugh)

"The shoot's over. Send the beaters home." The head 'keeper turned to supervise the day's count of gamebirds and animals.

We beaters, who walked the moors in a mile-long sweeping noisy line to drive the coveys of grouse towards the guns, could return to our accommodation. It was a bothy provided free by the Laird of Spittal during the early grouse season. We, mostly students on vacation from university, were intent on earning to contribute to our expenses when the semester resumed in October.

"Follow me, lads!" The 'keeper, who had in the early chill of that glorious 12th of August 1963 introduced himself to us as Willie Bogle, struck out over the featureless moor to guide us to our lodgings. We'd beat well over 20 steep miles on an estate of over 100,000 acres. The guns travelled back to the lodge in Land Rovers. Exhausted, silent, we followed Willie on foot over a treeless grouse-moor, purple with heather.

* * *

"I'll hae a gless o water." Willie entered the stone bothy, our temporary home.

"There's beer," offered one of the more generous students.

"Water'll dae fine." Willie filled a cup from the tap and sat down. Some screwed the tops off dark bottles of McEwan's Pale Ale.

"How come all you gamekeepers wear the same fancy dress?" The provocation, in the regional accent of northern England, came from an older post-graduate student.

Wille erupted in a blast of laughter. For that signature bark, he was known throughout the Grampians as *'The Keeper wi' the Lauch'*. Once heard, never forgotten.

"Your name?" Willie asked when he'd caught his breath, his sharp eye on the provocateur.

"Tom."

Willie's smile was steady but his eyes told he'd registered the sarcastic reference to the clothes worn by all gamekeepers on the estate – identical rough-spun, Harris Tweed jackets the colours of the grouse-moor, plus-fours buckled above lovat-green stockings and half-sprung, leather brogues to grip steep hillsides.

"So, Willie, what's the monkey-suit all about?" The student's English accent contrasted with Willie's Scots.

Eyes on the interrogator, Willie drew on his water as if to erase the affront. Then he switched from Scots to match Tom's Standard English.

"What's this all about?" He doffed the Harris Tweed deer-stalker cap and examined the warm, patterned shades. "This is the traditional estate tweed o' Spittal."

"They make you serfs dress alike?" The speaker was probing for a nerve.

"It's a tradition in the Highlands. Estates with a grouse moor, a deer forest and salmon streams have their own Harris Tweed. Keepers wear it. The Laird and his family wear it. Part for camouflage, part to show pride."

"Pride?" Tom's lip curled.

"Pride!" Willie affirmed. "Pride in our belonging, in our togetherness."

"You mean to show who you belong *to*?"

Willie exploded into another laugh, but his eyes never left the student's face.

"Belong? We aa belong somewhere, aye, and to someone. I was a stalker and a ghillie, first at Auch, then at Quoich till '39. Back from the War, I've rented myself out, like. Independent. A dozen estates seek me. The grouse, the ptarmigan, the stags, then the hinds. There's the culling and the heather-burning. The salmon. I'm here at Spittal for the early weeks of the grouse. The odd day's deer-stalking with a guest. Here, I'm proud to wear the Spittal tweeds." He paused, winked. "Saves wearin oot my own!" As if to underline his joke, Willie erupted into laughter.

"Independent, you say? Absentee landlords and rich London toffs pay you bugger-all to do their bidding *if* and *when* it suits them."

Willie's tone remained even though his eyes seemed to measure the very soul of his provoker. "The landowners, *toffs* you say, but lairds for generations, pay my fee. I take what suits me."

"Exploitation!" The student was annoyed at Willie's composure. "A working life away from home. Here, there and every-bloody-where! Your wife approve?"

Willie played with the cap in his hands, smiled, exploded into a barking laugh, then wiped his eyes. "Ma wife? Ma wife's used to ma ways. She aye cries me," and he smiled at the thought, "she cries me *a raikin' tink, a traivellin hoor!*" He burst into a great laugh as if his wife's description of him as *a wandering pedlar, an itinerant whore* was a source of humour.

Tom and other students from England, unfamiliar with the dialect, looked puzzled. I translated, and they laughed:

Willie, a wandering pedlar, a peripatetic whore!

"Would you be a student o' politics, maybe?" Willie addressed Tom.

"Political History. European; 20th century. Doing my doctorate with Professor Hobsbawm at Birkbeck."

"An just wha would Hobsbum o' Birkbeck be?" Willie's eyes twinkled.

"Erik Hobs*bawm*," Tom corrected. "Hobsbawm's only the most respected Marxist thinker in the country." His tone challenged contradiction.

"Marxism's a theory, is it no?" Willie scratched his head as if chasing a long-forgotten fact.

"Marxism's only the theory that explains why we plebs are walking the hills to drive grouse onto the guns of toffs from London for a capitalist landowner. Only the theory that explains how the bourgeoisie force us to work for bugger-all and live in this shite-hole while they're at the lodge drinking champagne."

Willie finished his water slowly. "Well, I'm grateful to you." He stood up and ran his mug under the tap. He smiled to us and was gone.

We beaters set about making supper. Tom, the doctoral student of Marxism from Birkbeck, pulled two grouse from inside his baggy jacket. "See? I'm gonna eat like these bastard toffs at the lodge."

There was nervous laughter. To pick up a grouse was forbidden. Labrador-retrievers served that purpose. For a beater to possess a grouse was tantamount to theft.

* * *

Come the weekend, I was alone in the bothy. The others had headed home or to meet friends working in the seasonal hotels of Braemar and Aberdeen.

On a walk, I fell in with Willie. He had a subtle way of finding out about a person without appearing overly curious. He learned that I was a Scot from Angus. I could speak a dialect similar to his own. I had nowhere to go at weekends and was content with my own company. I was not yet a student but had spent two years working since leaving school. Paying jobs first in the sunlit banana plantations on the island of Tenerife, then deep in the bowels of Ben Cruachan, helping excavate the miles of tunnels that served the pumped-storage hydro-electric power station based on the Snowy Mountains Scheme in Australia.

My status as a plantation worker, a tunneller inside the legendary Cruachan and especially my rank of *not-quite-yet-university-student*, appealed to Willie.

"A'll learn ye how tae get a hare for yer supper."

For the rest of the afternoon he showed me how to successfully set a braided brass-wire snare on a bare hillside to kill a running mountain hare instantaneously.

In his quiet way, Willie taught me about the Scottish Highland estate. Nature manages itself, he let me know without ever repeating himself, in ways that satisfy the needs of the animals whose natural home it is. The predated-upon evade or fail to evade the predators. An equilibrium is reached. Golden eagles, ravens, hooded crows and foxes are predators; mountain hares, rabbits, ageing deer, old ewes and even lambs are the prey. The passing of the wolf made the culling of the Red Deer necessary and helped finance great estates. The gamekeeper's job included the duties of deer-stalker, salmon-ghillie and protector of grouse and ptarmigan. Together, the varied tasks combined to assure a balance. Weaker stags were culled, controlled burning encouraged fresh heather that provided tender shoots for grouse and grass meadows for black-face sheep. Such balance assured paying guests weeks of demanding shooting and fishing. In this way, the estate, its moors, its grand lodge, its scattered bothies and the access tracks across miles of desolate hills and bridges over tumbling streams, could be maintained and the land preserved as it had been for centuries.

* * *

One evening the following week, Willie accompanied us back to the bothy from a long and difficult beat so that we wouldn't get lost. As before, he sat down with a mug of water and Tom once more took up his self-appointed task of trying to provoke Willie.

Tom talked of how injustice was the foundation of the Highland estate; that we workers must repudiate absentee landowners and their corrupt institutions; how inherited privilege supported exploitation and inequality;

how the Laird was humiliating us by making us walk the moors for a measly £2 a day to satisfy the appetites of his bloodthirsty toffee-nosed guests.

Willies weekly visits persisted. Because Willie listened serenely, often laughed, thanked us and left, Tom tried harder to hit the bull's eye. He talked of how estate workers like the 'keepers, stalkers and gillies were no better than 18th century Russian serfs; how Britain's workers had emerged from the War with losses but no gains; how a vague *'we'* must take revenge on the bourgeois capitalists who had tricked us into the war; how the real heroes of our time were Kim Philby and his like – who bravely repudiate the country they were born into along with its traditions and values.

But Willy continued simply to listen, laugh, and then leave after he thanked us.

* * *

One Friday evening, Willie invited me to accompany him. "The Laird needs a salmon for tomorrow's dinner with his guests. Our job's to catch him one." He carried a split-cane fly-rod.

"Here's the pool." Willie and I stood in the short heather looking into the dark water. The wide stream, whisky-amber from the scattered peat-bogs, spilled over rocks to tumble down into the glen. Bright scarlet Rowans hung over the opposite, higher side making casting impossible.

The great salmon lay in the brackish deep, gills pulsating. He refused to acknowledge the variety of flies that Willie's accurate casting coaxed by his hooked jaws.

After a fruitless half-hour, Willie reeled in his line. "Sunrise tomorrow. We'll get him."

The following morning, we returned without the rod. Still, the great fish rested on the bottom of the pool, head into the current.

Willie picked up a flat rock and threw it into the middle of the pool with a great splash. The salmon disappeared. Willie took off his jacket, waistcoat and tie, then rolled up his sleeves. Lying down on the bank, he stretched his arms under the overhang and into the water. His body jerked and his shoulders contracted. With a smooth roll and a flip, he cast the salmon over his back to land in the heather where it could not spring back into the stream. Willie removed a *priest* – a short club – from his 'poacher's pocket' and dispatched the salmon with one blow.

"There's aye a way!" He laughed. Willie was a man who found a solution to every challenge.

As we walked back to the lodge to deliver the 25-pound salmon to the cook, Willie told me of a variety of ways – both legal and illegal – that could be employed to take a salmon.

* * *

Weekend after weekend, when the other beaters had left, I learned many country skills from Willie Bogle, *the Keeper wi the Lauch.*

And for one night each week we listened to Tom pontificate on what he had learned from his Marxist mentor Professor Hobsbawm of Birkbeck College: that the capitalist industrial economy was doomed, that it produced an egregiously unequal society; that the property-less proletariat was the sworn enemy of the bourgeoisie who cornered land and money along with the better things of life that rightfully belonged to the working man.

Invariably, Willie listened with a smile on his face. When he'd finished his water, he stood up, thanked Tom, smiled and left.

* * *

As our time as beaters was running out, Tom made a final effort to provoke Willie.

"So, Willie, what do *you* think?"

"Aboot what?"

"About the things I've been saying. Professor Hobsbawm's history of the working class. The Communist Party. Class war. The need for the exploited to mount a revolution."

"What do I think of your Hobsbum and his Communists? Ye want to know, Tom?"

"I do!" Tom sensed triumph and grinned.

Willie's voice was so quiet that we strained to hear.

"From whit I've seen, yer average communist's a resentful man with a double tongue. With his revolution, he does what he can to wreck his inheritance but has nae sense o' what to put in its place save a bonny picture o' a Shangri-la that'll never be."

We were silent. This was the first response to Tom's political preaching we'd heard Willie utter.

Immediately, Tom returned to the attack.

"From what *you've* seen? *You?* Up here on a highland estate owned by a capitalist toff? How does *that* experience give *you* the right to come up with a bunch of anti-revolutionary shite like that? You've been brain-washed, Wille." Tom grinned.

Willie threw his head back and released a noisy burst of laughter.

Now, we thought, *Willie will rise, thank us politely, and leave.* But Willie sat stock still. When he finally spoke, his voice was quiet, his eyes on a distant place we innocents could not begin to imagine.

"*Experience*? You want my *experience*, Tom? I've seen shameless brutality and destruction by your Hobsbum's communists. If I tellt you the details ye widna sleep for the horror o' it. Aye, and I've listened to their apology that claims the ends justify the means. But, after half a century and more, the workers they rule over live in daily fear and their gulags are burstin' at the seams."

"Where could *you* have seen that?" Tom gestured to the surrounding mountains and moors, incautiously refusing to disguise his derision.

Willie's smile vanished.

"Where? Me? Ye ask me where I've seen that?"

Tom was rocked back in his chair by the challenge in Willie's voice.

"Ye say ye're a historian, eh? The 20th century. So you'll know all about the War?"

"Right." Tom's voice was losing some of its certainty.

"You'll've heard of the LRDG then?"

"The Long-Range Desert Group? Fought in North Africa. No communists there! Ha, Willie?"

"Richt you are, Tom. But efter we threw the Gerries out o' North Africa, ye ken what our platoon did?" He didn't wait for Tom's answer. "We parachuted into Yugoslavia. To help the partisans harass the Germans, stop them gettin back to the West too fast, like. Aye, and more than one of our officers and some of our men were born into estates like Auch, and Atholl, Quoich and Spittal. Today, I work, *choose* to work, for some of these very men – the lucky ones, like me, who got to come home wi aa their bits an' pieces intact. Oh, I know, Tom, to you and your Hobsbum o Birkbeck, they're *toffs*. Braw homes in London. Lodges in the Highlands where they shoot grouse, stalk deer, and cast fly for the salmon with their friends. They'll drink champagne or a braw single malt. I do the same myself when I get the chance! But make no mistake, laddie, these are patriots, leaders of men who love tradition, men who've never lacked bravery or failed in their loyalty to their country, aye, nor to naebody."

Tom was quiet now. Willie had earned our fixed attention.

"I helped Yugoslavs no matter who they were. I've organised and fought alongside nationalist Chetniks, aye an' wi communists wha bore no loyalty to anything or anyone except the Party. And what did I see, Tom?" Willie paused. No one spoke. "I saw the Communists strangle the life out of all the beliefs that their communities had lived and loved by – their own country and their own families, their faith, their traditions, aye, very law and order itself. All in the name of your Stalin's Marxism and your Hobsbum's communism where there's no law but what the Party says it is for its own convenience at any given moment."

Willie paused again.

"I watched the communists create a class war, watched them put down the middle class and degrade, aye and kill, any educated soul who could think for himself – the teacher, the lawyer, the doctor, the businessman – anybody and everybody who'd striven, studied and showed respect for their country and all that it had stood for, for generations."

"But the communists won!" Was Tom rallying?

"With Russian help, the communists won."

"So, class loyalty is stronger than patriotism."

"In the name of your class loyalty I saw countries – whole countries – wiped off the map, joined up by force under a new name like they'd never existed. It'll no last, Tom! It'll no last. Marx's class war's a handy lie but it canna explain aa the differences that make up this world."

Willie stopped. The anger that had driven his response to Tom's goading visibly drained from his face. He smiled again, threw back his head and laughed hard.

No longer was Willie harassing the retreating German Army or watching his back for the sudden communist dagger, he was a Highland gamekeeper at peace with himself, his employers, his family, his country, the entire, complex natural world around him and most of all with his place in this world.

Willie smiled at Tom and then at each of us in turn. He stood up, adjusted his Spittal Estate tweed deerstalker cap as if preparing for inspection.

"I'm grateful to you gentleman, one and all! Ye've learnt me a lot in the past four weeks. Aye, and ye've given me a lot tae think aboot!"

On his way to the door, he put his hand on my shoulder and winked. Then, straight-backed, Willie marched out into the gloaming as if to the skirl of a lone piper.

I too, thought I could hear the piper.

A Scottish Blackface Ram

In Caring for my Ficus
by Liliana Amador-Marty

"... And if my life is like the dust that hides the glow of a rose,
then what good am I..."

This Bitter Earth, performed by Dinah Washington

That winter the pitiful ficus sat sadly on the windowsill begging for care. An acquaintance had rescued it from a trash bin on a frozen sidewalk. What was a tropical plant doing so far away from its Mediterranean soil? And what made this person think I could care for this abandoned thing? It was pitiful. The dying plant just stared at me with three spindly branches reaching for help. What could I do for it? I knew nothing about plants and besides, I could barely take care of myself. I too was far away from the Caribbean waters of my birthplace in this cold, dark nordic city. We shared this in common. I had sentenced myself to three years of graduate school in the coldest, most homogenous place I had ever lived.

"What do you want from me?" I exhaled, "I have nothing to give you."

I could not know it then, but breathing so close to its three budding leaves was enough to bring it back from the dead. Just talking out load to the plant was reviving me too as I clung on to the pot, my head resting on the window, its large glass filling the room with the glaring yellow glow of the sun. It would soon be spring and as I sat in the burning sunlight, I was grateful for the heat on the nape of my neck. I often sat this way for hours studying this living thing I held in my hands. I envied its simplicity. Dependent only on water and light, it refused to die even when exposed to frigid conditions foreign to its tropical nature. But now it was in this warm place protected from the cold behind glass and it needed me to keep it alive. It felt good to be needed in this way, like a mother caring for her child. But first I needed to care for myself. I had survived a dark period of dark thoughts and was emerging on the other side of this tormenting and frightening inner turmoil.

In an attempt to find the part of myself that seemed lost, that spring I went to Barranquilla, Colombia, the place where I was born. Barranquilla is a portal city on the Northern coast of Colombia in South America surrounded by the Caribbean Sea. On the crowded dirt streets of this city, foreign to me because I was not raised there, I felt the unmistakable sense of home.

Everything about Barranquilla felt familiar, even though my parents had immigrated to North America when I was two years old. These Colombian strangers looked liked family. We were all the same: our wavy black hair, our dark brown almond-shaped eyes, even our size was *normal* in my birth country. At five foot nothing, I was average height for a woman in Barranquilla. Even my name, *Liliana*, so rare in the United States, was as common as *Mary* in Colombia. We all ate *arepas* for breakfast, said *carajo* when we got upset, and danced c*umbia* in the evenings after dinner, the same meals my mother cooked back home in Paterson, New Jersey. In the Caribbean sun, my body sweat in the heat and humidity cleansing the toxins from my insides and the negative thoughts that poisoned me. My skin glistened radiantly. My hair was shiny, replenished by the natural oils that had dried up on my scalp. Though constantly drenched in perspiration, this climate felt right. I returned from my pilgrimage with a renewed sense of strength and recovered identity. I had a new perspective, a second perspective that I needed to fully understand myself.

When I returned to the Midwest, it was summertime and my ficus was parched, its soil cracking. All the tiny leaves that had begun to grow had now fallen off. I left simple instructions for my roommates,

"Water it every day and talk to it occasionally."

I guess this was too much to ask. I felt as though someone had chopped off one of my limbs. I grabbed it from its home on the sill, filled the tub with warm water and bathed it, talking to it gently,

"It's going to be okay, you'll see, everything's okay now," reassuring words that I needed to tell myself.

Like a sick child of mine, I watched my ficus for weeks as it began to bloom again in its sunny spot near the window, misting it with nutrients and fertilising its soil. Occasionally I read Shakespeare aloud to my plant. We carried on this way until fall, when we both feared the dread of approaching winter. But by now, its leaves were dark green and plump, filling me with a sense of accomplishment. The branches had exploded with many veins in the budding leaves and the roots were gripping the earth within its shrinking pot. I had also grown with a renewed strength. I felt hope again and like the stems of the ficus tree, my spine re-appeared in my awareness, planting me firmer into the ground.

My ficus had been my companion for the past seven years at that period in my life. It was with me the winter I broke off my relationship with the college boyfriend I lived with, listening to me cry in the sunroom where the ficus grew the fastest. It lived with me when I took an apartment alone grieving my loss, filling my void with roses I gave to myself and the sweet smell they left behind even in death. That was when I cut the lower branches, braiding the stems into a trunk so it could stand upright and firm. I braided my long hair the same way when it was damp. That same year though, I chopped off my long hair. I was changing, transforming. We both survived our last winter in this freezing midwestern state, turning the bathroom into a sauna so that my tropical skin and its tropical bark could replenish their moisture. My ficus moved with me to New York City in the back of a U-Haul for three cold nights and almost died again. All of its leaves fell off by the time we arrived in Manhattan, but at the very top of one branch was one tiny, green leaf reaching towards the light. Hope. When spring arrived, I placed it on the fire escape where it grew with a renewed desire to live. My ficus was resilient, flexible and strong. I was like my ficus.

I often joined my plant on the fire escape that summer writing in the morning sun and sitting in rainstorms, letting the large drops trickle down my face as the darkened warm skies thundered above us. There was a time as an adult when thunderstorms found me huddled, afraid of myself. Now I felt overjoyed at being alive, feeling the water pouncing my eyelids, witnessing lightning bolts rip through the dark clouds photographing my tree and me, freezing that moment in my memory. Back then, I dreamt of someday taking my plant to warmer soil, freeing it from its restrictive pot, so its roots could spread out, deep into the earth. I hoped someday my ficus would reach towards a tropical sun growing tall, limitless, its trunk thick, strengthened by warm breezes tossing its branches about, having found its power in its journey to a better place. And if dark clouds should hover over me again, I can look back on my competency in caring for my ficus and know that I too am resilient, flexible and strong. Perhaps I would peer outside my window at my ficus in the ground, my face reflected in the glass and see the two lives I saved.

My ficus

American Cemetery
by Neal Atherton

D-Day 6th June 1944 and a poignant visit to Normandy

I confess that I have a love of history and especially in the period of time in France that covers the occupation and the D-Day landings. It is not my intention to go over all that the story encompasses. That has been well told many times by far better historians and been reviewed extensively quite recently with the fascination of the 75th anniversary of the landings. All my writings are done with a desire to inspire you to visit the places we have loved over the years. What I hope to achieve is to convey a sense of the atmosphere to you and the way these sites have an impact on us as visitors. With the war sites in Normandy, the feeling that these are places we have loved is perhaps not the correct expression. You can love Provence. You can love Paris. You cannot love a cemetery at a place where so many lost their lives. You can however be moved.

The Normandy American Cemetery and Memorial in France, Cemetiere Americain, is located in Colleville-sur-Mer, on the site of the temporary American Saint Laurent Cemetery. This was established by the US First Army just two days after D-Day, on the 8th of June 1944. It is worth a pause for thought that many military personnel who left the south coast bases of England were buried just a few yards into occupied France before the week was out. By definition of its location, this was the first American cemetery on European soil laid out in World War II.

The approach to the cemetery and memorial is quite unusual and unexpected. As you get close to Colleville-sur-mer on the D514 you come upon a roundabout that is well tended and rather than driving on a well-used coastal road you feel in another place altogether. You could be at the approach to an upmarket Golf and Country Club, reminiscent of where the Masters is played in Atlanta, USA. What this sudden change in the landscape impels you to do is to turn left and not to carry on. You cannot just drive past this place, a site that is the most visited memorial site for Americans in the world. Turn left you must do and after going through the wooded area you can park your car and take what is one of the most extraordinary walks you will ever make.

There is a new visitor centre here now that was opened in 2007, but that was some three years after our visit. The new centre tells the story of D-Day and Omaha Beach and gives the visitor a place to reflect and hear the recollections of many participants bringing those dreadful days to life once again. On our visit we just had the cemetery and memorial to contemplate, but be assured that was more than sufficient to bring those days back into vivid perspective.

As you walk across into the cemetery you are confronted by row upon row of stark, brilliant white crosses. Every single one is perfectly laid out in unison so that whichever way you look down the rows they are in line, standing to attention. Initially this affecting sight is just too much to take in and you sort of want to turn away and try not to look. We found ourselves drawn over to the memorial at the head of the cemetery that faces down a long straight manicured lawn leading the eye between the two sides of the grave site. In front of the memorial is a reflective pool. There is not a sound, even the birds seem to have caught the mood and are silent, somehow knowing it would be disrespectful to find a landing place.

The memorial is made up of a semi-circular colonnade that has a large inscription running around the upper curved part. Attached at either side of the memorial there is a loggia, and these contain large maps and narratives of the D-Day military operations and the subsequent breakout into the Normandy countryside. At the centre of the semi-circular structure is a bronze statue, "Spirit of American Youth Rising from the Waves." You cannot help but reflect that sadly the place is dedicated to and contains the generation of American youth whose rise ended so abruptly and tragically just yards from this statue.

On the Walls of the Missing, constructed in a semi-circular garden to the east side of this memorial, you will find inscribed 1,557 names of those who never had a last resting place. Some have been found and identified in the years following the construction of this memorial, and those are marked by a Rosette against their names. I found this especially poignant as my great uncle Alan Atherton also was never found after being killed in the similar Allied landings at Salerno a few months earlier.

The cemetery site in front of you covers over 170 acres and contains the graves of 9,385 American military dead, most of whom lost their lives in the D-Day landings and the operations that followed as the Allies broke out from the beachhead. The whole cemetery spread out before you is so impeccably laid out that it is somewhat dreamlike. Can this be real? In many ways it should not work as a memorial, it is too pristine and so far removed as an image from the bloody horrors of those landings. Yet, it is that starkness, that total contrast with the events themselves that cause you to be so moved by the experience. It stuns you into silence. I have never been in a place with so many other people and not been aware of any sound. No one speaks; they just silently walk through the paths, occasionally looking at the graves – but not too often.

There is one more place that you have to visit and to do so you have to leave the flawless cemetery behind you and step through to an observation point overlooking Omaha beach. At its centre there is an orientation table that gives a battle view on a map of the scene as it was on the 6th of June 1944. The cemetery was very affecting, but it is here overlooking the beach that you feel deeply the emotion of this poignant site. As you look out down to the beach over the grassy knolls, you get a sense of the actual deadly dangers those young men faced. The beach is not wide, but it is wide enough to know that it would seem a very long way to a soldier running towards a machine gun at the site of this observation point. It is then that it finally hits you that the men in those graves behind you are buried within yards of where they fell. This is as far as they got. It is that realisation which moves you to tears.

This American Cemetery at Colleville-sur-Mer is a place that I would say affected me almost as much as anywhere else I have ever visited. The only other memorial site that I find more intensely moving is The Mémorial des Martyrs de la Déportation at the eastern tip of the Île de la Cité in Paris, located in the small park behind Notre Dame. That memorial in Paris differs in that it has a personal resonance for me, so it should and does have a deep effect on me whenever I visit Paris. Unlike Paris, the Normandy Cemetery does not have a personal connection, but it is a place that stirs the emotions, and I will never forget it. Nor should I.

American Cemetery

Luxury Limo Surprise
by Robyn Boswell

It was a phone call that you would usually only dream about.

"Good morning – am I speaking to Robyn Boswell?"

"Sure are."

"Did you recently join the Christmas Club at the Kensington supermarket?"

"Sure did."

"Well, I'm phoning to tell you you've won a prize."

Wow! My mind started racing – worst-case scenario would be a meal in a good restaurant, but maybe, just maybe, it would be a tropical holiday in Rarotonga or Fiji. I held my breath.

"Congratulations – you have won a trip to the supermarket in a limousine."

My heart dropped. I lived by myself, I drove myself the ten minutes to the supermarket every week. As a total introvert I couldn't imagine anything more embarrassing than having a limo turn up in my shared driveway – actually I don't think there was anyway a limo could even turn around there – and why on earth would I want to do my every day grocery shopping by limo by myself?

"Um, thank you for the offer, but I don't think that will work out for me. It's not really my scene. Can you give it to someone else who might appreciate it?"

The tone turned somewhat frosty. I was obviously turning down what the marketing folk had seen as a grand gesture. The caller tried a little more to convince me, but I dug my toes in. In the end, she gave me a day to think about it. I didn't need to think – there was no way I was going to put myself through that humiliation.

The next day in the staffroom at school I told my colleagues about my weird, disappointing experience. Most people thought it was a hilarious proposition.

One of my friends said, "But I would have gone with you!"

I noticed a few more heads nodding around the room. Uh-oh – had I made a wrong decision?

That night I ate humble pie and rang the supermarket to see if the limo would come to school and take a carload of passengers shopping during a lunch hour. They were only too happy to oblige, so the next day I threw the invitation open to my colleagues. I still wasn't all that enthusiastic myself, but from the excited way some of them acted, you would think they had been invited to accompany the Queen on a Royal Tour. I soon had a carload of eager limo riders ready to take up the invitation.

The much-anticipated day finally arrived. Those of us who were embarking on the luxury tour to the supermarket spent our morning tea break in our drama room wardrobe and managed to dredge up some elbow-length white gloves and absurdly ornate hats that had done duty in one of our stage shows. The men grabbed boaters and bow ties. We didn't tell the kids what was happening so that it would be a surprise for them all. At lunchtime, we emerged in our finery and attracted a growing group of very curious kids.

Suddenly, to my surprise, a car pulled up alongside us in the parking area. My cousin, Raymond, in real life a very important mining consultant in Toronto and a very keen amateur photographer, was in town for a few days and had decided to get into the swing of things. He hopped out in his pristine trade-mark white linen suit and panama hat with a ubiquitous carnation in his buttonhole; produced his camera, which he had decked out with the longest lens he owned and started snapping off photos. Even my colleagues were startled – they had never met him before, and his Canadian accent added to the intrigue. I didn't enlighten them right away, and it sure added to the atmosphere.

Suddenly, a highly polished, stretched black limo slid smoothly down our long driveway. It was the only one in town, and most of the kids had likely never seen it before. It was like the Pied Piper as it attracted an ever-increasing stream of excited kids who skipped and danced down the driveway behind it.

The driver, replete in suit and chauffer's hat, got out and tried to swat away some of the sticky fingers that were testing out the shininess of the gleaming doors and bonnet. He opened the door and ushered us in with a bow. He was a very dour individual and I've never figured out if that was his usual mien or if he was simply overcome by the unexpected crowds of ebullient kids and the 'photographer' clicking away. He certainly didn't join in the frivolity and laughs and didn't chat to us at all during our adventure, despite our trying. Maybe he was embarrassed about the whole idea as well.

One of my colleagues in particular, the one who had precipitated my asking them to come to school, was so excited she was fit to burst. The rest of us were just out for some laughs. We glided off up the driveway, still pursued by a tail of enthusiastic kids. The first thing we noticed was a chilled bottle of bubbly and some glasses. Hmmm – it was lunch hour and we had to go back and teach for the afternoon. Did we dare? Of course, we did – six people and one bottle of bubbly wasn't going to harm anyone.

As we drove through the traffic lights at the main intersection in the middle of town, sipping on our glasses of bubbly, our most eager passenger wound down the window, stuck her white-gloved hand out and did a perfect rendition of the Royal Wave. There must have been quite a few puzzled people in the street who had a story to take home that night.

We eventually arrived at the supermarket to find that Raymond had got there before us and was once again doing his paparazzi act, much to the puzzlement of the few people who were going into the store. I'd like to say that we were received with great fanfare and showered with gifts, but strangely, as we piled out and stood there waiting to be greeted, no one even came out to meet us. We wandered around the supermarket getting very strange looks from the few customers who were there at that time of the day; bought a few snacks for lunch to eat on the return journey and settled back into the luxurious seats for the fifteen-minute drive back to school.

As we reached the street where our school was, we could hear cheering. We turned down the driveway to find our colleagues who were still at school had arranged a welcome back for us. The driveway was lined with all the kids in the school who were waving and cheering as though their favourite pop idols had come to visit. It was a perfect fun end to a crazy experience.

When I saw how much joy it brought to my friends and colleagues and how much amusement we'd got from the whole experience, I was glad I'd been able to get over my initial curmudgeonly reaction to give my colleagues plenty of laughs and an entertaining tale to tell their families.

Life Changing Moments
by Ronni Robinson

While I have had many incredibly huge moments in my life, including getting out of an abusive marriage, finding and marrying the love of my life and having two beautiful, healthy children, there are two life-changing moments that I feel helped empower me and define me as a woman.

The first life-altering moment was the evening I discovered I had an eating disorder for over thirty years of my life.

From the age of nine, until just shy of 40, I stuffed my face nonstop with food on too many occasions to count. I lived to eat and thought of food obsessively.

Talking to friends at a party was merely tolerated until I could get to the dessert table. Hovering around the dessert table, then hoarding the treats off in a corner was my main objective.

When we threw parties, I couldn't wait for the party to be over to scarf down leftover desserts. Then I would lie and say I stuffed the desserts down the garbage disposal or threw them away outside.

I wore clothes that stunk because throwing them in the wash after numerous wearings would shrink them, and I couldn't afford to buy new clothes.

The self-loathing I felt was immense, but I was powerless to stop eating. It controlled me.

Looking at my undressed self in the mirror each night, I swore at myself and promised that I would do better and eat less the next day. Sadly, that rarely happened.

The night I randomly heard the words "compulsive overeater" on television was my "ah-ha" moment. I believe that ideas are presented to you for a reason at certain times in your life. When you are ready to accept it, you hear the idea.

Upon listening to those words, I went to my laptop and started Googling. I quickly found myself on the Overeaters Anonymous website. The website prominently asks – Are you one of us? It asks questions such as, "Do I go on eating binges for no apparent reason, sometimes eating until I'm stuffed or even feel sick?" "Do I have feelings of guilt, shame, or embarrassment about my weight or the way I eat?" "Do I eat sensibly in front of others and then make up for it when I am alone?" I answered yes to these and so many more of the questions.

It hit me – I am a compulsive overeater. I have a sickness. I have a mental illness. I need help. From that moment on, I attacked this eating disorder relentlessly. I went to OA meetings and therapy. I read books about recovery and penned an anonymous blog. I committed to recovering and am now over 12 years recovered.

It wasn't easy, but I went from a life of being controlled by food and living to eat, to eating to live, and I am profoundly grateful and changed for the better.

The second life-changing moment came about two years into my recovery. I had always been an athlete when the world of triathlon came knocking on my door in the form of a fundraiser. For those who don't know, a triathlon is a race of different swimming, biking, and running lengths, always in that order. While I had been a runner for over a decade, I had never seriously biked or swam. I decided to step out of my comfort zone.

I started with the sprint, or the shortest triathlon distance. I had a friend who mentored me in running years prior, who also happened to do triathlons. She pointed me how to get a training plan and gave me a lot of direction on proceeding into the sport.

I found that I loved training and the structure I was required to follow. The sprint distances were over in less than two hours, so after two summer seasons of sprints, I decided to move up to longer distances, which required more training and more endurance, which appealed to me.

A couple of years after that, I opted to do the longest race – a full distance Ironman, which includes a 2.4-mile swim, a 112-mile bike ride, and a 26.2-mile run, one right after the other.

If you asked me five years earlier if I would ever attempt a full Ironman, I would have said you were out of your mind. But I loved everything about triathlon. It filled me in mind, body, and spirit. It helped cement my recovery because I quickly learned that whatever I ate ultimately affected my training or race performance. It also gave me a passion that took up a lot of brain space, pushing food out. It touched my competitive spirit and changed my body with all the training I did.

My first full Ironman was in June 2015. It was so hard. Though we swam in a bay, there was still a strong current, making what should have been calm waters very challenging. The bike portion was known for its flatness, which is wonderful for a beginner. However, powerful headwinds made the 112-mile ride ever more laborious than it already was. During the last few miles, I told myself I was never going to do this again.

When I got into the changing tent after the ride, to get ready for the run. I sat down and caught my breath. I had an internal dialogue going on in my head.

I'm done, I can't do this anymore.
But your husband, kids, and so many friends are already stationed along the run to cheer you on.
I know, but I'm so tired, how can I possibly run a marathon now?
Don't quit, you'll regret it.
Quitting would be sweet relief.
Ronni, you are not a quitter. Everyone is waiting for you out there.
You can do this.
No, I'm not a quitter. Yes, I can do this.

Off I went onto the run course. I saw my family and friends. Each time was glorious because I got to stop and give them sweaty hugs. I could feel the blisters forming on my feet, I knew I was dehydrated, and my legs hurt from doing so much work. I told myself – one and done, just finish.

And I did. And it was amazing to be done.

A few days later, when I was back to 100% physically, I finally was able to absorb the enormity of what I had done fully. It felt so empowering. I took on a big, hairy goal and nailed it. It wasn't pretty, but I had done it. I realized that if I could finish an Ironman, I could do anything I set my mind to and reiterated those words to my children. I know that today, the same as the day I finished.

With my eating disorder behind me and having the knowledge that I can do really hard things; nothing can hold me back in pursuing my dreams.

Finishing the Ironman

Mom – Some Thoughts and Memories
by Syd Blackwell

At the age of twenty-four years, one hundred thirty-five days, Kay Blackwell became a mother for the first time. She would give birth to three more boys in the next seven years, and a daughter fifteen years later. My own recollections of my mother began about four years later.

I was a sickly child. My most serious ailment was rheumatic fever that occurred during my fourth year. My earliest recollections of my mother were of her caring for me during these ailments that plagued my pre-school years. Also, at this time I began piano lessons from elderly Mrs. Langdale who lived behind our home. Mom had been advised that I should not participate in active sports because of a heart murmur from the rheumatic fever, and piano lessons became the alternative. I continued for about ten years but was never really any good. I also lived an active, robust, adventurous 1950s' boy life despite the heart murmur.

Before my teen years, I did not think about my mother very much, but she was the person that was always there, doing everything. In the early years when we heated and cooked with coal and wood, she was up before six, to get the house heated (in colder seasons), dad breakfast and off to work, and then kids up. Her days were spent in cleaning, shopping, preparing, cooking, washing, ironing, mending, sewing, gardening, budgeting, and so much more. She was always there. She was the first person we saw each morning and usually the last we saw each night. We all took her work for granted. We helped only occasionally and then usually whined and complained throughout.

By the time I had turned into a teenager, I was really starting to understand and appreciate how much my mother did. I also observed her through her last pregnancy, a most interesting life experience for a teenage boy. I had a great deal of friction throughout my teen years with my father. My mother became my guide and counsel. Even some of my friends talked to her about their problems. She also became proficient at giving her sons haircuts. Some friends even came for one too.

I left home for university in September 1965. I would return for employment four of the next five summers, but I resided in Victoria. Unlike most of my family, I would never again live in the Kootenays. It would be 29 years before I got close. I only knew of the intervening years through sporadic messages and infrequent visits. My mother was not often a part of my active life. It would be years more before I understood that she was always with me.

She was there for my wedding in 1970... and for my wedding in 1983... and for my wedding in 2003. Motherly duty!

In late 2006, Gundy and I visited Uruguay and quickly made a decision to retire there. Gundy sold her business and left in March 2007, but I had difficulty selling my business. I was excited when mine finally sold in September. I drove to Rossland for a visit with my mother. I left two days later.

FARE THEE WELL

Summer lingered a little longer
than usual this year
By the last day of September
autumn golds, oranges and reds
had not yet captured half
of summer's deciduous greens
A steady rain fell as I waved farewell
to my mother in the upstairs window
now knowing when I might see her again
or what condition she might be in then
or even if there will be a when
I dried my misted eyes
and began the rise
up the highway to tomorrow
quickly reaching fog
before rain turned to snow
summer letting go
me getting to go

Hope Slide Viewpoint
30/09/07

For most of the next year and a half, our communication was by telephone and occasionally by mail. I received frequent updates from my sister, Nancy. I heard of her continuing physical deterioration and the signs of mental problems. By the end of 2008, it was becoming clear that her time in her own house was nearing an end. She already had considerable assistance, and the coming year would see that escalate. On Christmas Eve, Nancy arranged a Skype call where mom could be present. Our conversation was difficult. I felt strongly that I needed to send a letter to my mother, while she could still understand. I could see that time was slipping away.

Casa Inspiración
Sunday, January 18, 2009

Hello Mom,

I need to write to you. I've known this for some time; particularly since I spoke to you on the phone on Christmas Eve.

However, I want first to talk to you about the card that Nancy chose for you to send to me on my birthday. I know there was divine guidance in the choice of that card. I have never read or seen a card like that and know that it was where it was in the store so that Nancy would find it for you so you could say what you really wanted to say. I'm sure you don't remember all of it, but here is what it said:

"Dear Son,

There are lots of things I meant to tell you before you grew up and journeyed out into the world. I suppose by now you've learned some of them for yourself. But there are things you need to know and words you'll only hear from someone who's known you from the start. Someone who heard your first heartbeat, who held you and looked into your eyes with amazement. Someone who relives the wonder and special meaning of this day every year. I want you to know that you're as deeply loved now as you were in my heart back then. And wherever life takes you, that love will forever go with you."

I began my journey out into the world such a long time ago. Your home was my home only until I was 18; that was 44 years ago. I have always been a traveller. We have spent a long time at a distance. However, I have never doubted or never stopped feeling that you loved me and that I loved you.

Now that the physical distance is greater than it has ever been, it has become stressful to you. However, physical distance is not very important. Even when I was a lot closer, I didn't see you very often. There were times in those years when I didn't see you for more than a year. I know it's now been longer than that since we last saw each other. I also know that you are concerned about when we will see each other.

However, I have become a spiritual person. I am sure that I always was. I am sure we all are. I just didn't know it when I was younger. I have had more time, since I stopped working, I have done more thinking about my spirituality. We are all spirits having a human experience; not humans having a spiritual experience. We are forever connected, you and I, and we have always been so. We will continue to be so. Nothing can prevent that. No distances change that. Whether we are here in this human world or when we pass again into the spiritual world, we will still be connected. We are spirits together.

I have always known this and felt this. I have been awakened to my spirituality, but I have always known about our love. The difference is now I can see and understand and talk about it as I never could when I was younger. I know that the distance is only a human distance and that the spiritual distance is non-existent. It is the only distance that really counts. I cried when I left Rossland to move to South America because I too focused on the great physical distances and the uncertainty of the future. But the future is always uncertain in human terms. It is only certain in spiritual terms.

So, for this time in our humanity, we only talk on the telephone. It is a human way of communicating a lot of things that generally are not so important. It is also a way of reconfirming in a human way our love – a love that is universal, eternal and uncompromised by the simplicity of our humanity.

I'll call you again around the end of the month. I hope you will have received this letter by then. If not, we'll talk anyway, and I'll know that you will know that I love you and I will know that you love me.

By August 2009, phone conversations had become disjointed.

FURTHER THOUGHTS FROM AN EVOLVING MIND

The characters of my dreams
come from here and there
cast together on stages
of my creation
it matters not how or when
I first knew them
for they have new roles
to perform

new relationships to form
age and manifestation
my manipulation

I do not sleep the deepest sleep
I travel about in a world I keep
separate from waking

But that difference
is not now so clear
to my mother dear
who can do the same
in the middle of some story
we share on the telephone

Not that she was always so gifted
but she is now
and somehow I understand
there isn't much difference between
that and how I dream

Casa Inspiración
09/12/08

By October, they were worse.

PHONE CONVERSATION WITH MY MOTHER

I was out last night over on the other side of town
she said
but when I asked her where she couldn't remember
at Nancy's I asked
well if it was it sure didn't look like her she said
of my sister

and I know it's come to this

I heard of my brother's new house
twice in fifteen minutes
and about the flowers he brought
like poinsettias she said but couldn't remember a name
asters I asked thinking of a fall flower
and she said that's it

177

and I know it's come to this

Then she told me John Hart had phoned
but she couldn't remember his name or where he lived
and when I guessed who she was talking about
she said yes that's the one
he's just like a son
but moments later she forgot his name again

and I know it's come to this

And when I said it was spring down here
she suddenly flew back seventy-five years
to tell me once again of a Christmas turkey dinner
in the blazing summer heat of Australia
her only visit to the southern hemisphere
showing some thoughts still connect

and I know it's come to this

And once again I heard about how
they've taken her car away
and she only had one little dent in it
and she can drive okay but they took it away and sold it
not at all recognizing the walker she needs to walk
and the chairlift she needs for the stairs

and I know it's come to this

And when as I have done
I think that it has been a long time since I saw her
and wonder if I ever will again
I have to remember that even if I did visit
it might well be as last night

and I know it's come to this

Casa Inspiración
12/10/09

June 23 (2013) – Sunday

We breakfasted with Nancy and Don on excellent breads and jams and bowls
of fruit and thick yogurt. Wonderful!

Around noon, we will visit our mother. Nancy sees her all the time; Tom also visits her regularly. I last saw her at the end of September 2007. I never thought I would see her again. She is now 91, wheelchair-bound, incontinent, unable to self-feed and fully into Alzheimer's. I had no expectations that she would know me in any way.

We found my mother at one of the tables for residents who cannot feed themselves. Nancy visits once or twice a week, mostly at lunch so she can feed mom. We appeared and she recognized Nancy. Don, Gundy and I stood back. She does not know Nancy as her daughter, but as someone who comes to visit her often.

Suddenly, she focused on me. Everyone else also noticed this. She stared intently at me and then smiled. She had recognized me in a way that she had not done with other family members who had visited. She did not say anything, but there was no question that for a few moments there had been recognition.

Soon the food appeared, and Nancy fed mom. From time to time, she looked at me briefly. She also looked at Gundy a few times. After her meal, I leaned in close to her head and she spoke to me in a low, slow voice.

"I haven't seen you in a very long time."

Then the moment was gone. She was somewhere else. However, I was fighting back tears. The initial recognition, the fleeting glances, and this amazing statement had never happened with anyone else since she slipped down the Alzheimer slope.

There would be no more moments.

Kay Blackwell passed away in her sleep on March 22, 2018.

My Mother's Last Gift
by Tina Wagner Mattern

It was 1993, and I was 43 years old when my birth mother and I were finally reunited; a reunion that became the foundation for our relationship, which would last for 2 decades. Once a year for the next 20 years I would fly from my home in Portland, Oregon, to Clearwater, Florida to spend a week getting to know my mother. They were weeks of revelations for both of us; weeks of questions answered, confessions, forgiveness and tears. But they were also weeks of delight; of recognizing in ourselves the off-the-wall sense of humor we shared. We learned the simple joy of just being together, whether it was playing bingo at her condo's clubhouse, putting together jigsaw puzzles over a glass or two of wine in the evenings, or taking an occasional road trip.

And as those years of weekly visits passed, my mother and I bonded anew... this time not so much as parent and child, but as beloved friends.

* * *

On a hot summer day in early July 2013, I got a call from Sharon, my half-sister in Florida that would shake me to my core; our mother was in intensive care. Within days, I was on a plane.

Sharon had told me on the phone that Mom was very ill—double pneumonia, congestive heart failure and anemia due to internal bleeding somewhere—but she had battled most of these health issues before and had triumphed. Nearly 81, she was our family's indomitable Energizer bunny. So, when the pulmonologist broke the news that our mother was not going to live, Dana, my half-brother, Sharon, and I were stunned and heartbroken.

Entering her room in ICU, I looked down at my funny, bossy, inexpressibly lovable mother and wondered: how can anyone so alive be terminally ill? There she was, hooked up to beeping machines and wearing a CPAP with the highest saturation rate of oxygen available, but unlike the other patients in ICU, she was her usual silly self, making faces, teasing the nurses, joking and laughing. Even after the doctor had explained the dire prognosis to her, her irrepressible attitude didn't falter. "You know," she told us, "I would've thought that hearing I was going to die would make me a basket-case, but strange as it seems, I'm really at peace about this." We, her children, of course, were not.

"Don't cry," she said, wiping our tears. "I know where I'm going after all. Heaven's going to be wonderful." We did our best, but heaven seemed so far away.

Throughout her days in the hospital, Mom had a positive spirit that became infectious; she entertained and inspired family, friends, neighbors and loved members of her church; each visitor was treated to her absurdly delightful sense of humor and uplifting faith. As long as her pain was kept under control, she was the sassy, often hilarious life of the party. Visiting hour rules in the intensive care unit limited callers to two at a time, but there were rarely less than 6 in Mom's room. The wonderful attendant staff, captivated by this high-spirited, anything-but-ordinary patient, smiled, and looked the other way.

One afternoon, Janet, Mom's best friend and long-time comrade-in-shenanigans, came for her daily visit. This time she brought her twelve-year-old granddaughter, Kimberly, with her. Janet and Mom tossed insults and droll comments back and forth as Kimberly and I alternately laughed and rolled our eyes. After a few minutes of this, though, Janet grew serious and handed Mom an envelope. "Here, I brought you something," she said. "Open it and read the note."

Mom smiled, drawing out the folded sheet of paper, and began to read out loud a lovely little poem about angels. "Oh, that's sweet," she said, when she finished.

"Now, look in the envelope," Janet instructed. Pulling it open, Mom peeked inside and chuckled. "It's a feather!" She held the tiny white plume up for us to see. "Must have been a small angel, huh?"

Kimberly and I laughed.

Janet, smiling through suddenly teary eyes, leaned forward and grabbed Mom's hand. "Listen, you—this feather is important. When you get to heaven, I want you to send it to me to let me know you got there."

Mom laughed. "You don't want much, do you? Okay, I'll see what I can do."

During the week to come, our family and Mom's dearest friends stayed close by her side, treasuring every second, cherishing every wisecrack, every laugh, every tender, reassuring hug. Each of us imprinting on our hearts the moments spent with her.

Much too soon, however, the day came when I had to return to Portland. Saying goodbye was agonizing. How could I leave knowing I wouldn't see her again? I offered to change my flight, despite the exorbitant fee, but Mom, with her unshakable faith, hugged me and whispered, "Go home, Tina. I love you. This isn't goodbye, sweetheart, it's 'see you later'." My last memory of my mother is of her grinning her irresistible grin and blowing me kisses through her oxygen mask.

Early the following Monday morning, I got the call: surrounded by her children, grandchildren and dearest sister and brother, Mom had slipped gently from their arms into God's.

On Tuesday afternoon, my phone rang; it was Janet. We had been checking in with one another throughout the weeks leading up to Mom's death, so I assumed she was calling to see how I was doing. Instead, her voice brimmed with excitement. "I have something to tell you," she said. Intrigued by her unexpected tone, I asked, "What's up?"

"My granddaughter, Kimberly, stayed with me last night," Janet said. "We finished watching a movie and were just sitting there on the sofa, when I looked over and saw Kimberly's arm go up in the air. 'What on earth are you doing?' I asked her. She turned to me, all wide-eyed, and held out her hand, 'Grandma, look!'"

Janet's voice dropped to an awed whisper. "It was a little white feather, Tina. Right out of thin air!"

My arms broke out in goosebumps and an ecstatic smile spread across my face as I pictured my mother entering heaven, pointing to the nearest angel and saying, "Hey, I need to borrow one of those feathers!"

"Oh Janet," I said with a lump in my throat, "She made it! I never doubted that she would, but what a sweet miracle!" Janet sniffled, "Amen."

Mom, who had always delighted in giving her loved ones presents, had given us one last gift... a feather from heaven.

Nervous Night in Nevada
by Leslie Groves Ogden

Returning home after a 1976 Idaho camping trip, my husband Barry and I were tired of driving the same monotonous roads in Nevada or navigating the crowded Interstates in California. Ordinarily we drove through long stretches of unpopulated Nevada, or alternatively, we battled Bay Area traffic west of Reno. We couldn't avoid all the aggravation, but perusing our map, we did discover a turnoff on our usual route that would take us onto a new stretch of highway and through some areas we had not seen before.

As we left the Sawtooth Wilderness, we entered Nevada and turned west. Near Reno we planned to turn south on Highway 395, enjoy the unexplored landscape, then join the scenic route along the eastern Sierra Nevadas. With suitcases, pillows, sleeping bags and our three children sharing the back seat and cargo area, with camping gear stashed in an overcrowded top carrier, our big Chevy station wagon lumbered along I-80 toward Reno. It was getting dark when the exit appeared, and rather than attempt to fight traffic and find a motel in the big city, we drove on through, thinking that Carson City would be a less confusing place to find suitable overnight accommodations.

The neon lights of Carson City, however, flashed by on both sides of the highway, and by the time we spotted motel signs we had passed the corresponding exits. Twice we left the highway only to encounter gas stations or dark residential streets instead of motels. Eventually we found our way back onto 395 while I pulled out the Nevada map and a flashlight. I assured the family that before too long we would be coming to a little town called Minden and soon after that, Gardnerville. It looked like 395 reverted to a two-lane road as it passed through the two small towns. Surely, we would find something convenient and adequate for just a single night's stay. Although the cooler had been packed with snacks and drinks, and pillows and sleeping bags made for comfy and cozy travel, all of us felt restless, hungry, and tired. We had wasted almost an hour driving in circles in Carson City. Night had fallen. We really needed to stop and get some sleep. Tomorrow would be another long day of travel.

Fifteen miles later, the highway became a rural road as we entered the outskirts of Minden. We slowly traversed the main drag, observing the dimly lit buildings and quiet sidewalks. Finding a motel there seemed unlikely.

After eight or nine blocks, the buildings dwindled, and the road widened. We sped up, hoping for better luck in Gardnerville.

Entering town, the road narrowed, the speed limit decreased, and buildings appeared. Occasionally a car cruised by in the opposite direction. Porch lights illuminated a few small houses. Gardnerville seemed even more quiet than Minden. Then, passing through the main business district, we noticed a neon glow ahead and country music appeared to be originating from an old two-story clapboard building. As we approached, the music grew louder, mingled with rowdy voices emanating from an open doorway. Driving slowly by, we saw a blinking neon sign that advertised, "Hotel and Bar".

Should we stop? Barry and I discussed it as he drove around the block. A quick look at the map showed no towns ahead until Bridgeport, California, another 65 miles away. The thought of spending another exhausting hour or more in the car with complaining children was enough to persuade us to circle back and park in front of the brightly lit windows. Barry took a deep breath, got out of the car, and walked in.

A few minutes later, he returned with good news: a room was available above the bar. We gathered a few overnight essentials, collected our sleepy offspring, locked the car, and traipsed inside.

A long bar dominated the right-hand wall, the high stools occupied by seedy-looking characters right out of a Hollywood western. The music continued to blare, but as we entered, the cacophony of voices dropped to a low, interested murmur. Cigarette smoke formed a cloud overhead, and the stale smell of spilled beer permeated the room. All eyes followed us as we escorted our brood past the bar, across the wood floor, around battered tables, and along tired booths lining the far wall, where we reached a steep stairway ascending to second-story rooms.

Pausing at the landing, we noted a short corridor interspersed with a half-dozen doorways. A threadbare carpet stretched the length of the hallway, ending at an open door to a shared bathroom. Barry wielded the old-fashioned room key to number 4, manipulating the worn lock. Gratefully, we entered our safe haven, eager to scarf down a few peanut butter crackers, locate pajamas and toothbrushes and get the children into bed. Our momentary relief, however, did not last. Room 4 was small, dark, and smelled like burnt tobacco and stale sweat. Feeling our way inside, we discovered the only light came from a naked bulb hanging from the ceiling, which Barry illuminated by yanking a chain. As the light glowed dimly, we surveyed our hastily booked accommodation: peeling linoleum floor, dingy gray walls, two sagging double beds and a curtainless, screenless window overlooking the street below. The room was hot and stuffy, and when we opened the window, music and laughter from the bar drifted up and in.

Out of options, we made the best of it. While I checked the worn sheets for fleas or other unwelcome residents, Barry escorted the kids down the hall to the bathroom. Careful not to touch grimy surfaces, they took care of bedtime ablutions quickly and all three dropped gratefully onto the shabby mattresses. Despite the noise wafting from below, they slept soundly. Finally, Barry and I squeezed into the beds among their sprawling arms and legs and attempted to get some rest.

Sometime in the wee hours, the bar closed. We had been asleep a short time when the commotion of patrons leaving awakened us: drunken shouts, raucous laughter, a loud argument, car doors slamming, engines revving. We heard people stomping up the stairs and heavy footsteps passing our door. When the racket outside finally died down, a more sinister conversation became audible. Creeping over to the open window, we looked down to find a group of shady-looking characters peering in the windows of our car, while others poked and prodded at the top carrier on the roof. Clearly, they planned to break in. And it did not seem like there was much we could do to stop them.

We watched anxiously as they discussed what to do. We listened to an animated argument; grim voices accompanied by forceful gestures. Eventually, the disagreement gave way to reason. They must have decided the potential spoils were not worth the effort. After all, as they gazed into the back seat and cargo area, only the detritus of a camping trip was visible: pillows, blankets, an old cooler, a few scattered toys and books, tent poles and well-used lawn chairs. And how likely was a top carrier to contain anything valuable or expensive? With a sigh of relief, we watched them slowly disperse and fade into the dark night.

We didn't get much sleep after that. Up and dressed at first light, we used the communal bathroom as quickly as possible, gathered our belongings, and escaped down the stairs and out the door. Our car was intact, although we found many fingerprints in the dusty paint.

Friends who travel tell me that Gardnerville is no longer that backwater redneck town we encountered in 1976. It has apparently grown into a respectable suburb of Carson City, and if you search Expedia or Kayak you will find at least three chain hotels in town. When I googled *"hotel with bar in Gardnerville"*, up popped a photo of a building that probably was the site of our unsettling experience. Over the years the place has improved, at least from what I can tell from the picture. If we ever take that route back to Idaho, maybe we will pay a visit.

Hotel with bar in Gardnerville

Unto the Haven
by Ronald Mackay

Brittle frost that coated the meadow-grass caught the low winter sun, breaking its light into shards of stained-glass on a cathedral floor.

O give thanks unto the Lord for he maketh the storm to cease, so that the waves
therof are still.

Then are they glad, because they are at rest: and so he bringeth them unto the
haven where they would be.

Hugh Bentley had often read these words aloud in the long nights of off-shore patrol work. He found them rousing at times, always reassuring. As commander of the tiny Royal Navy corvette *HMS Balmuir*, he was charged not only with the physical safety of his seamen but their moral well-being too. Hugh took both charges seriously. Most of his able seamen had been enlisted as teenagers from Scottish farms and factories. But U-boats cared nothing about the age of those who manned a wartime patrol vessel.

Early morning sunlight invariably brought back memories of these years of trial, of occasional victory and deep sorrow. Unsought memories would assault when frost refracted a beam from a spikey white blade of grass or an overnight spider's web and unexpectedly caused it to erupt into the rainbow's spectrum. The spectacular flash of colour within which his command had exploded from under him, sucking most of his crew into the North Sea. A U-boat's triumphant conning tower, bridge and periscope sank beneath the waves in search of its next victim.

Strong arms had gripped and dragged him onto floating debris. Together, they had struggled to reach and rescue the few – so few they failed to match the numbers on one hand. The pair worked as yoked horses might, accustomed to drawing together in synchronised silence.

Then, when hope of more survivors was gone, they'd spoken reverently. Throughout the night they'd kept each other awake, aware of being officer and able seaman but conscious too of a deeper bond, although their pre-war lives would have been unlikely to bring them together. Shared survival after violent danger, binds souls.

Hugh had confided that he was a career officer deemed just experienced enough, in these needy times, to command the smallest naval warship charged with keeping vital sea-lanes open. The boy had listened in silence.

"You?" asked the commander.

"Under pressure," the boy admitted.

"How so?" Hugh was puzzled.

"It was prison or the Navy!" The boy glanced away. He still remembered the judge looking at him in bewigged seriousness. *"It's your choice. Which is it to be?"*

Hugh had nodded, understanding now.

"Your offence?"

"Poaching."

"Poaching what?" Hugh's had long been a landed family. They knew the nuisance of poachers, their covert practice despite the law. Hugh also knew the consequences for repeat offenders. Not a rap on the knuckles nor a ruinous fine, but time in jail for an adult, in a reform school or a borstal for a minor.

"So, not your first time?"

The boy shook his head. "Like my faither learned to poach at his faither's knee, so mine taught me. It's in our blood." His soft voice was tinged with seriousness and pride, as he quoted a universal truth in his Angus dialect:

"It's a poor man that canna keep his own pot boilin'."

Clasped to the floating detritus reeking of scorched oil, alongside the young man who had dragged him aboard and with whom he had striven to save others, Hugh had reflected on the laws of chance. *If the boy's father hadn't taught him to poach, if the boy hadn't learned how to snare a rabbit, if the landlord hadn't reported him, if he hadn't been prosecuted, found guilty and given the choice between jail or the Navy, the boy might never have been aboard the Balmuir. Hugh might never have survived.*

"It's a poor man indeed who can't look after the needs of his own family." Hugh pondered the meaning of the boy's words knowing them to be true; knowing that his life had been saved by someone brought up not only to embrace that wisdom but also to act on it in part from necessity, part custom. Life is not easy.

* * *

The commander, the boy and the four wounded were spotted by an aircraft from RAF Leuchars, then picked up by an Arbroath trawler that same day. Hugh never saw the boy again, but he never forgot him, nor what he had made of the option offered him by an enlightened judge. *Prison or the Navy?*

By War's end, Hugh commanded a sizeable frigate, faster and more powerfully armed than the *Balmuir*. Standing securely on her bridge in sweater and duffle coat, he had accompanied scores of transatlantic convoys as part of a flotilla of protection. Sometimes they failed, often they were successful. At least he never ended up in the sea again, nor had to be hauled aboard a shard of oily flotsam by a teen-aged able-seaman.

* * *

Over the years, Hugh's family circumstances changed. His elder brother died of wounds sustained in battle. Hugh married. When his father died, Hugh abandoned his career in oil and gas exploration to manage the family estate.

* * *

Now, on this winter morning, as he watched the lad crouch down to remove the rabbit from the snare, he recalled, in his mind's eye, the poacher on the raft in the swell of the North Sea.

The boy stood up and killed the rabbit with a single blow. He pulled the snare and the stake out of the ground and walked down the fencerow looking for signs of another rabbit-run where he might reset them profitably.

Hugh had spotted the set snares and the occasional drop of blood, but this was the first time he'd caught a poacher red-handed. He waited till the boy was hemmed in by the angle where the tall hedge met the fast-flowing Dichty Burn before breaking cover.

The boy froze. Sharp young ears had heard the crisp crackle of a boot on frosted grass. He looked up, saw he was cornered and stood stock-still, rabbit held by its hindlegs in one hand, snare in the other. All the evidence that a judge would need for a successful prosecution.

"What do you think you're doing?" Hugh was conscious of the officer in his voice.

The boy didn't move. Then he raised both hands, displaying what they held.

"It's a poor man that canna keep his own pot boilin'." Only the slightest hint of belligerence.

Hugh had to grasp the top rail of the fence to prevent himself from reeling. *It's a poor man indeed who can't feed his own family.*

The boy noticed the stumble and called out, betraying concern.

"You all right, Surr?"

It took Hugh a moment to bring himself back from the day his world erupted and a torpedo hit his *Balmuir* amidships with the loss of most.

"Pickin up a wee rabbit for me and my mither." Expressionless, the boy held the lifeless rabbit higher and let the snare fall to the ground.

Hugh fought to regain control. "Where do you live?"

"Kirkton." He gestured towards the subsidised municipal housing beyond the estate boundaries towards the encroaching suburbs of the city.

"Why are you not at school?"

"School?" The sound was dismissive.

"Why are you not working?"

"Because I can't get a job."

"There's work enough."

"Not if you were at the Baldovan."

Baldovan Approved School was the borstal where offenders were sent, too young to withstand the barbarism of prison.

"Why Baldovan?"

"Gee Bee Aitch."

Hugh looked at the face pinched white with cold, the skinny frame dressed in hand-me-downs, at cracked shoes glistening wet from the frost.

The boy must have felt the silent disbelief in Hugh's eyes. *"How could a poor specimen like you be capable of inflicting Grievous Bodily Harm?"*

"I used a knife." Offered without emotion or apology.

Hugh wondered if he was carrying the knife now, but asked, "Do you want a job or do you prefer to steal?" He heard the superiority of the officer in his own voice. A superiority he didn't feel inside himself but a trait that had developed early – naturally – and had become a habit first as a naval officer and then as a captain of industry.

"Tried that."

"Where?"

"Docks, ship-yards, the jute mills." He gestured towards the port on the river.

"And?"

"Nuthin. Soon as I say *Baldoven*, it's: *We don't need the likes of you!*" After a pause he added, "See?" as if he felt a need to check if Hugh understood the endless challenge of a borstal reputation.

Hugh remembered the night on the North Sea. *Yes, he saw.*

"Your name?

There was a hesitation, then: "Reilly."

Hugh waited.

"Willy Reilly."

The diminutive, Hugh realised, was what this boy's mother must call him: *Willy*. He hadn't yet, neither in body nor in soul, grown into "Will" for her. Maybe not for anybody. Not even in his own mind. *Willy*.

"Do you want a job, Will?" Hugh used the adult form intentionally.

The boy hesitated, caught off-balance. Here he was, discovered red-handed by the toff himself, the estate-owner, the Laird, and he heard himself being addressed by his adult name for the first time. The very first time in his life. Was this a question? Or was he being baited? Baited for amusement and benefit or so that the toff could share more damning evidence with the judge: *The poacher said he preferred stealing to working, your Honour.*

"This is my family's place. This estate." Hugh gestured to the fields, trees, to the walled garden and to the chimneys of the big house among the chestnut trees in the distance.

"I know."

"You know?"

"Seen you drive to toon. Big shiny black car."

"No doubt." The pre-War Daimler attracted attention.

"You've passed me when I've been walkin into town to look for a job. Or walkin back."

"Without one."

"That's right." The anguish of repeated failure glistened for a moment in the lad's eyes.

"So, Will, here's your chance. I need a good man for our market garden. A man who knows wildlife and the land, a man who can keep the rabbits out of my cauliflower and cabbage fields. A man who can use a knife to clean the rabbits so I can take them into Nicholson's." Hugh chose his words carefully, wanting the boy to feel more like a fellow-man than a miscreant; to know that his skill with a knife could be channelled to good use.

"Mr Nicholson takes my extras too."

Hugh had to subdue a smile. Canny old Nicholson, the best butcher and poulterer in the city! Buying from whoever, not caring where the rabbits, hares, wood-pigeons or pheasants came from. The Laird's legitimate game hanging alongside the poacher's. For the same price.

"You serious, Surr? About the job?"

The *Sir* took him back to the raging North Sea, the heaving grey Atlantic. Formal discipline essential in the face of war. Conduct that can pull success from the ravening jaws of failure.

"Dead serious, Will. Five pounds a week. Start at eight, finish at five. One on Saturday. Sundays off. Arrive at the back door of the big house at 7.30 every morning and cook will give you porridge in her kitchen."

* * *

Over the months, in front of Hugh's battle-bruised eyes, the boy turned into a young man. He worked hard; grew and filled out with the porridge; learned additional useful skills; how to stand up straight, speak man-to-man with respect for both himself and others; how to complete well, a job unsupervised.

Hugh watched him with quiet satisfaction, watched without saying just how proud he was to see him grow. He allowed the increasing demands he made on Will and the increasing responsibilities he charged him with to speak for themselves. From rabbit-trapper, fence-maker and odd-job-man to game-keeper responsible for hatching and raising the pheasants for the shoot. An estate had to rely on revenues from a broad range of sources – cattle, forage, corn and cash-crops, seasonal vegetables, raspberries and soft-fruit, and of course sport-shooting.

In time, Will courted and then married the daughter of a ploughman at Claverhouse, a few miles to the west. Hugh renovated a small cottage on the estate and offered it to the couple at nominal rent.

* * *

One Saturday in spring, as Hugh handed Will his wage-packet, Will thanked him then asked:

"Surr, I have somethin to say to you."

"Then say away, Will."

"It's not just me. It's Lizzie, too. Could we speak to you this efternoon? Both of us?"

Despite the spring birdsong, Hugh's spirits chilled. He'd imagined the day might come when Will would move on. Here, he was part game-keeper, part general farm-worker. It was natural for the young man to want to advance. But he had hoped that the cottage might offer an incentive to stay.

* * *

Will and Liz arrived at his office at three. Candles of ivory flowers graced the horse-chestnut trees outside his window. Both visitors were bathed and dressed. Will had shaved. Lizzie stood shyly, her coat unbuttoned. Will carried his bonnet in both hands. Hugh had prepared himself for what was coming.

"Surr," began Will, then stopped. Lizzie looked at her husband. A man now, though barely 20.

"It's like this, Captain Bentley." Then she stopped too.

"Out with it!" Hugh heard impatience colour his voice. One failing among others that he had promised to rid himself of after his wartime command ended, after he retired from industry. But he never had.

"I'm gonna have a baby, Surr. We think it's gonna be a boy." Lizzie's face was radiant.

Will smiled at her, proud, loving, then turned to Hugh. "So, we want – we're askin your permission, Surr, to call our son *Hugh*."

"*Hugh*, like yoursel. For all ye've done for Will, Surr. All ye've done for both of us." Lizzie smiled.

Hugh nodded briskly, giving his assent, not trusting himself to speak. They thanked him and left.

Hugh remained at his desk, head bowed, for a very long time.

When he was finally ready, he rose and went upstairs to share this honour with his wife *and give thanks that they, theirs and all for whom they had been made responsible, had been brought unto the haven where they would be.*

Family Love and a Dog named Bruce
by Carolyn Muir Helfenstein

Let's get the cows!

That's all Bruce would need to hear and out the laneway to the back pasture field he'd race, knowing he had only a limited amount of time to enjoy sniffing out mice and moles in the fence rows before his work began. He kept his eyes and ears on Harry. Bruce was an Australian Shepherd farm dog.

"OK, Bruce. Get the cows!" Bruce responded, and Harry needed only to wait. Like a bullet released by the pull of a trigger, Bruce would begin what came so naturally to him. Taking a wide swath to the left, around our herd of Holsteins, he began his routine. These cows knew exactly what was about to happen, but they pretended to ignore him.

It was as if Bruce were drawing a huge string around the entire herd, pulling it tighter and tighter. Back and forth he'd weave a pattern, to the left and then to the right, snipping at the heels of any cow that dared not move along with the rest of the herd. Like liquid black and white, the wary Holsteins would finally begin the inevitable plodding journey to the barn. It was milking time.

Bruce had arrived at our farm as a Christmas present, an unforgettable day. Harry was sitting in the family room of our farmhouse in his very own lumpy chair that I'd reupholstered with my awkward, unskilled city-raised fingers, the year before. Our hundred-year-old yellow brick farmhouse had been our home since 1963.

And on that wintery day just one day before Christmas in 1975, our three children, our eleven-year-old twins Suzanne and Robert, and David, age five, had a surprise for their dad.

"Dad, Merry Christmas!" Their combined voices reverberated throughout the old house. Our twins decided David should be the one to carry the surprise into the room where their dad was sitting. The twins lifted the wiggling puppy from David's outstretched arms, and like passing a basket of freshly laid eggs, the two together placed the fluffy ball of grey, bronze and black on their father's lap.

"Dad, we got you a puppy for Christmas!" David got right to the nubbins of the matter.

Harry laughed, his face a mirror of utter surprise, his huge, rough hands holding the puppy, his index finger scratching the seven-week-old ball of fur behind the ear, an action that must have felt to the puppy somewhat like his own mother licking him with her all-knowing tongue, to calm his thumping heart. "Well, little fella, you and I are going to be buddies, are we?"

"Yes, yes, he's yours!" Again, David speaking up.

"Do you like him, Dad?"

"He's beautiful, Suz. I should know what breed he is…?"

"Dad, he's an Australian Shepherd. They're great cattle dogs. This dog will work. You won't have to get the cattle anymore." That was Rob adding the details.

"Dad, what will you call him? He's your dog." Suzanne adored her father and seemed always able to read his mind. By now all three children were cuddled around Harry, getting as close as a family can get. What a scene. I leaned against the doorway into the family room where the staircase led upstairs to our bedrooms. I sighed. My heart filled with family love, knowing this would be a Christmas scene cherished forever. I hugged myself with the joy of it. Oddly enough, no camera appeared to capture the moment, however my mind's eyes had, and will have forever. An old red leather chair, their dad and his children; and his puppy.

Christmas doesn't get much better than that.

"Hmmm, let me see, a name for this puppy. Hmmm. Well, I'll tell you." He looked at his three children.

"When I was a little boy in England, your age, David, I had a dog named Bruce." The puppy looked up at Harry and the children were quick to pick up on that.

"Dad, did you see that? Did you see that? He likes the name." Suzanne said.

"I agree," added Rob. "Hi Bruce." The puppy looked at Rob.

David clapped. "Smart dog!"

"Dad, maybe I should take Bruce outside for a minute." Suzanne, always the practical one, scooped up the puppy and with Rob and David in close pursuit, she led the little parade out the back door and gently placed the puppy on the snow. Before many minutes, the excited puppy left a yellow mark on the blanket of snow that now covered the landscape. Bruce County could almost always provide snow by Christmas Day. All three piped up, "Good dog, Bruce." The training had begun.

We soon recognized when Bruce was happy. His long tongue would be hanging out, his ears would be on the alert, and he would be on the move. Aussies are busy creatures. He was never really trained, he just knew.

As Bruce settled in as a member of our family, we learned that he hated thunder and lightning, in fact he would crawl into the darkest hole to avoid it or find one of us for protection. We all remembered the stormy afternoon in particular, when Bruce found himself locked out of the barn as the sky blackened and the wind moaned through the trees. Farm dust swirled around him and must have blocked his vision, and that would have frightened him. He knew Harry had disappeared down the farm laneway in the family van. We could only guess later that Bruce must have sniffed at the split wooden door, the only way into the barn, hoping miraculously it would open for him. That split door, as old as the barn itself, probably built by the Ballagh family of Belmore some 50 years before, would not keep Bruce from his hiding place.

It was Suzanne who happened to look out the window. She ran to the door. "Bruce, come in, you look terrible, poor dog. Why aren't you in the barn?" Another boom shook the earth. "Bruce. I know. A storm, come on in." She put her farm jacket over him and went back to her homework, but not until she'd found a leftover hot dog in the refrigerator, a treat that he gobbled down gratefully. He must have sensed that at last he was safe from the dreaded thunder and lightning. Suzanne never thought to look out toward the barn, so she didn't know the story about Bruce's attempt to get in with the cattle, a sure place to find safety.

When Harry returned from town, the storm had moved on and the sun was peeking out from behind the receding storm clouds. He backed the family van right up to the split door. He was glad to be home and looked forward to the cup of tea he knew I'd have brewing. It was then he found himself staring at what appeared to be an attack on the split door by something as strong as a bear. The bottom foot or so of the wooden door had been ripped away.

He wondered...

Entering the kitchen and seeing Suzanne's jacket resting on Bruce, Harry guessed he was looking at the culprit. "Bruce, old buddy, that was terrible thunder, wasn't it?" Harry scratched his sad-looking dog behind the ear, and then sat down at the familiar pleasure this kitchen table and chair always brought, his cup of tea already waiting for him.

Suz appeared. "Dad, I saw Bruce standing out in the rain. You know how he hates thunder. He looked sick. I had to let him in. He's been lying in that corner ever since. Poor dog, but I'm sure he's not sick."

Meanwhile, Bruce, his chin on his paws, his eyes focused only on Harry, was a picture of abject misery and if a dog could produce tears, this dog of ours was indeed next to tears.

"Hi Kiddo," Harry looked at me, his cup in hand, and knowingly I refilled it. He smiled, a twinkle of thanks in his eye.

"Guess what? Something attacked the old split door to the barn while I was away. There's a hole in it big enough for a raccoon to get in, but I can't imagine a raccoon being stuck in that little passageway of ours with three doors to choose from." Harry was referring to the fact the little entrance way opened up into the milk house, the cattle barn and then of course the outside by way of the old split door.

We all turned to Bruce. Their dad was sure of the culprit now.

Bruce stayed put, flat out on the new kitchen tiled floor, his chin still remaining on his front paws; but he had begun his favorite method of pleading forgiveness. We all recognized this routine of his and we muffled our laughter. Bruce would lift one eyebrow as his eyes turned to Harry and then next, he'd lift the other eyebrow and his brown eyes would look to me, pleading for understanding. Again, and again, those eyebrows rose and fell, and we all thought he was the cleverest dog in the world!

We understood his dilemma. He'd scratched his way through the old wood of the door into the passageway, every crash and bang of the thunder and the lightning making him more and more frantic, making him scratch harder and harder, only to find the inner doors were locked. Checking Bruce's paws for proof, Rob discovered that two of the nails on each front paw were broken off and that horrified the whole family. "Dad, Bruce must have squeezed back through the hole he'd made to make a dash for the house."

Bruce became so much a part of our family history that when our children grew up and went off to college, the stories about Bruce went with them. When the city friends came for a farm weekend, the first questions were, "Where's Bruce?"

"Bruce loves to play football," Rob would warn the friends with a grin, "Once he catches the football, he never, ever, gives it back."

"Hup, ten, fourteen, twenty-three, go!" All the complicated routines of a major league football game, all said in jest, and the half-boys, half-men would weave in and out across the horse field. Suzanne, now a very athletic university student, was often as not the captain for one team and a lead player, and Bruce was always in hot pursuit, hoping to nab the ball from whatever team had it. Of course, that meant the two teams would make a great fuss of chasing Bruce around and around the field, his quick feet and keen eyes allowing him to be just far enough ahead of the desperate runners that they would fall on the grass exhausted. Then Bruce would simply drop the ball and return to the players, nosing their faces and giving the giggling teens sticky licks on their cheeks. I often saw those happy college visitors lie on their backs out there in that field, exhausted from play, looking up at the blue sky and the sun, no doubt wondering if life could get any better than living on a farm.

I knew how much Bruce meant to our children and was not surprised that they became storytellers of the finest order. The object of their affection, of course, was Bruce.

For example: "Yes, that was the house plant Bruce chomped on, Mom's special house plant! It caused his face to blow up like a balloon. Allergic reaction," they'd add with the wisdom of a farm vet. Another time: "That's the field where he and our Old English Sheepdog, Pepsi, hunted groundhogs together; that's where he placed the groundhog bodies, and yes, over there, in the curve of the creek? That's where Bruce almost died." Everyone would just look serious. Our three knew how to catch the attention of their listeners. And it was a black day for all of us. I found myself telling the same story on many occasions:

It was Rob who came running into the kitchen that morning to tell me.

"Mom, Mom, Bruce is in trouble, he's going to die!" he said. It was a school day in March when the ice on our creek that ran by the barn and house was just beginning to break up. "He's on the ice, well really, he is in the creek! He's hanging on to the ice, but he can't get out! I've told Dad, and he warned us not to try to get him; but Bruce is going to drown. He's going to die!"

"Where is Suzanne?" I demanded.

"She's out there. I don't know what she's going to do. I think she went to get Bruce, but I don't know!" Rob now had two to worry about, a sister and Bruce.

I knew Suzanne would disobey her father and go to the rescue. That girl saw things in a straight line and at the end of the line that very morning, was her Bruce! Rob left again. I was out the door in a flash. David followed. His jacket was wide open, as per usual.

By now, however, their Dad had left the cows and was carrying a long ladder across the barnyard. Suzanne ran to me and I hugged her. We all could see Bruce, well, we could see his head and his two front paws; and we could hear him barking. He was in the middle of the creek. The water under the ice was running high, so there was no way he could touch bottom. It was obvious to us he could not attain purchase on the ice to haul himself out. Our three were frantic, but seeing their Dad rushing across the soggy, flooded field despite the weight of the heavy ladder, gave them courage that he would save Bruce. Of course, he would save Bruce. He was Dad.

Far off, down at the corner, the big yellow school bus came into view. It was the one our three took to the nearby school. The kids looked at their dad, now struggling as he drew closer and closer to Bruce. The bus was steadily making its way to our stop. Next it would be at the end of our laneway. The children began the journey to the bus stop, refusing to take their eyes off their dog. Bruce had stopped barking by this time. Our children could see their Harry placing the ladder across the creek. Then their hero began the crawl out to the spot where he could latch on to the slippery fur of Bruce's back. By now the bus was at our mailbox. It had stopped.

The bus driver held steady, not moving the bus one foot forward until Harry had grabbed the dog, pulled with all his might, no doubt pleading with Bruce not to wiggle, and with one powerful heave, had Bruce on safe ground. The bus started up, the driver tooted the horn, and our three heads and arms out the windows yelled at the top of their lungs, "Thanks Dad! Thanks!"

Harry lifted Bruce into his arms and the three of us raced back to the house as fast as we could despite the clumps of thick grass sticking up through the heavy wet snow and creek water that had flooded the entire field. Truth be, it was Harry and I who raced, Bruce hardly moved; the shock of the entire horrible experience was beginning now to take hold.

In the house Bruce did not argue in the least when Harry and I dried him off vigorously with a ready supply of old towels and wrapped him in a big blanket, all the time telling him what a great dog he was. It took several more blankets and more fresh towels before he began to relax. Harry looked at me knowingly. I phoned the school to tell the principal that I had good news for our three children. The principal, understanding the importance of a farm dog to farm children and the danger of spring floods, told each class that Bruce was recuperating.

Bruce stayed in the house all day and when David, Rob and Suzanne burst through the kitchen door at 4:15 pm, there was Bruce smiling at them, tongue out, both eyes shining, eyebrows twitching as he looked from one to the other. Bruce, our farm dog. A special breed.

I often recall those stories; I can see those precious moments of living on a farm and I know today our grandchildren are told those same stories and to them a farm is a very special place. And I sense no story is more exciting than the one where they get to say, "Get the cows, Bruce!"

Dog named Bruce

The Cyprus Affair (Final Scenes)
A Screenplay by Susan Joyce

Adapted from Susan's book, The Lullaby Illusion

How to read a Screenplay

The script is a blueprint for the story that appears on the screen, including essential physical cues like location, time of day, general environment, etcetera. A good screenplay is both interesting to read and well-constructed, in terms of format and layout and allows for the reader to "watch" the film in their mind's eye.

Script writing is visual writing. Scripts vacillate wildly from large blocks of text to simple pared-down lines of dialogue. Writing a good screenplay that allows a reader to "see" the movie as they read it is a challenge.

A script shows the SCENE ACTION and location appearance. The first thing you should understand when reading scene descriptions are the terms INT. and EXT. Those mean "interior" and "exterior" and denote where the scene takes place. The last word in the scene description tells the reader when the action happens, day or night.

EXT. CARS PARKED ON RISE NEAR HIGHWAY – NIGHT

A script also shows CHARACTER ACTION and what is happening around characters. The tense for such sentences is present tense. Example: "Susan turns the radio on at low volume."

The next thing that throws some people off is "(O.S.)" or "(O.C.)". If either of those descriptions appears next to a character's line, the mean they are "off camera" or "off screen." Another common abbreviation you will find is "(V.O.)" for "voice over."

Parentheticals are the words that appear in parentheses directly under a character's name, telling you something essential about the character's behavior. This something should use language that's visceral and visual. For instance, "(smiles)."

Hope you enjoy my script!

Scene 96

EXT. CARS PARKED ON RISE NEAR HIGHWAY – NIGHT

Susan and Charles sit in their car and watch as others climb into their various cars parked near the highway.

Ronit waves at them and gets into her friend's car nearby.

Ilene and Josh get into their family car parked in front of them.

Susan gets into the back seat of the convertible. Charles stretches his large body out across the two front seats.

Random explosions sound from across the pass.

An abrupt spark discharges behind their car.

CRACK! SNAP! BANG!

Susan sits up and utters a loud SHRIEK.

Charles remains stretched out on the front seats.

> CHARLES
> Probably ammunition left behind. The car's
> as safe a place as any. If we die, we die. Try
> to relax.

Susan sighs, clasps her hands together.

> SUSAN
> We will survive.

CRICKETS' CHIRPS and Charles' SNORES keep her awake.

She overhears a conversation between Ilene and her son Josh from the car parked in front of them.

> JOSH (O.S.)
> Are we going to die?

> ILENE (O.S.)
> I don't know love. If we do, we'll die
> together as a family.

Susan wipes tears from her eyes.

SUPER: "WEDNESDAY, 24 JULY 1974"

Scene 97

EXT. CARS PARKED ON RISE NEAR HIGHWAY – DAWN

Susan turns the radio on at low volume.

> BFBS ANNOUNCER (V.O.)
> The British ships are waiting off the
> Northern coast of Cyprus to rescue foreign
> nationals in the Kyrenia area.

Excited, Susan jumps up and tries to wake Charles. He grunts, snores, and turns over.

She looks around to see if others are stirring; all is quiet.

No movement.

> BFBS ANNOUNCER (V.O.)
> Make your way to the nearest beach.
> Helicopters will comb the beaches.

She stops a UN SOLDIER walking past.

> SUSAN
> Have you heard the evacuation news?

> UN SOLDIER
> Yes. We must wait on clearance from the
> Turks to lead a convoy through the area. It
> will happen soon. We will run two convoys
> to the Six Mile Beach, east of Kyrenia.

The sun rises. People move about. Ronit joins them and gets into the back seat of their car.

Car engines start and cars move forward to form a convoy.

Scene 98

EXT. CYPRUS MOUNTAIN HIGHWAY – DAY

Two UN armored scout cars and two Land Rovers lead the way to steer cars clear of any explosives left along the road.

More UN jeeps and armored cars follow in the rear. The convoy turns left onto the main highway and winds its way north, down the mountain pass to Kyrenia.

Susan gazes sadly at the smoldering tree stumps and dead bodies visible off the highway.

The lead UN vehicles drift back and forth, guiding cars around huge shell casings and unexploded devices (some over three feet long) scattered along the buckled, twisted road.

KA-BOOM! POW!

A powerful explosion sends shock waves through their bodies. Susan jumps. Ronit shrieks. Charles slams on the brakes.

KA-BOOM!

A car ignites and bursts into flames a few hundred feet off the road.

HORNS BLAST. BRAKES SQUEAL as cars come to a screeching stop.

A UN SOLDIER motions drivers to stay back.

Dazed, Charles, Susan and Ronit sit in silence and watch the fiery combustion shoot skyward.

LATER When the fire stops crackling and becomes embers, the UN soldier motions for cars to move forward.

After a slow and bumpy ride with many zigs and zags, they reach the village of Kyrenia.

Scene 99

EXT. KYRENIA MAIN STREET – DAY

Mouth open, Susan inhales in horror at missing corners, walls, and rooftops of beautiful old villas. Gaping holes in buildings reveal burned out interiors.

Scorched bodies litter the sidewalks. Susan covers her mouth and shakes her head.

Ronit chokes back tears.

Fragments of twisted vehicles lie scattered along the streets alongside lifeless bodies torn apart by bombs and bullets.

When they near the corner where they would turn right to drive home, they see neighbors wave to them.

The convoy travels through the town; now a twisted reality of death and destruction.

They pass building after building punctuated with blackened holes, smashed windows and doors.

Dead animals and humans lie scattered across the morbid landscape.

Susan sits and stares in stunned disbelief; then weeps with convulsive gulps for air in a high-pitched wail.

Charles and Ronit reach out and pat her.

Susan sobs loud and long. Ronit gently strokes her shoulder.

At the main intersection the convoy turns right and heads east, toward the Six Mile Beach.

Scene 100

EXT. SIX MILE BEACH – DAY

Approaching the entrance to the "SIX MILE BEACH" road, the convoy stops.

A UN SOLDIER directs drivers to park their cars near a closed beachside restaurant.

Charles parks the car. They get out and remove their small suitcases from the trunk. A UN soldier approaches.

> UN SOLDIER
> We are collecting car keys and will drive
> your vehicles to the UN facility for
> safekeeping.

Charles shrugs and looks at Susan.

> SUSAN
> We have all that matters. The car's not
> important. Thank you!

Charles hands him the keys.

They join others waiting in the shade of a grape arbor covering the restaurant's patio and help themselves to clusters of grapes hanging overhead.

Refugees mingle and wait in line for helicopters to airlift them to the waiting ships.

A TELEVISION CREW roam the area interviewing people.

They move toward Susan.

JOURNALIST
(to Susan)
Good morning! We're from a Swedish
television station and would like to ask
about your experiences during the war.

SUSAN
I'm just grateful to be alive.

JOURNALIST
Are you European?

SUSAN
No, American. My ancestors were.

JOURNALIST
Where were you when the coup started?

SUSAN
Nicosia at the airport. And, I was in my bed
in Kyrenia when the Turks dropped their
first bombs on the village.

The journalist motions for the cameramen to move in closer, as he
interviews her.

SUSAN (CONT'D)
So many lives lost. So much destruction. It's
sad and senseless. War has stripped Cyprus
of everything. For what?

Susan wipes away tears.

Scene 101

EXT. SIX MILE BEACH - FURTHER DOWN – DAY

Refugees line up ready to board the evacuation helicopters.

A BRITISH ROYAL NAVAL OFFICER waves the women and children to the
front of the line. Men stand towards the back.

> BRITISH ROYAL NAVAL OFFICER
> Women and children first. The landing
> helicopters will take you to the British ships
> anchored offshore.

Susan and Ronit wait in line and watch helicopters land and lift off.

WHOMP! WHOMP! WHOMP!

Susan observes the whirling blades rotate.

The British Royal Naval Officer motions Susan and Ronit to move to the front of the line.

Susan turns to the UN SOLDIERS standing by.

> SUSAN
> Thanks for keeping us safe!

The soldiers wipe tears from their eyes.

Scene 102

EXT. SIX MILE BEACH FURTHER DOWN - HELICOPTER LANDING AREA – DAY

A BRITISH ROYAL NAVAL OFFICER checks passports of the women and children in line.

Susan hands him her passport. A nervous Ronit smiles and holds up her hands.

> RONIT
> I... I don't have mine. I'm Israeli.

He nods and motions her forward.

Ronit presses her hands against her chest.

> RONIT (CONT'D)
> Thank you!

They run, heads down, toward the huge helicopter.

WHOMP! WHOMP! WHOMP!

The whirling blades chop fast overhead.

In one swift swoop, sailors lift Susan and Ronit onto the helicopter, into a seat, and lock safety belts.

The engine SCREAMS as the chopper lifts straight up off the ground.

They look at each other and laugh out loud.

As they soar above the blue Mediterranean Sea. Susan points to the Kyrenia Castle.

> SUSAN
> (loud voice)
> Still standing tall.

Ronit points to the beachside Zephyros Hotel. Half of it is missing.

Scene 103

EXT. HMS HERMES SHIP - DECK – DAY

The helicopter carrying Susan and Ronit drops straight down.

SAILORS rush forward to unfasten seat belts. One swoop lowers Susan and Ronit onto the deck.

The sailors corral them with other refugees into a painted square.

> HMS HERMES SAILOR
> Stay within the lines. It's a lift to lower you
> to the decks below. Keep arms down.
> We're descending.

In an instant, the platform plunges downward. With a THUNK, they land in the belly of the enormous ship.

Scene 104

INT. HMS HERMES SHIP - LOUNGE – DAY

A bevy of smiling SAILORS greets them.

ONE SAILOR hands them a HAPPY HERMES t-shirt and a boarding pass.

> HMS HERMES SAILOR ONE
> Welcome to the HMS Hermes! Please move
> forward to the waiting cots. Your boarding
> pass tells you where you will sleep for the
> night.

ANOTHER SAILOR offers English biscuits and tea.

Susan bursts into tears.

HMS HERMES SAILOR TWO
(smiles)
It's all right, Miss. It's English tea, you
know.

They sip tea and nibble on biscuits.

SUSAN
(to Ronit)
I hope Charles got on board. How will I find
him?

Ronit smiles.

RONIT
Probably in the cafeteria.

Susan laughs.

SUSAN
Good place to search for a hungry man.

Ronit hesitates.

RONIT
Tell me about that dream you had before
the war started?

SUSAN
It was profound. I drove our convertible
down a steep mountain road. Without
warning, the two right tires came flying off.
A calm voice told me to just trust myself
and steer to safety.

Ronit smiles.

RONIT
And you did.

SUSAN
We had a bumpy landing, but we're safe
now.

They listen to an announcement.

SHIP'S PA (V.O.)
Anyone who requires medical attention
should proceed to the ship's hospital.

Ronit nudges Susan.

RONIT
Let's go! You need to have your eye
checked.

Scene 105

INT. HMS HERMES SHIP - HOSPITAL ROOM – DAY

A DOCTOR (40) puts drops into Susan's eyes.

DOCTOR
A scratched cornea. It will heal... with time.

SUSAN
Only a scratch? I'm lucky.

DOCTOR
Others, not so. One young lady, on her
honeymoon, lost her leg to gangrene.

Susan goes quiet for a second.

SUSAN
Was she in the car that turned left to
Kyrenia instead of right with the convoy?

DOCTOR
(words catch in his throat)
Yes. A terrible choice.

RONIT
Good news; we're alive and healthy.

Susan sighs.

SUSAN
The bad news... paradise is a convenient
illusion.

Eyes wide open, the doctor looks at her, then nods in agreement.

MONTHS LATER

SUPER: "OJAI, CALIFORNIA, SPRING 1975."

Scene 106

EXT. OUTDOOR PATIO TABLE – DAY

Susan sits in jeans and a t-shirt at an outdoor table in a garden.

She opens her sketchbook and a large portable watercolor palette, then dips a thin paintbrush first in water, then in a light blue color, and quickly sketches the Kyrenia Castle with its four Byzantine towers from her memory.

INSERT - A sketch of Kyrenia Castle

BACK TO SCENE

With confidence, she dips the pointed brush tip into water and then dabs a variety of rich watercolors and finishes painting the castle rising above the intense blue hue of the Mediterranean Sea.

She paints the reflection of a setting sun of gold and red and billowing white clouds with silver linings moving in from the sea.

She stands and admires her memory of the majestic castle which stands guard over the Kyrenia harbor.

INSERT - Finished painting of Kyrenia Castle.

FADE OUT.

Beach Evacuation – 1

Beach Evacuation – 2

CONTRIBUTORS

ALISON ALDERTON   215

AMY BOVAIRD   216

ANDREW KLEIN   217

CAROLYN MUIR HELFENSTEIN   218

DENIS DEXTRAZE   220

ELIZABETH MOORE   222

FRANK KUSY   223

IRENE PYLYPEC   224

LALLY BROWN   226

LESLIE GROVES OGDEN   227

LILIANA AMADOR-MARTY   228

MALCOLM D. WELSHMAN   229

MARY MAE LEWIS   230

MIKE CAVANAGH   231

NEAL ATHERTON   232

PATRICIA STEELE   233

PATTY SISCO   235

ROBYN BOSWELL   236

RONALD MACKAY   237

RONNI ROBINSON   238

SUSAN JOYCE   239

SUSAN MELLSOPP   240

SYD BLACKWELL   241

TINA WAGNER MATTERN   242

VAL POORE   243

VERNON LACEY   244

Alison Alderton

Alison with Buster

Alison Alderton was born in Chichester, West Sussex, and educated in the county, studying art, design and photography at the West Sussex College of Design in Worthing and later creative writing with NEC, Cambridge. For over 20 years she has been a freelance writer-photographer working mainly for boating associations and inland waterways publications.

Alison has cruised extensively through the inland waterways of England, Ireland, Northern Europe and Scandinavia on her Dutch barge Lily, contributed to several books and written over 120 articles for various publications. Accompanied by her beloved Buster on many voyages these exhilarating travels are the subject of her debut book *Boating with Buster – the life and times of a barge beagle*, which was published in 2018.

Boating with Buster Amazon Link: https://bit.ly/38qDfOz

After living and travelling overseas for the past 12 years, Alison and her husband along with their beagle puppy, Maksi, have recently returned to the UK where they are currently planning for the next chapter in their lives.

Alison does not blog but the travels of 'Lily & the barge beagles' are recorded and offer a rare glimpse into the world of those who dare to be different:

Website: http://alisonalderton.com/

Amy Bovaird

Amy Bovaird, world traveler, ghostwriter, two-time bestselling author and inspirational speaker thrives with sight loss. She educates and entertains her readers with humorous anecdotes of coping with ongoing sight and hearing loss. Bovaird earned her M.A. in Bicultural – Bilingual Studies from the University of Texas at San Antonio and is a lifelong learner, whether it is vision, writing or language related. She has written three faith-based, often humorous, memoirs. She calls herself the "low vision motivator with high expectations" because she feels everyone can and should live a rich full life. Bovaird lives in northwest Pennsylvania. Every day she negotiates for the upper hand with her three kittens, and on most occasions, fails miserably.

In 2016, her first memoir, *Mobility Matters: Stepping Out in Faith* received the Distinguished Medal of Literature by Ohio Valley University, her undergraduate institution, along with the Outstanding Alumni award.

Her other two memoirs in the Mobility Series are *Cane Confessions: The Lighter Side to Mobility* and *Hitting a Home Run: Blind and Thriving.* Her books are available in regular and large print paperbacks, eBook format and audio.

Website: https://amybovaird.com/

Andrew Klein

Andrew Klein spent fifteen years trekking the globe. During this time, he would share great adventures with fellow travelers he met in the most remarkable places. He lives with his family north of Atlanta, where he writes the *Oliver Phenomena* children's book series.

Carolyn Muir Helfenstein

1955 At the age of 17 Carolyn Muir began her teaching career in a one-room rural school, near Toronto. Attending Toronto Teachers' College to complete her certification followed. She received the highest academic standing award that year.

After a period of teaching and marriage to British-born Harold Helfenstein, they fulfilled a dream to farm. And they had three children. Many of Carolyn's short stories come from that era.

1986 The opportunity to buy the local newspaper arrived in the mail; her answer — *Why not?* CBC-TV learned of *the farmers who bought a newspaper.* Well-known entertainer Wayne Rothstad and CBC-TV crew spent three days filming the scenes and the interviews and the *Teeswater News* went prime-time in "Out Your Way".

Carolyn was elected to the Board of the Ontario Community Newspaper Association; and eventually sat as president.

1991 The News produced an *Extra* that helped in saving a seniors' home from being relocated. The community revolted. Another 1st prize provincial win.

1993 After reading of the government's decision to close institutions for adults unable to live independently, Carolyn wrote *Belonging*. Her readers began to understand all they wanted was to belong and local communities made that happen. *Belonging* won 1st prize, provincial competition.

2008 Carolyn's memoir *Why Not?* was published, filled with stories about running the Teeswater News. Her readers say they can follow the experiences, the laughter and the tears, as they read.

2010 Carolyn knew she wanted to regain her connections with Newfoundland where she was born. She learned that Waterloo University's three-year Independent Studies Program would help her research. But she was 73... She graduated with a Bachelor of Independent Studies in 2013. Both *Rock Solid* and *Why Not?* are now in the Newfoundland Folklore Archives of Memorial University, NFLD. And Carolyn has regained her Newfoundland identity.

For more info— Google: Carolyn Muir Helfenstein -Spirit of the Hills

Denis Dextraze

Canadian born Captain Denis Dextraze started traveling internationally at age 18 when he hitchhiked around Europe during the summer break. After graduating from two U.S. universities, he specialized in international high-tech marketing which took him around the world. He retired early to enjoy sailing his 45 ft. ketch. Between his career and his port-o-calls on Aventura, he visited more than 80 countries.

Once upon a time in Cuba is being written so that an interesting two-year capsule of Cuban history, starting in May of 1998, will not be lost forever. All events reported in this book really happened no matter how ludicrous, illogical, or incredible they appear.

These years were times of changes and uncertainty for the Cuban authorities. They wanted our money but did not want us because we were "contaminating" the communist indoctrination of their controlled population. We were living interesting times, sharing the docks in Marina Hemingway with an array of adventurers not representing any normal and organized society in the world. They ranged from millionaires, drug smugglers, Hells Angels members, pedophiles, smugglers, tough Vietnam vets, world class sailors, escaped refugees. We were pioneers living interesting times and loving it!

During those days as it is still today, the Cuban society was segregated into two categories. On the 0.3% upper side, the communist ruling party composed exclusively of militaries whether in uniforms or not were living in incredible luxury ironically just like their ousted predecessors of the Batista regime. On the downside were the other 11 million slaving Cubans living in desperate conditions. We, as visiting foreigners, were odd-balls in this two-class system. Since we did not belong to either class, we were tolerated and generally allowed privileges that were reserved to the Cuban military elite and forbidden to the population.   dextraze@yahoo.com

Elizabeth Moore

Elizabeth has lived in Australia all her life. She is happily married, a mother of two, grandmother of five and devoted assistant to one very bossy tortoiseshell cat named Lucy. Her working career began as a speech pathologist and later morphed into the totally unrelated field of retail manager in a university science centre and planetarium.

Travel has always been a focus and yes – there has always been a bucket list. This was brought into stark relief when she was diagnosed with breast cancer and following treatment, a travel timetable began to take shape. Guam was first, followed quickly by European and North American adventures. Illness nudged another long-held interest to the fore and Elizabeth began chronicling her trips with extensive photography, promising herself she would also write about her exploits.

Frank Kusy

Born and raised in the fog-shrouded streets of 1960s London, and with more than 30 years of travel writing experience under his belt, aspiring Buddhist and incorrigible cat-lover Frank Kusy is a SUNDAY TRIBUNE RECOMMENDED AUTHOR and a four-time Gold Medal Winner on the Harper Collins Authonomy site.

Frank has been awarded the AIA Awesome Indies Seal of Excellence for his flagship book *Rupee Millionaires* and has been a featured author on several promotional sites, including BookBub, Pixel of Ink, Indie Book Bargains and FreeBooksy. His books have received international press acclaim and have made the Kindle Top 100 List several times. His first published book, *Kevin and I in India*, climbing as high as #5. In 2015, his children's book *Ginger the Gangster Cat* won a Gold medal in the prestigious Wishing Shelf Independent Book Awards for 6 to 8 year olds, though both his cat books (the second one is *Ginger the Buddha Cat*) appeal as much to adults as to children.

Check out Frank's book store at: frankkusybooks.weebly.com

Irene Pylypec

Irene Pylypec suffers from Peter Pan Syndrome, but she's fine with that. After spending an idyllic childhood on a self-sustaining farm on the Canadian prairie, Irene left the country life for university. When she realised a Fine Arts degree wasn't likely to lead to a job, she switched to a college course in graphic design.

A self-professed daydreamer and adventurer, she backpacked solo throughout England, Scotland and Ireland upon graduating in the mid-seventies. This is when she caught the travel bug. Besides her native Canada and trips to USA, her passion for travel took her on numerous adventures to Soviet and modern-day Ukraine, Russia, Hong Kong, Mexico and Cuba.

Not satisfied with the nine-to-five lifestyle, Irene never stayed in one place very long and consequently worked at many and diverse places. Her jobs included waitress, seamstress, printing press operator, print shop scheduler, marketing assistant, meat packer and electronics assembler.

Professional careers included graphic design, technical illustration, photo re-touching (i.e. manual Photoshop), proof-reading, teaching ESL and coordinating an ESL program. Irene is also a businessperson. A lay-off notice resulted in her providing graphic design services at a time when home businesses were new and not that well received. She was also the owner of an ecommerce site when online storefronts were in the pioneering phase.

But above all, Irene is a storyteller. She loves to share her travel stories with her readers. The goal in her first memoir (published in 2018) is to take the reader on a journey back in time to walk side-by-side with her on her many adventures and misadventures. Her blog, meanwhile, tells humorous anecdotes of prairie life.

These days, she writes, reads, gardens, and looks forward to spending more quality time with her young grandchildren.

Oh…and to imbibe in fine wine. Preferably with chocolate.

Website: https://www.irenepylypec.com

Lally Brown

Born and bred in Yorkshire, England, Lally embraced the Swinging Sixties with naïve enthusiasm. As a teenager in search of adventure she trekked overland to war-torn Israel, working on a small kibbutz driving a tractor and picking oranges to earn her keep. She managed to hitch-hike around the country staying in Haifa, Jerusalem and Acre. This amazing, and occasionally dangerous experience was the spark that ignited her lifelong love of adventure and travel.

Lally has lost count of the number of homes she has had over the years but says her most memorable are those on remote St. Helena Island where ex-Emperor Napoleon Bonaparte was imprisoned and where he died; Montserrat in the Caribbean when the volcano erupted, Turks and Caicos Islands and the British Virgin Islands.

Now, in her twilight years, Lally is writing about her adventurous life using the journals she kept at the time. Her books prove that truth can indeed be far stranger than fiction, with erupting volcanoes, hurricanes, earthquakes, evacuations, abduction, drug smugglers, people smugglers, armed robbery, hangings, stowaways, bribery, corruption, political intrigues, riots, and much, much, more.

Leslie Groves Ogden

I am a retired elementary school teacher who enjoys going through all my old journals, travel diaries and photographs in search of possible story ideas. I have written about several true but unusual experiences and shared those stories with family and friends. In the future, if enough interest is generated, I may compile these stories into memoir form and seek publication. For now, I am content to keep writing as a hobby. I find that now is the ideal time to get serious about putting my experiences into story form, since we are quarantined at home here in California and my days are uneventful with few diversions. Writing adds interest to my stay-at-home hours. I hope you enjoy my story.

Liliana Amador-Marty

Liliana Amador-Marty is a Colombian-American writer. She has been journal writing since the age of ten, honing her writing skills at Bates College in Lewiston, Maine where she earned a Bachelor of Arts degree and a Master of Fine Arts from the University of Minnesota in Minneapolis. Liliana continued post-graduate work in *Memoir Writing* at The New School in New York City, where she wrote her first story, *In Caring for my Ficus*. Currently living in London, United Kingdom.

Amador-Marty writes personal narratives, travel stories and poetry, meeting weekly with an international collective of women writers, *Primrose Pens,* where she develops her work. Her travel story, *Blood Memory* was featured on Fred's Blog, 2019 Authors Showcase, and was selected for the anthology, *40 Memorable Life Experiences* in 2020 edited by Robert Fear. Liliana's personal narrative, *Gypsy Curse*, is published on the web at www.thecreativesoulcollective.com. Her latest travel story, *Return Trip* about her visit to Havana, Cuba, will be featured in a new writing blog, www.unwrittenpoetry.com. Liliana Amador-Marty is currently working on a Memoir.

Malcolm D. Welshman

Malcolm with Dora

Malcolm Welshman is a retired vet and author. He was the My Weekly vet for 15 years and has written many features for magazines such as She, The Lady, The People's Friend, Cat World, Yours, and newspapers such as The Sunday Times and the Daily Mail.

He is the author of three pet novels, the first of which, *Pets in a Pickle*, reached number two on Kindle's bestseller list. His third novel, *Pets Aplenty*, was a finalist for The People's Book Prize 2015. His memoir, *An Armful of Animals* – published September 2018 – was long-listed for the Dorchester Literary Festival's local author prize. His fourth pet novel, *Pets are a Pleasure*, was published in February 2020.

Malcolm is also an international speaker on cruise ships, having completed 50; and he has talked at over 40 WI, Rotary, Probus and retirement associations' meetings. He is a bi-monthly contributor to a local community radio, Keep 106 in Dorset.

Website: http://malcolmwelshman.co.uk

Mary Mae Lewis

Mary Mae is author of the novel *Where There's a Will, There's a Woman* and has had success with short stories; she came runner-up in North Staffordshire's TOO WRITE adult fiction competition in 2017 and was highly commended in THE POTTERIES PRIZE for flash fiction in 2018. She contributed to Robert Fear's *Travel Stories and Highlights* 2019 and his *40 Memorable Life Experiences* anthology 2020.

She's also been published in the *Telegraph* and is a published poet.

A retired teacher, Mary came late to becoming a writer and her work is based on true life experiences.

She has been married for over 50 years, has 3 sons and 4 grandchildren.

She has travelled extensively, including living in Grand Cayman for four years and Malawi for five. She now spends half the year in Spain, where she does most of her writing, and half in Newcastle-u-Lyme, Staffordshire UK.

She blogs on her Facebook page *Where There's a Will, There's a Woman* and has just finishing her memoir *Don't Stop the Fiesta*, which will be published, and available on Amazon, in the New Year (2021).

Website: www.author-marymaelewis.co.uk

Mike Cavanagh

Mike Cavanagh is now in his sixties and has no idea how that happened. He lives with his wife, Julie, adult son, Dan, and two black cats in Bateman's Bay, Australia. Mike writes various stuffs, plays guitar, composes music, is doing research on rock-wallabies, and spends way too much time playing computer games.

He thought he knew who he was until a diagnosis of high-functioning autism in his sixties gave him pause to rethink who he thought he was, and how he got here. So, he wrote a memoir, then another... as you do. Info on Mike's writing and music lurks here: https://oneofitslegs.org/home-page/

Neal Atherton

Neal is a travel writer with a particular passion for France and French wine. His love of history also comes to the fore in his writing. He has travelled extensively in France over many years and often spends time in Paris. He has written four books on France and conveys his feelings for that country and the people he and his wife have met with warm affection. The stories are many and varied but always told with humour and a wish to inspire you to follow his footsteps. Neal loves to help with the travel plans of others and his friends always look forward to his bountiful return from exploring the cellars and vineyards of France. All his books are on Amazon including Kindle Unlimited along with one about family history written from a military perspective.

Neal now lives in Somerset although he is a Lancastrian and spent most of his life in that county. He talks like a Lancastrian and you may have to agree writes like one. He loves the English game of cricket, golf, soccer, photography, walking and cooking. Of course, he loves to travel also.

His books can be found at: http://getbook.at/FrenchTravel

More information is on Neal's website: www.nealatherton.com

He is happy to be contacted via the contact details on the website.

Patricia Steele

Patricia Steele was born in Woodland, California to an English/Dutch mother and a Spanish father. Patricia's writing career started from a very early age—and on toilet paper! Her aunt watched her poking her pencil lead through it and promptly gave her a paper tablet. Patricia has been writing ever since, following in the footsteps of her maternal grandmother, who was a prolific writer, linguist and poet.

Patricia studied creative writing at Marylhurst University and became involved with three different writer's groups. Several of her poems were published in *An Anthology* through the Oregon Writer's Colony. Patricia retired in 2011 and was then able to write full-time. Her first paid writing was a magazine article *Living with Cystic Fibrosis,* which was published in My Health magazine. Patricia has written *Fairydust to Daffodils*, a memoir about her daughter Chrissy, who lost her life to Cystic Fibrosis in 1978 at a very young age.

Patricia followed short articles with her first book, a work of fiction, entitled *Shoot the Moon*. Since then she has a whole array of books. Two travel memoirs: *A Roundabout Passage to Venice* and *Mind the Gap in Zip it*

Socks, her new memoir *Fairydust to Daffodils*, more fiction books: *Tangled Like Music, Wines, Vines and Picasso, Thorny Secrets and Pinot Noir, Cloisonné, Flamenco Strings Uncorked,* and a very unique cookbook titled *Cooking Drunk* Three of her books are available as audiobooks.

Besides writing, her other passion is Genealogy. She researched her Spanish heritage and her ancestor's trek walking across the miles of Spain, through the flowers and sugar plantations of Hawaii and into the state of California. She wanted to explore the reasons why her grandmother and her grandparents left Spain in 1911. *The Girl Immigrant* and *Silvan Leaves* are Book One and Two of her *Spanish Pearls Series*. The series is based on her grandmother; Spain and Hawaii come alive and encompass five generations. A Book Three is in progress. She writes this series under the name Patricia Ruiz Steele.

Patricia lives in Casa Grande, Arizona.

Website: http://www.patriciabbsteele.com/

Patty Sisco

Patty Sisco is a teacher, counselor, writer, and crafter. She lives with her husband, her two grandsons, a dog, and three cats in Grand Prairie, Texas. She enjoys movies, reading, sewing, creating home decor, blogging, and being a grandmother to her six grandchildren; she hates to cook. She is currently working on a sequel to her memoir, *Another Cheesy Family Newsletter*, written under the pen name of Elizabeth Silva.

Robyn Boswell

I live in the beautiful far north of New Zealand surrounded by beaches and forests. My family have lived here since the earliest days of settlement in New Zealand.

I love travelling and have been lucky to have explored many fascinating parts of our wonderful world. I've visited America many times and stayed with wonderful friends I have made. I lived and worked in Scotland, the land of my ancestors, mostly clearing tables and washing dishes in a slightly questionable restaurant, a million miles from my job as a teacher in New Zealand.

My greatest adventure was 3 months camping and 20,000 kms around the Outback and Tropics of Australia. Nowadays it's all about rediscovering my own beautiful country and discovering the joys of cruising. Travel has truly broadened my mind.

Ronald Mackay

Born in Scotland in 1942, Ronald worked in international development intended to reduce rural poverty.

After retiring from Montreal's Concordia University in 2002, he and his wife Viviana, whose grandparents moved from Italy to South America after WW1, farmed avocadoes, wine grapes and olives in Argentina and Chile for 10 years.

Ronald segued from technical and academic writing into more creative forms. He has written two memoirs. *Fortunate Isle, a memoir of Tenerife* (2017) tells of his life and work in the Canary Islands in the '60s when Francisco Franco was dictator. *The Kilt Behind the Curtain* (2020) is about his two years in Romania under the communist regime of Nicolae Ceauşescu in the late '60s.

Ronald writes drama for the theatre as well as short autobiographical pieces based on his own life.

Ronni Robinson

Ronni Robinson is a writer and indoor cycling instructor in the suburbs of Eastern Pennsylvania, where she lives with her husband in their newly minted empty nest, as both kids are off to college.

Ronni has been freelance writing since freshman year in college (a long time ago) and has appeared in aSweatLife, Ravishly, The Temper, 50 Shades of Aging, Healthy Women, The Philadelphia Inquirer, the Courier-Post, The New Brunswick Home News, and Parents Express magazine.

Ronni's passion is helping others who are struggling with eating disorders. She lives on Instagram, but you can also find her on the Facebook page "Overcoming Food Nonsense," where she serves as an administrator. She also does public speaking about eating disorders and emotionally abusive relationships. She has competed in dozens of triathlons, including three IRONMAN triathlons and four half distance IRONMAN triathlons. When not writing or perched in front of her laptop, you can find Ronni in the gym. *Out of the Pantry* is Ronni's first book, but hopefully not her last.

You can read more of Ronni's writing on her website https://www.ronnirobinson.com/ or buy *Out of the Pantry: A Disordered Eating Journey* here: https://bit.ly/3b2fayU.

Susan Joyce

Born in Los Angeles, California, author Susan Joyce spent most of her childhood in Tucson, Arizona and returned to LA as a young working woman. Inspired as a child by postcards from her globe-trotting great aunt, Susan left the United States at age 20 to see the world. She planned on being gone for a year but ended up living in Europe and the Middle East during her 20s and 30s. Her travel adventures inspired Susan to become a writer.

An award-winning author and editor of children's books, Susan's first adult book in her memoir series, *The Lullaby Illusion—A Journey of Awakening* is a travelogue of the politics of the Middle East, Europe, the United States, and Israel during a twelve year 'roller-coaster' period of her life. Susan's heart led her to a new, fun, and exciting chapter in her life when screenwriting spoke to her. A book or a film originates in the writer's imagination first. Once the writer writes her version on paper, the script begins a new life when others involved in the production process; the editor, the director, the producer, the cameraman, etc share how they imagine it. Like magic, the ultimate creation becomes a dance shaped by the keen observation of others from different angles.

Susan is also writing a TV series set in a jazz club in Germany where expats gathered to make new friends in their adopted homeland. Stay tuned.

Susan Mellsopp

Susan with Jay

Susan Mellsopp is happily retired and lives in Hamilton New Zealand with her new guide dog Maya, a cream and gold Labrador. She also has her retired guide dog, a golden retriever named Jay. Much of her life has been spent as a dairy farmer, and also working as a librarian, archivist, and accessible transport researcher.

She runs a writers' group and is constantly being challenged to write in genres other than travel and memoir. Susan has published two school histories, written for an alumni magazine, and writes for a national magazine which is published monthly. She is a voracious reader, loves to travel, listen to classical music, cook, spend time with friends and use modern technology.

Syd Blackwell

I was born in a little ski town that used to be a gold mining town in the mountains of southeastern British Columbia. I also lived on the coast, on Vancouver Island, in the north, and even in northern Alberta for a decade. I visited every province and territory in Canada, and more than 40 other countries. I was an educator, an innkeeper, and an assisted living facilitator. My life was rich with experiences before I left Canada less than two months before my 61st birthday.

Uruguay has been our home for more than a decade. My wife and I share our home with our five dogs. Prior to 2020, we had international visitors every year. We also continued to travel, particularly in South America. In fact, we returned from a vacation in Brazil in March, re-entering Uruguay five minutes before the borders were closed. They have not re-opened. We will just have to remain in our wonderful home in our adopted country for the time being.

Tina Wagner Mattern

Tina and her husband Fred

Tina Wagner Mattern is a 69-year-old Portland, Oregon writer. She has been published numerous times in anthologies such as *Chicken Soup for the Soul*, *The Maine Review*, *A Cup of Comfort* and most recently (and gratefully) in Robert Fear's *40 Memorable Life Experiences*. She dabbles in short, humorous fiction but her main focus is on finishing her memoir-in-progress, *Butter Side Up, Thank God.*

Val Poore

Val Poore was born and raised in England but at the end of 1981, she moved to South Africa where she and her family lived for nearly twenty years. She loved South Africa and all its people, but had to return to Europe in 2001 for personal reasons. Since then, she's been working as a freelance ESL writing skills teacher and trainer in the Netherlands.

Val shares her time between a 120-year-old barge in Rotterdam and a cottage in Zeeland, both of which seem to take an inordinate amount of time to maintain. She loves writing and as a distraction from teaching, she wrote her first memoir about her much-missed former home in South Africa in 2006. Bitten by the writing bug, she now writes articles for magazines and blogs as well as publishing her own books.

Vernon Lacey

Vernon grew up in Cheshire, England and studied Applied Linguistics and Literature at Liverpool University. He qualified as a teacher and worked in schools in Liverpool and London before setting off for Barcelona to learn Spanish and teach internationally.

He now lives in Munich where he has taught English and Philosophy. He is currently taking paternity leave and studying classical guitar with the German virtuoso Johannes Kreusch, fulfilling a long-standing musical dream. He is married to a German native and they have three children, two girls and a boy.

Thank you!

I trust you have enjoyed this brand-new collection of Inspirational True Stories.

If you did, then please leave a review on Amazon, even if it is only a few words. Thank you!

Please check out the fd81.net blog for Authors Showcase updates throughout the year. You can also e-mail me at fd81@assl.co.uk with any questions or to get advance notice of upcoming features and new releases.

Many thanks to everyone who has contributed and given their whole-hearted support to this publication.

Travel Stories and Highlights Series

A great way to spend coffee breaks for weeks to come.

176 Stories

156 Highlights

111 Authors, Writers & Poets

getbook.at/TS-Series

getbook.at/TravelStories2017

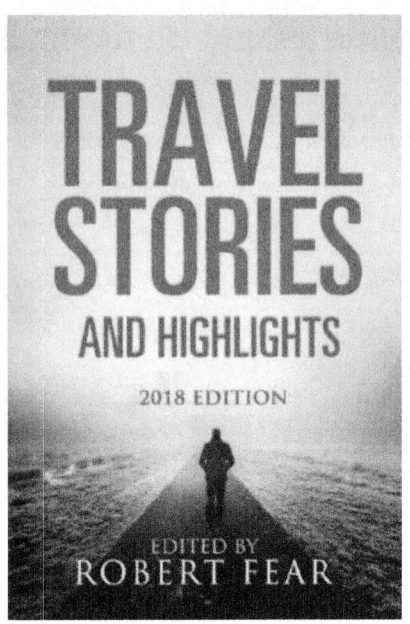

getbook.at/TravelStories2018

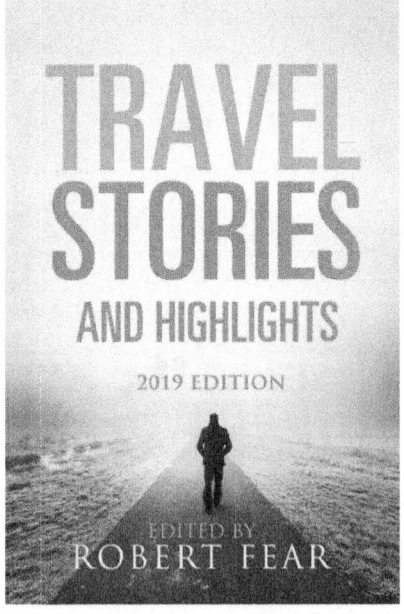

getbook.at/TravelStories2019

40 Memorable Life Experiences

Each life is a journey…

…and for good or bad, the stories captivate.

Inspiration awaits.

In this anthology, 21 writers have shared their experiences and produced 40 short stories. Young and old, these writers have been living their lives. Now, they've put those stories down to help others.

From each joy and tragedy there is a lesson to be learned.

The best adventures can be found in the biographies of others. When the stories are true, they hold so much more power.

What can you find out about yourself…

…by looking at life through their eyes?

You'll love this thought-provoking collection, because these stories run from light-hearted to heart-breaking and have plenty of amusing, witty moments to make your day.

getbook.at/40MLE

About the Editor

Robert Fear has lived in Eastbourne, on the south coast of the UK for half his life. He moved there to be with Lynn, his future wife and is still there with her over thirty years later. As cat-lovers, they have taken on several rescue cats over the years and are currently owned by three.

For his day job, Robert works as a self-employed software consultant. In his spare time, he writes, edits and self-publishes books, and organises annual writing features on his blog.

Robert's interest in travel goes back to his twenties when he spent most of his time abroad. His experiences included a summer in Ibiza, hitch-hiking around Europe and touring the USA & Canada. His most eventful trip was in 1981 when he travelled around Asia.

Born into a religious sect known as the Exclusive Brethren, his father John took the brave step of leaving it with his young family when Robert was nine years old. Robert never saw his grandparents again but is thankful for being able to grow up outside this restrictive group. His life has been full of adventures that he would never have experienced otherwise.

Books by Robert Fear

Summer of '77: Beaches, bars and boogie nights in Ibiza

A holiday can change everything... it did for Fred.

He went on a two-week break with three friends to the Spanish island of Ibiza in July 1976. It was so enjoyable they all vowed to come back for the following season.

In April 1977, Fred returned to Ibiza, alone, in pursuit of his dream.

Behind him, he left his family, his girlfriend, and a promising career in banking.

Challenges lay ahead. This would be no holiday.

He needed a place to stay and to find work that would sustain him through the next six months.

This true to life memoir follows 21-year-old Fred's adventures as he acclimatises to living abroad. In a time before instant communication, he keeps in touch with family and friends by letter. They are his lifeline to home.

getbook.at/Summerof77

Fred's Diary 1981: Travels in Asia

Have you ever wanted to read someone else's diary?

Would you like to experience travelling in Asia without leaving home?

Then this book is for you. Fred's Diary 1981 is a fascinating insight into a young man's travels around Asia in the early 1980s. This is a unique opportunity to delve into Fred's daily diary, which details the 158 days he spent travelling around Asia.

Follow Fred throughout his extensive travels to Hong Kong, Thailand, India and Nepal.

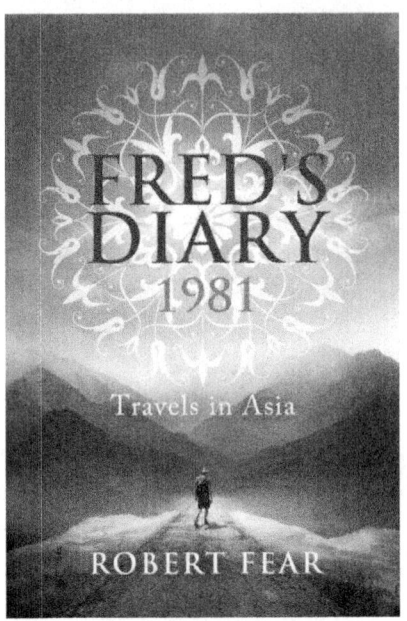

getbook.at/FredsDiary1981

Exclusive Pedigree: My life in and out of the Brethren

John Fear was born into a religious sect known as the Exclusive Brethren. This sheltered him from the outside world as he grew up but could not hide him from its influences. A struggle began in his mind that led him to leave the Brethren, along with his young family.

This is a story that was always meant to be told. During his later life, John Fear had prepared a lot of the book, along with notes for chapters that he knew would not be completed. It is only now, over twenty years later, that the book is finally being published. It contains original content written by John, along with diary notes, letters and magazine articles. The final chapters are written by his second eldest son, Alastair. The memoir is introduced and edited by his eldest son, Robert, as a tribute to his father's amazing life.

getbook.at/ExclusivePedigree

Printed in Great Britain
by Amazon